Chalcedon in Context

Church Councils 400–700

Translated Texts for Historians, Contexts 1

TRANSLATED TEXTS FOR HISTORIANS, CONTEXTS

TTH Contexts is a new occasional series developing the work of Liverpool University Press's distinguished Translated Texts for Historians. TTH provides scholarly translations, with introduction and notes, of sources for all aspects of political, social, cultural and intellectual history for the period 300–800. TTC locates these texts in the framework of the latest scholarly debate with edited papers by leading researchers who have met to discuss problems and prospects. TTC volumes present wide-ranging analyses of texts published by TTH, providing an essential resource for scholars and students working on the formative period of Late Antiquity and the Early Middle Ages.

Editors
Gillian Clark, University of Bristol
Mark Humphries, University of Swansea
Mary Whitby, University of Oxford

Chalcedon in Context

Church Councils 400–700

Edited by
RICHARD PRICE and MARY WHITBY

Liverpool
University
Press

First published 2009 by
Liverpool University Press
4 Cambridge Street
Liverpool
L69 7ZU

British Library Cataloguing-in-Publication data
A British Library CIP record is available

ISBN 978-1-84631-177-2

Typeset by XL Publishing Services, Tiverton
Printed and bound by the MPG Books Group

TABLE OF CONTENTS

ABBREVIATIONS

ABAW.PH	Abhandlungen der Bayerischen Akademie der Wissenschaften, Philosophisch-historische Abteilung
ABAW.PPH	Abhandlungen der Bayerischen Akademie der Wissenschaften, Philosophisch-philologische und Historische Klasse
ACO	*Acta Conciliorum Oecumenicorum*
ACO II	*Acta Conciliorum Oecumenicorum*, Series Secunda
AHC	*Annuarium Historiae Conciliorum*
Byz	*Byzantion*
ByzF	*Byzantinische Forschungen*
ByzZ	*Byzantinische Zeitschrift*
CCSL	Corpus Christianorum, Series Latina
CRAI	*Comptes rendus des séances de l'Académie des Inscriptions et Belles Lettres*
DOP	*Dumbarton Oaks Papers*
DTC	*Dictionnaire de théologie catholique*
ep./epp.	*epistola/epistolae*
EThL	*Ephemerides Theologicae Lovanienses*
FilMed	*Filologia Mediolatina*
GCS	Die griechischen christlichen Scriftsteller der ersten drei Jahrhunderte
GOTR	*Greek Orthodox Theological Review*
GRBS	*Greek, Roman and Byzantine Studies*
IMylasa	*Die Inschriften von Mylasa*
JÖB	*Jahrbuch der österreichischen Byzantinistik*
JRS	*Journal of Roman Studies*
JTS	*Journal of Theological Studies*
MGH	Monumenta Germaniae Historica
NF	Neue Folge
OCP	*Orientalia Christiana Periodica*
OGIS	*Orientis Graeci Inscriptiones Selectae*
PG	Patrologia Graeca
PL	Patrologia Latina
RBen	*Revue bénédictine*
RHE	*Revue d'histoire ecclésiastique*

RThL	*Revue théologique de Louvain*
SBAW.PH	Sitzungsberichte der Bayerischen Akademie der Wissenschaften, Philosophisch-historische Abteilung
SC	Sources Chrétiennes
StP	*Studia Patristica*
TTH	Translated Texts for Historians
TU	Texte und Untersuchungen
ZKG	*Zeitschrift für Kirchengeschichte*

LIST OF CONTRIBUTORS

Averil Cameron is Professor of Late Antique and Byzantine History at the University of Oxford and Warden of Keble College, Oxford.

Catherine Cubitt is Senior Lecturer in Early Medieval History in the Department of History, University of York.

Thomas Graumann is Senior Lecturer in Early Church History in the Faculty of Divinity, University of Cambridge.

David Gwynn is Lecturer in Ancient and Late Antique History at Royal Holloway, University of London.

Judith Herrin is Professor Emerita and Senior Research Fellow in Byzantine Studies at King's College London.

Andrew Louth is Professor of Patristic and Byzantine Studies at the University of Durham.

Fergus Millar is Emeritus Professor of Ancient History and a member of the Hebrew and Jewish Studies Unit at the Oriental Institute, Oxford.

Richard Price is Senior Lecturer in the History of Christianity at Heythrop College, University of London.

Charlotte Roueché is Professor of Classical and Byzantine Greek at King's College, London.

Michael Whitby is Professor of Classics and Ancient History, University of Warwick.

INTRODUCTION

Averil Cameron

The publication in three volumes in the series Translated Texts for Historians of a complete English translation with notes of the materials relating to the Council of Chalcedon (AD 451) by Richard Price and Michael Gaddis[1] is a major event. For the first time this priceless dossier becomes readily accessible, and in English translation. This means that professional historians, theologians and students alike can have to hand in convenient form a collection of material which is of the utmost importance for understanding both the history of the Church and the history of late antiquity. Its publication coincides with the appearance of other works by historians dealing with church councils, in particular Fergus Millar's Sather Lectures, published in 2006, and related articles by him.[2] Several recent works on the role of bishops in late antiquity, as well as many publications on the separation of the miaphysites, or non-Chalcedonians, in the sixth century, and on questions of orthodoxy and heresy, also underline the centrality of the negotiations and rivalries

1 Richard Price and Michael Gaddis, *The Acts of the Council of Chalcedon, translated with an introduction and notes*, TTH 45, 3 vols. (Liverpool University Press, 2005).
2 Fergus Millar, *A Greek Roman Empire: Power and Belief under Theodosius II (408–450)* (Berkeley and Los Angeles, 2006) and the articles listed on p. 69 below; see also Ramsay MacMullen, *Voting about God in Early Church Councils* (New Haven, 2006); Peter Norton, *Episcopal Elections 250–600: Hierarchy and Popular Will in Late Antiquity* (Oxford, 2007). Averil Cameron and S.G. Hall, *Eusebius, Life of Constantine* (Oxford, 1999) was the first English translation since the nineteenth century of the *Vita Constantini*, containing Eusebius' version of the Council of Nicaea, and has a detailed historical commentary; it has been followed by several other translations into different languages. The great series of editions of the acts of the ecumenical councils initiated by Eduard Schwartz, the *Acta Conciliorum Oecumenicorum*, has in recent years been continued by the very important work of Rudolf Riedinger on the Lateran Synod of AD 649 and the Sixth Council of AD 680–1; see Riedinger, *Kleine Schriften zu den Konzilakten des 7. Jahrhunderts* (Turnhout, 1998). The appearance, at the same time as this volume, of an English translation by Richard Price of the materials relating to the Fifth Council (Constantinople II) of AD 553 (TTH 51) will be a further important contribution to the topic, as well as to the growing revisionist literature on the reign of Justinian.

surrounding the 'ecumenical' councils of the fourth century and later.[3]

The Church began from a very early date to resolve internal disagreements by means of meetings whose proceedings were in one way or another recorded; the earliest example is of course the debate within the Church of Jerusalem in the first century. In the context of a growing new religion which felt its mission to be universal, once the decision to proselytize among the gentiles had been made, local meetings ('synods') were ways of establishing communion, imposing order and designating hierarchy. A precedent was set in the early fourth century when the Council of Elvira issued a set of canons aimed at regulating Christian behaviour, but as Constantine discovered, local synods did not prevent the development of wide discrepancies of practice and indeed belief. His first intervention in church affairs resulted in a meeting being called in Rome, and then a council being convened at Arles in AD 314, but the Council of Nicaea held under his aegis in AD 325 was the first such meeting of bishops which claimed to be universal; this was so even though the balance of participants was anything but even between east and west, and a myth quickly grew up according to which the number of those attending matched that of the servants of Abraham (318) as reported in Genesis 14:14. The stakes were immediately raised: the emperor himself called the council, put state resources into its arrangements, and clearly intended it to settle the awkward fact that the Church which he had decided to support was divided, and potentially seriously so. Present at the council but not yet a bishop was Athanasius, who was himself exiled in AD 336 and who was to appeal again and again in a series of tendentious and partisan writings to the Council of Nicaea as the cornerstone of orthodox faith. Eusebius of Caesarea, the contemporary who was its first historian, has left for reasons of his own an account which omits all the highly contentious issues and yet which makes it clear once and for all how crucially important it and its successors would be in the future.[4]

3　See Claudia Rapp, *Holy Bishops in Late Antiquity: The Nature of Christian Leadership in an Age of Transition* (Berkeley and Los Angeles, 2005). On the miaphysites see, for example, Lucas van Rompay, 'Society and community in the Christian East', in Michael Maas, ed., *The Cambridge Companion to the Age of Justinian* (Cambridge, 2005), 239–66.

4　Eusebius, *Life of Constantine* III.4–22. For Athanasius see D.M. Gwynn, *The Eusebians. The Polemic of Athanasius of Alexandria and the Construction of the Arian Controversy* (Oxford, 2007).

Although the Council of Nicaea was never revoked, what had perhaps seemed a simple and even straightforward matter of achieving consensus and moving forward from an agreed position turned out over the next centuries to be a source of enormous division and struggle. Far from ending the matter, the Christological formulae in the statement of faith agreed at Nicaea and confirmed by the First Council of Constantinople in AD 381 were bitterly fought over by the next generations.[5] In the west, the Council of Chalcedon in AD 451 has been felt to have settled the profile of catholic Christianity so firmly that in many quarters the patristic period is still seen as ending then. But in the east, many felt that Chalcedon had gone too far, and the valiant efforts of later emperors were not sufficient to prevent the non-Chalcedonians from forming their own churches.[6] By the seventh century despairing emperors resorted to simply ordering an end to theological argument, naturally without success. The disputes and shifting alignments before, during and after the ecumenical councils were the nearest thing to politics in this period. They involved not only the Church and its bishops but also the political elite, the emperors, monks and indeed also Christians in the street who at times resorted to actual violence in the expression of their rivalries and enthusiasms.[7]

As the papers in this volume demonstrate, the circumstances surrounding these councils – their preliminaries, organization, attendance, documentation and eventual reporting in official or unofficial documents – are currently a major subject of study. In all cases the critical editing and indeed the translation of the surviving records are fundamental. Fergus Millar has recently shown the degree to which historians of the Council of Chalcedon and the fifth century have still to draw on all the riches that the documentary evidence contains; the evidence from the Council of Ephesus for the religious policy of Theodosius II and the role played by his sister Pulcheria has also received considerable attention lately, though some basic questions remain

5 See, for example, Lewis Ayres, *Nicaea and its Legacy: An Approach to Fourth-Century Trinitarian Theology* (Oxford, 2004).
6 The extent of Justinian's investment in achieving some kind of ecclesiastical unity is vividly revealed in the papers edited by Celia Chazelle and Catherine Cubitt, *The Crisis of the Oikumene: The Three Chapters and the Failed Quest for Unity in the Sixth-Century Mediterranean* (Turnhout, 2007).
7 See the paper by Michael Whitby below, with Michael Gaddis, *There is no Crime for those who have Christ: Religious Violence in the Christian Roman Empire* (Berkeley and Los Angeles, 2005).

disputed.[8] Problems about the reliability of some council acts as a record of the actual proceedings have been explored, notably in relation to Ephesus I (see Thomas Graumann's essay in this volume) and the Lateran Synod of AD 649, where Rudolf Riedinger's work has revealed the editorial role of Maximus the Confessor and the Greek monks in his entourage. Similarly the materials from the Sixth and Seventh Councils in AD 680–81 and 787 (though the latter still awaits its critical edition) are of extraordinary interest, not only for the actual debates but also for their lists of bishops attending, and for the precautions taken to guard against the citation of forged documents and authorities – which is at the same time clear evidence of the extent to which the practice was taking place.[9] By focusing on one manuscript containing one of the many florilegia drawn up for use in the ecclesiastical battles which surrounded the later councils in the series, Alexander Alexakis has strikingly revealed the extent of manipulation as well as the amount of effort and energy that went into their preparation and into the arguments that surrounded them.[10] At one level, indeed, the classic problem of Byzantine iconoclasm can be seen to depend in important ways on a veritable war of texts.

It would be impossible to overestimate the importance of the ecumenical councils of late antiquity. Once set on this road, the complexities of procedure inevitably increased, and so did the determination of the various groups and individuals to secure their desired outcome. Insofar as what was aimed at was a verbal definition of the faith, with all the problems such an attempt implies, it has been argued that the endeavour was a fatal step in the wrong direction: there is more to religion and more to Christianity than forms of words, and the search for verbal definition was doomed to failure. Indeed the ecclesiological and disciplinary problems with which the councils also struggled proved to be as recalcitrant as the doctrinal ones. Yet Constantine could hardly have left the Christians in different parts of the empire to go their own way, and there were good precedents for recourse to imperial authority for the settlement of disputes. Nevertheless, the intervention of

---

8 See R.M. Price, 'Marian piety and the Nestorian controversy', in R.N. Swanson, ed., *The Church and Mary*, Studies in Church History 39 (Woodbridge, 2004), 31–8.

9 See on this Susan Wessel, 'Literary forgery and the Monothelete controversy: some scrupulous uses of deception', *GRBS* 42 (2001), 201–20.

10 Alexander Alexakis, *Codex Parisinus Graecus 1115 and its Archetype* (Washington DC, 1996).

emperors in church affairs was a fateful step. Michael Whitby has recently emphasized both how much state effort was put into achieving the desired results at the Council of Chalcedon, and how recalcitrant determined ecclesiastics could be.[11] Emperors were never able to 'control' the Church, and the precedent set by Constantine in fact initiated centuries of struggle. It is for good reason therefore that current work by historians on the councils, as can be seen from the papers in this volume by Fergus Millar, Richard Price and Catherine Cubitt, focuses on the difficulties of achieving the formulations agreed by the councils, on the methods and strategies that were adopted by interested parties, and on the lengths to which partisan reporting resorted; but the fact remains that these councils, and arguably the Council of Chalcedon most of all, shaped the subsequent history of both the western and eastern churches, centuries before the so-called Great Schism of AD 1054. Indeed, the Council of Chalcedon and its reception have informed and are still powerfully felt in the ecclesiastical development and traditions of the western churches, the eastern orthodox churches and the non-Chalcedonian oriental orthodox churches of today.

The rulings of these councils also covered moral and ethical questions, and matters of church order, including the primacy of sees. As Judith Herrin's paper shows, the late seventh-century Trullanum, or Quinisext Council, concentrated on filling the gap in rulings on such matters left by the failure of its two most recent predecessors to issue such canons. Gradually, by a complex process and only over a considerable period the canons issued by ecumenical and other councils were gathered together and eventually formed the basis of 'canon law', an ecclesiastical legislative system which ran parallel to that of the state.[12] This topic also involves the much discussed question of the legal or quasi-legal authority of bishops following on from the initiatives taken in that direction by Constantine. Legal procedures were also crucial to conciliar decisions, and many bishops were themselves legally trained; in terms both of record-keeping and legal procedures it is no coincidence that the

---

11 Michael Whitby, 'The role of the emperor', in D.M. Gwynn, ed., *A.H.M. Jones and the Later Roman Empire* (Leiden, 2008), 65–96, at 84–6.

12 The *Synagoge* or 'collection of fifty titles', compiled by John Scholasticus, patriarch of Constantinople in the late sixth century, represents a key stage in this process. See Caroline Humfress, *Orthodoxy and the Courts in Late Antiquity* (Oxford, 2007), chapter 7, 'Forensic practice and the development of early canon law', 196–213; Hamilton Hess, *The Early Development of Canon Law and the Council of Serdica* (Oxford, 2002); Norton, *Episcopal Elections*, 18–38.

Council of Chalcedon followed not long after the promulgation of the Theodosian Code.[13]

As is shown in the paper by Charlotte Roueché below, the study of the councils leads us into questions of procedure and popular and elite decision-making. Perhaps most of all, however, in recent scholarship on late antiquity, the evidence of the councils, and not least that of Chalcedon, is fundamental to the large body of work that has been published on the definition of 'heresy'; for 'heresy' is the other face of orthodoxy. One way of explaining the emerging understanding of orthodoxy is to say that it becomes clear through the condemnation of the heresies by which it is challenged at different times; another, of course, is to say that the concept of 'orthodoxy' itself is a construction which depends on the labelling of other doctrines as heretical.[14] Many techniques were employed in late antiquity as part of this process, and conciliar definitions and conciliar debates and their recording were certainly among them. It is hardly surprising then if by the early Byzantine period ecclesiastical writers began to appeal to the cumulative weight of the councils in their attempts to summarize what constituted orthodoxy, or that the councils took on a new life of their own in Byzantine iconography and even acquired their own liturgical commemoration.[15]

The papers in this volume have their origin in a one-day conference held at Corpus Christi College, Oxford on 18 November 2006, organized by Mary Whitby, which revealed the range of current interest in this material. The contributors address some of the many issues which surround the history of these councils, and demonstrate how immensely important they were, and what a fruitful topic they provide for current and further research. The conference was held to mark the publication in TTH of the Price and Gaddis edition of the Acts of the Council of Chalcedon; it is very appropriate that this volume, which inaugurates a new series, TTH Contexts, should have been edited jointly by Richard Price and by Mary Whitby in her capacity as a General Editor of the TTH series.

---

13 See Caroline Humfress, 'Law and justice in the *Later Roman Empire*', in Gwynn, ed., *A.H.M. Jones and the Later Roman Empire*, 121–43, especially 139–40. Humfress remarks that A.H.M. Jones 'took it for granted that late Roman legal structures and processes could not be analysed apart from ecclesiastical and religious developments'; the converse is also true.

14 Humfress, *op. cit.*, chapter 8, 'Defining orthodoxy and heresy', 217–42.

15 Christopher Walter, *L'iconographie des conciles dans la tradition byzantine* (Paris, 1970); idem, 'Icons of the First Council of Nicaea', in his *Pictures as Language: How the Byzantines Exploited Them* (London, 2000), 166–87.

THE COUNCIL OF CHALCEDON
AND THE DEFINITION OF
CHRISTIAN TRADITION

David M. Gwynn

'Few councils have been so rooted in tradition as the Council of Chalcedon.'[1] The words are those of Aloys Grillmeier, from the conclusion
of the first volume of his monumental work *Christ in Christian Tradition*, and they are words with which the bishops who gathered at
Chalcedon in 451 would have wholeheartedly agreed. Yet what do we
mean by 'Christian tradition'? How did that tradition develop over
time? Who had the authority to determine what would come to be
regarded as traditional? All of our contemporary sources for the great
controversies that divided the Christian Church in the fourth and fifth
centuries appeal to the authority of the one true and unchanging Christian tradition. Yet at the heart of those controversies lies a debate over
the very nature and interpretation of Christian tradition itself. In this
short paper I wish to explore the place of the Council of Chalcedon in
that debate and the evidence of the Acts of Chalcedon that have now
become so much more accessible through the superb new translation
and commentary that Richard Price and Michael Gaddis have brought
before us.

In its broadest sense Christian tradition embraces everything handed
down by the Church from the time of the apostles onwards, including
doctrinal teachings, ethics, customs and liturgical practices. More
narrowly, tradition represents the expression of the faith of the Church,
preserving the Christian message revealed by Christ for later generations.[2] In western patristic studies a 'traditional' outline of the
development and definition of the Christian faith down to the fourth and
fifth centuries is structured around the fixed points provided by the

---

1 Grillmeier (1975), 550.
2 '"Tradition" refers simultaneously to the process of communication and to its
content. Thus tradition means the handing down of Christian teaching during the
course of the history of the Church, but it also means that which was handed down'
(Pelikan 1971, 7).

creeds and canons of the first four ecumenical councils – Nicaea (325), Constantinople (381), Ephesus (431) and Chalcedon (451) – and around the writings of the Fathers whose teachings underlie and interpret those councils. Within such a framework, it is all too easy to view Christian tradition as something fixed and static and to assume that the great councils and Fathers already held in their own times the authority that they would acquire for later generations. Yet tradition is neither fixed nor static but is constantly redefined as new controversies arise and contexts change. The status of the councils and creeds of Nicaea, Constantinople and Ephesus and of the writings of Fathers like Cyril of Alexandria was by no means universally agreed at the time of Chalcedon, and still today significant Christian denominations refuse to accept the authority of Chalcedon or the vision of Christian tradition that Chalcedon upheld.[3] In the Acts of Chalcedon we thus possess an almost unique opportunity to observe the debates over the nature and interpretation of the Christian tradition taking place at a council which would itself play a crucial role in the definition of previous tradition and in turn attain traditional status for many future generations.

From Nicaea to Ephesus II

The Christian message rests upon the historical event of the Incarnation of Jesus Christ, and the highest authority of the Church lies in the scriptures which proclaim that original message. From the deaths of the apostles onwards, the early Church placed great emphasis on the continuity of her faith in the apostolic teachings preserved in the scriptures. That continuity was protected by the principle of the apostolic succession of bishops, already visible in Irenaeus of Lyons in the late second century and laid down in detail by Eusebius of Caesarea in his *Ecclesiastical History*, and it was Eusebius who first described those whom he regarded as authoritative teachers as 'Fathers of the Church'. By the

---

3 For an introduction to the differing attitudes of the non-Chalcedonian churches towards the various great councils of the fourth and fifth centuries see for the Church of the East (long wrongly identified in western scholarship as the 'Nestorian Church') Aprem (1978), Brock (1985) and Bruns (2000), and for the miaphysite or Oriental Orthodox Churches (traditionally and inaccurately described as 'monophysite') Sarkissian (1965), Samuel (1977) and the papers collected in Gregorios, Lazareth and Nissiotis (1981).

early fourth century there had thus already developed a strong Christian sense of the importance of tradition in maintaining the connection between the contemporary Church and the world of the apostles. In the years following the conversion of Constantine (306–37), the first Christian Roman Emperor, this emphasis on tradition gained a new significance. Complex doctrinal debates divided the expanding Church on a new scale, debates in which all those involved appealed to Scripture and the issues at stake could not be decided on scriptural terms.[4]

It was in an attempt to settle the greatest conflict to divide the fourth-century Church, the so-called 'Arian Controversy', that Constantine summoned the Council of Nicaea in 325 that condemned Arius and declared the Son to be *homoousios* with the Father.[5] Nicaea was the largest Christian council held down to that time and the first council since the age of the apostles that could plausibly claim to represent the entire Christian body. Henceforth the debate over Christian tradition would rest not only on the words of Scripture but on the statements of great councils and of those who came forward to interpret those councils. Yet the question still remained just which councils should possess authoritative status and who were the 'Fathers' who would be recognized as the true interpreters of the tradition. As is well known, the ecumenical authority of Nicaea and its creed was by no means immediately accepted within the fourth-century Church.[6] There was nothing resembling an initial consensus on the meaning of the 'Nicene faith', for different bishops could and did interpret the Nicene Creed in very different ways,[7] and for several decades after 325 the creed was widely ignored. Only in the 350s did Athanasius of Alexandria begin to

---

4 The following pages offer only a very brief survey of the crucial years that separate Constantine and the Council of Chalcedon. A far more thorough examination of the role of tradition and the appeal to the Fathers in the formation of Christian identity in the fourth and early fifth centuries is provided by Graumann (2002), while for the initial reception of the early ecumenical councils and their creeds see also the important article of de Halleux (1985).
5 The standard modern account of the 'Arian Controversy' is that of Hanson (1988), although see also now Ayres (2004) and Behr (2004).
6 For the origins of the title 'ecumenical council' see Chadwick (1972). The title was first applied to Nicaea by Eusebius of Caesarea (*Life of Constantine* III.6) and in the Encyclical Letter circulated on behalf of Athanasius of Alexandria by the Council of Alexandria that met in 338 (quoted in Athanasius, *Apologia Contra Arianos* 7).
7 Ayres (2004), particularly 85–100.

proclaim the primacy of Nicaea over all other councils in his *De Decretis Nicaenae Synodi* and *De Synodis* and to uphold the Nicene Creed as the true symbol of orthodoxy sufficient to refute every heresy.[8]

The arguments of Athanasius exerted increasing influence as the fourth century wore on, and the rising status of Nicaea is reflected in the emergence of the legend that 318 bishops attended the council (the original number was closer to 220).[9] The sufficiency of the Nicene Creed as a refutation of all heresies was taken up by the Cappadocian Basil of Caesarea, who like Athanasius appealed to the bishops at Nicaea as 'fathers'. Indeed, for the Nicene Creed to be upheld as representative of orthodoxy it was essential to define Christian tradition through the authority of the council and the Fathers as well as through Scripture, for Scripture of course could not justify the inclusion of the unscriptural term *homoousios* in the creed. However, Basil was also fully aware that further doctrinal clarification was still necessary, particularly in relation to the Holy Spirit who had barely featured in the creed of 325: 'We can add nothing to the Creed of Nicaea, not even the slightest thing, except the glorification of the Holy Spirit, and this only because our fathers mentioned this topic incidentally, since the question regarding him had not yet been raised at that time' (Basil of Caesarea, *Letter* 258. 2). It was in order to justify his apparently novel teachings against the charge of innovation that Basil attached to his work *On the Holy Spirit* the first detailed florilegium, a compilation of extracts drawn both from the Fathers and from Scripture, and he also appealed to the place of the Spirit in liturgical custom.[10]

Basil's teachings underlay the expanded statement on the Holy Spirit that appears in the creed traditionally associated with the 150 bishops who attended the Council of Constantinople in 381.[11] Although commonly known today as the 'Nicene Creed', this Niceno-Constantinopolitan Creed differs significantly from the creed of 325 both in its

---

8 'What need is there of councils, when the Nicene is sufficient, as against the Arian heresy, so against the rest, which it has condemned one and all by means of the sound faith?' (Athanasius, *De Synodis* 6). There is an assessment of Athanasius' presentation of the Nicene fathers and his appeals to patristic tradition in the *De Decretis* in Graumann (2002), 119–41.

9 Aubineau (1966). For a tentative reconstruction of the original signature lists of Nicaea see Honigmann (1939), 44–8.

10 Graumann (2002), 200–31.

11 On the council of 381 and its creed see Ritter (1965), Kelly (1972), 296–331 and de Halleux (1982).

enlarged reference to the Holy Spirit and in general wording, while also omitting the anti-Arian anathemas of Nicaea. The only explicit authority for the association of the Niceno-Constantinopolitan Creed with the Council of Constantinople in 381 is in fact the Council of Chalcedon, a point to which I will return, and the bishops who gathered in 381 explicitly upheld the authority of Nicaea. 'Neither the faith nor the canons of the 318 fathers who came together at Nicaea in Bithynia are to be annulled, but shall remain valid, and every heresy is to be anathematized' (canon 1, Council of Constantinople 381).

The status of the Nicene Creed as a statement of the traditional faith of the Church was therefore firmly established before the outbreak of the fifth-century Christological controversies in the conflict between Cyril of Alexandria and Nestorius of Constantinople.[12] In his Second Letter to Nestorius Cyril invoked 'the great and holy synod' of 325 in support of his doctrine of the hypostatic union of the human and divine natures of Christ, a doctrine upheld at Chalcedon where Cyril's letter was recognized as the authoritative interpretation of Nicaea. Nestorius in his reply rebuked Cyril for failing to understand the teachings of the Nicene fathers and cited their authority to justify his own emphasis upon the distinction of the two natures within the single person of Christ. As this exchange demonstrates, the Nicene Creed like the scriptures could not in fact settle the question of the relationship of the human and divine natures of Christ, for Cyril and Nestorius each cited the creed on their own terms. In his abrasive Third Letter to Nestorius to which were attached the Twelve Anathemas Cyril insisted in uncompromising terms on the undivided unity of the Incarnation, foreshadowing Eutyches' later teaching of one nature in Christ after the union. Cyril refused to accept that Nestorius could prove his orthodoxy by appealing to Nicaea, for Nestorius' interpretation of Nicaea was itself false. 'It is not enough for your Reverence only to agree in confessing the symbol of the faith previously set out in the Holy Spirit by that holy and great synod formerly gathered in Nicaea, for you have not understood or interpreted

---

12 For recent assessments of the controversy see McGuckin (2004) and Wessel (2004), while for a more detailed analysis of the appeals of Cyril and Nestorius to the Fathers and to tradition see Graumann (2002), 278–342. As Wessel (p. 302) observes, throughout these controversies 'the formation of Eastern Christian doctrine thus proceeds not according to the ineluctable structures of dogmatic history but according to a complex historical and cultural process fuelled by the claims of adversaries competing to appropriate the Christian past.'

it correctly, but have perverted it even though you may have confessed it verbally' (Cyril of Alexandria, Third Letter to Nestorius).[13]

This was the judgement that Cyril sought to prove at the First Council of Ephesus in 431. At the council the letters of Cyril and Nestorius were read out in turn and compared to the Nicene Creed, reinforcing the central importance of Nicaea as the standard by which orthodoxy should be judged. Cyril's Second Letter to Nestorius was acclaimed and effectively canonized as a true interpretation of Nicaea. The need for such an interpretation and the importance by 431 of the appeal to the authority of recognized Fathers in addition to the scriptures is well encapsulated in the words at Ephesus of the presbyter and notary Peter of Alexandria. Four weeks after the approval of Cyril's Second Letter and immediately following another reading of the Nicene Creed, Peter declared that 'it is right that all should assent to this holy creed, for it is pious and also sufficient to benefit the world under heaven. But because certain people, while pretending to profess and accept it, misinterpret the force of the ideas according to their own pleasure, and distort the truth, being sons of error and children of perdition, it has become absolutely necessary to set out statements by the holy and orthodox Fathers that can show convincingly in what way they understood the creed and had the confidence to proclaim it, so that, evidently, all who hold the correct and irreproachable faith may also understand, interpret and proclaim it accordingly' (quoted in Acts of Chalcedon I. 915). The florilegium that follows, drawn from works cited by Cyril himself, includes writings of Peter, Athanasius and Theophilus of Alexandria, the three Cappadocians, Cyprian of Carthage, Ambrose of Milan, Atticus of Constantinople, Amphilochius of Side and Julius and Felix of Rome (the letters of the latter two, as is well known, in fact originated with the followers of Apollinarius of Laodicea).[14]

Having thus proclaimed both the authority of the Nicene Creed and its correct interpretation by Cyril and the other approved Fathers, the council of 431 then proceeded to pass what has become known as canon

13 For the significance of Cyril's appeal to Nicaea and his use of Athanasius' anti-Arian rhetoric against Nestorius in this letter to establish himself as the new champion of orthodoxy see Wessel (2004), 126–37.

14 The most famous Apollinarian text cited by Cyril is of course the formula 'one nature (*mia phusis*) of the Word incarnate' which he believed to be Athanasian. For a fuller analysis of the texts associated with the First Council of Ephesus and the importance of patristic citation in 431, on a scale not visible in earlier councils, see Person (1978) and particularly Graumann (2002), 349–409.

7 of Ephesus. 'The holy council laid down that no one is allowed to produce or write or compose another creed beside the one laid down with the aid of the Holy Spirit by the holy fathers who assembled at Nicaea' (quoted in Acts of Chalcedon I. 943).[15] By Nicaea the bishops in 431 meant the creed of 325, for there is no mention of the Council of Constantinople in 381 or its creed in the Acts of Ephesus I or in the writings of Cyril, and this canon was to exert an important influence on subsequent debates. The Formula of Reunion in 433 that reconciled Cyril with the Antiochene supporters of Nestorius led by John of Antioch recognized that the Nicene Creed still required further clarification, as had the council of 381 and Cyril in his Third Letter to Nestorius. But the Formula made no claim to replace Nicaea. 'We must state briefly (not by way of addition but in the form of giving an assurance) what we have held from the first, having received it both from the divine scriptures and from the tradition of the holy Fathers, making no addition at all to the creed issued by the holy fathers at Nicaea. For, as we have just said, it is sufficient both for a complete knowledge of orthodoxy and for the exclusion of all heretical error' (The Formula of Reunion, quoted in Cyril's Letter to John of Antioch, in Acts of Chalcedon I. 246).

The status of Nicaea and the tradition of the Fathers remained a central concern for the two men whose teachings and actions played a crucial role in the resumption of the controversy after the Formula of Reunion: the archimandrite Eutyches and Dioscorus the successor of Cyril. In 448, Eutyches was condemned by Flavian of Constantinople and Eusebius of Dorylaeum at a synod in Constantinople for teaching one nature in Christ after the Incarnation. Eutyches maintained that this teaching was in accordance with the faith of Nicaea confirmed at Ephesus and with the faith of the Fathers, especially Athanasius and Cyril. Such a claim had of course by now become customary, but Eutyches is then alleged to have declared that 'if it happened, as he said, that our Fathers have made mistakes or errors in certain expressions, this he for his part would neither criticize nor embrace, but examine only the scriptures on such questions as being more reliable' (quoted in Acts of Chalcedon I. 648). No comparable statement occurs in any of the acts of the fifth-century councils, and given Eutyches' emphasis elsewhere upon the authority of the Fathers he may have been denying the validity of certain patristic passages brought forward by his opponents rather than

15 For discussion of this canon see L'Huillier (1996), 159–63.

denigrating the Fathers *in globo*.[16] Possibly Eutyches was responding to accusers who pressed him with dyophysite quotations from the Fathers, for apparently he repeated his earlier judgement in denouncing those who taught two natures in Christ after the Incarnation. 'He said that he had neither learnt it in the expositions of the holy Fathers nor, if such a statement were read to him, would he accept it, since the divine scriptures, as he claimed, make no mention of natures and are superior to the expositions given in teaching' (quoted in Acts of Chalcedon I. 648). Eutyches' insistence on the superiority of the scriptures to the Fathers appears to have surprised his accusers, but his words were not directly challenged or cited in his condemnation in 448.[17]

Dioscorus defended Eutyches, and under his leadership the Second Council of Ephesus in 449 (often described in the words of Pope Leo as the *Latrocinium* or 'Robber Council') restored Eutyches to his office and upheld the latter's insistence that no addition could be made to the faith of Nicaea. At the council Dioscorus had canon 7 of 431 proclaimed once more, and then declared that 'if then the Holy Spirit sat together with the fathers, as indeed he did, and decreed what they decreed, whoever revises those decrees rejects the grace of the Spirit' (quoted in Acts of Chalcedon I. 145). Eutyches' accusers Flavian of Constantinople and Eusebius of Dorylaeum were themselves denounced for preaching a different creed (Acts of Chalcedon I. 962), and at no time does Dioscorus show any awareness of the creed later associated with the council of 381.[18] Throughout the proceedings and subscriptions of the council of 449 only two previous councils are ever acknowledged, Nicaea and the First Council of Ephesus, while the acclamations of the attending bishops affirm the authority of Cyril as the canonical Father

16 I owe this suggestion to Richard Price.

17 I have quoted here from the summary of Eutyches' argument read out in Constantinople in 449 when the minutes from the synod of 448 were re-examined at Eutyches' request. The slightly different account of Eutyches' argument originally recorded in 448 is preserved in Acts of Chalcedon I. 359 (see Price and Gaddis, I, 200, n. 220).

18 In a polemical letter written in *c.* 448, Theodoret of Cyrrhus asserts that Dioscorus rejected the council of 381 not because of its creed but because of its second canon which laid down that bishops should only act within their own diocese: 'When the blessed fathers were assembled in that imperial city in harmony with them that had sat in council at Nicaea, they distinguished the dioceses, and assigned to each diocese the management of its own affairs, expressly enjoining that none should intrude from one diocese into another. They ordered that the bishop of Alexandria should administer the government of Egypt alone, and every diocese its own affairs. Dioscorus, however, refuses to abide by these decisions' (Theodoret, *Letter* 86).

for the interpretation of Nicaea not only through his Second Letter to Nestorius but also through his Third Letter and its Twelve Anathemas.

Chalcedon

By the time the Council of Chalcedon was summoned by the emperor Marcian (450–7) in 451, therefore, all were aware that the question of the nature of Christian tradition and the interpretation of that tradition was of critical importance. All agreed that there was one true Christian tradition from which deviation indicated heresy. What was not yet agreed was just what that tradition should include. All recognized the authority of the scriptures and of the Nicene Creed, and the writings of Cyril were also held in great respect. But how the Nicene Creed should be interpreted remained a subject of debate, and so too did the question of which of Cyril's various writings were authoritative, a question that particularly revolved around the status of his Third Letter to Nestorius and the Twelve Anathemas. The bishops at Chalcedon, whose conception of their own role as a 'holy, great and ecumenical council' (Acts V. 30) was far stronger than that of the Nicene bishops in 325, had to decide these questions.

On one essential issue the council was indeed almost unanimous. Christian tradition, like any construct of identity, is defined to a significant degree in negative terms, confirming what is to be approved through the exclusion of those who lie outside the accepted limits. There was already an established canon of heretics condemned at previous councils, including Arius at Nicaea and Eunomius, Macedonius and Apollinarius at Constantinople in 381. Few of those present in 451 were prepared to protest against the addition of Nestorius (already condemned at the First Council of Ephesus) and Eutyches to that number, although the Egyptian bishops initially hesitated to anathematize Eutyches (Acts IV. 26) and Theodoret of Cyrrhus delayed long before condemning the teachings attributed to his friend Nestorius (Acts VIII. 5–13). The names of Nestorius and Eutyches thus joined those of Arius and other heretics as terms of abuse that could be and were directed against any position that a given individual wished to denounce in contrast to their own 'traditional orthodoxy'.

The positive question of what previous teachings could be upheld as traditional and orthodox was, as always, considerably more difficult to resolve. The authority of Nicaea was recognized by everyone at Chalcedon. The council was originally planned to meet in the city of Nicaea itself to symbolize this continuity, and although this plan had to be abandoned in favour of a location that enabled tighter imperial control on proceedings, acclamations and appeals to the Nicene faith recur throughout the council.[19] The Nicene Creed was read out before Chalcedon's own Definition in the fifth session, thereby introducing the controversial Definition in a form that all could accept, and the Definition was presented in accordance with canon 7 of 431 not as a new statement of orthodoxy but as an interpretation of the existing creed.[20]

Like the First Council of Ephesus in 431, the bishops at Chalcedon also tested other patristic writings against the truth of Nicaea, and approved Cyril of Alexandria as the authoritative interpreter of Nicaea. The Definition upheld 'the conciliar letters of the blessed Cyril' (Acts V. 34), particularly the Second Letter to Nestorius and the Letter to John of Antioch concerning the Formula of Reunion. More ambiguous was Chalcedon's attitude towards Cyril's uncompromising Third Letter to Nestorius and the Twelve Anathemas. This letter is not identified in the Chalcedonian Definition, and the proposal of Atticus of Nicopolis that it be read in the second session (Acts II. 29) was evaded without formal rejection, leaving the status of the Third Letter and the Anathemas open for later debate. Chalcedon also upheld the Tome of Leo of Rome, but despite western claims to the contrary it was Cyril not Leo who exerted the greatest influence in 451.[21] The Tome, which Leo wished to present as the definition of orthodoxy, was in fact judged by the eastern bishops according to its agreement with the teachings of Cyril (Acts IV. 9).

Far more problematic for the bishops at Chalcedon than the status of Nicaea or Cyril, however, was the demand that they accept the Niceno-Constantinopolitan Creed of 381. As we have seen, this creed was

---

19 The original imperial summons calling the bishops to Nicaea in May 451 is preserved in the emperor Marcian's *Letter to the Bishops* (Price and Gaddis, I, 98). Miaphysite writers like (Ps.-) Zachariah of Mitylene (*Chronicle* III. 1) and Michael the Syrian (*Chronicle* VIII. 10) attribute the failure of Marcian's plan to Divine Providence protecting the holy reputation of Nicaea.

20 For the presentation of Chalcedon as a restatement of Nicaea see Grillmeier (1987), 210–22, Norris (1996), 141–7, and Price and Gaddis, I, 56–8.

21 Against the older view which privileged Leo's Tome over Cyril as the crucial influence on Chalcedon (Grillmeier 1975, 543–4, still upheld by Pelikan 1971, 263–4, and 2003, 259), see among numerous studies Meyendorff (1969), de Halleux (1976), Gray (1979), Grillmeier (1979), 753–9, and McGuckin (2004), 233–43. There is a recent re-examination of the role of Leo at Chalcedon in Uthemann (2005).

apparently unknown to the council of 431, and is probably one of a number of creeds then in existence and accepted as revised versions of Nicaea. Certainly there is very little indication that the majority of the bishops in 451 were even remotely familiar with the creed of the 150 fathers, which was introduced by the imperial commissioners as a symbol of orthodoxy alongside the original Nicene Creed at the end of the first session (Acts I. 1072). Before this stage, the only bishop at Chalcedon to have shown detailed knowledge of the creed of 381 is Diogenes of Cyzicus in his account of the condemnation of Eutyches in 448. 'He [Eutyches] adduced the council of the holy fathers at Nicaea deceptively, since additions were made to it by the holy fathers on account of the evil opinions of Apollinarius, Valentinus, Macedonius and those like them, and there were added to the creed of the holy fathers the words "He came down and was enfleshed from the Holy Spirit and Mary the Virgin". This Eutyches omitted, as an Apollinarian' (Acts I. 160). As Price and Gaddis observe, Eutyches can hardly be blamed for not citing so poorly known a creed.[22]

In the second session at Chalcedon, the creed of 381 was then read out in full in succession to the original Nicene Creed. The responses of the bishops to the two creeds as recorded in the acts are enlightening. On the reading of the Nicene Creed, 'the most devout bishops exclaimed: "This is the faith of the orthodox. This we all believe. In this we were baptized, in this we baptize. The blessed Cyril taught accordingly. This is the true faith. This is the holy faith. This is the eternal faith. Into this we were baptized, into this we baptize. We all believe accordingly. Pope Leo believes accordingly. Cyril believed accordingly. Pope Leo expounded accordingly"' (Acts II. 12). The creed of 381 was then read out. 'All the most devout bishops exclaimed: "This is the faith of all. This is the faith of the orthodox. We all believe accordingly"' (Acts II. 15). No bishop was going to refer to the creed of 381 as the creed of baptism or as the creed of Cyril.[23]

Similarly, when the commissioners in the fourth session asked the bishops to bear witness to the harmony of the Tome of Leo with the

---

22 Price and Gaddis, I, 158, n. 113.

23 The respective attitudes that prevailed at Chalcedon towards the creeds of 325 and 381 are perhaps best encapsulated in the statement of the Illyrian bishops during the fourth session in their acceptance of Leo's Tome: 'We uphold the creed of the 318 holy fathers as being our salvation and pray to depart from life with it; and that of the 150 is in no way in disharmony with the aforesaid creed' (Acts IV. 9.98). A similar statement was made in the same session by the bishops of Palestine (IV. 9.114).

creeds of 325 and 381 (Acts IV. 8) the great emphasis in the acclamations that follow concerns Leo's agreement with Nicaea, which Constantinople confirmed. A few acclamations omit the 150 bishops of Constantinople entirely (Seleucus of Amaseia, IV. 9.12; Theodore of Damascus, IV. 9.14; and Polychronius of Cilician Epiphaneia, IV. 9.117), while Romanus of Lycian Myra alone among the bishops not only omitted to refer to the council of 381 but also questioned whether even the Nicene Creed could provide an adequate basis to judge later writings as orthodox. 'I agree that the two letters, that is, of Cyril of sacred memory and of the most devout Archbishop Leo, speak in accord, but the holy and ecumenical council at Nicaea did not discuss these matters' (IV. 9.131). One might legitimately wonder whether other bishops shared such concerns or whether there were at some stage during the council any explicit objections to the introduction of the apparently unknown creed of 381 into the debate. If there were, however, those objections have disappeared from our official record.

We can at least be certain that some of those at Chalcedon did refuse to adopt the 381 creed. This attitude was particularly strong in Egypt where the earlier silence of Cyril and Dioscorus concerning the Council of Constantinople and their rejection of any creed other than Nicaea remained highly influential. When Diogenes of Cyzicus in the passage quoted earlier from the first session condemned Eutyches for failing to recognize the clarification of Nicaea provided in 381, the Egyptian bishops immediately defended Eutyches and appealed to canon 7 of 431, exclaiming 'No one admits any addition or subtraction. Confirm the work of Nicaea' (Acts I. 161). The 13 Egyptian bishops in the fourth session who asked to remain outside the debates until Dioscorus, who had been condemned in the third session, was replaced likewise refer in their petition only to the creed of 325 (Acts IV. 25) and omit any reference to the creed of 381 as a symbol of orthodoxy. The strength of Egyptian feeling on this question was apparently recognized by the Emperor Marcian who in his Letter to the Monks of Alexandria in 454 (Documents after the Council 14) appeals solely to the faith of 325 and not (as in his other writings after Chalcedon) to the creeds of both 325 and 381.

The Egyptian hostility to the council of 381 was also shared in Rome. An important motive for the emphasis placed by the imperial commissioners at Chalcedon on the Council of Constantinople was that the exaltation of the earlier council reinforced the famous decree, later known as the 28th canon of Chalcedon, which proclaimed the privileges of Constantinople as 'New Rome'.[24] This decree was approved in the sixteenth session of Chalcedon[25] and led to immediate tension with Rome, where Pope Leo appears to have had no more knowledge of the council of 381 than the majority of his eastern contemporaries. Anatolius of Constantinople, in his efforts to justify the contentious decree, felt the need to identify the council of 381 and its leaders in his Letter to Leo in December 451 (Documents after the Council 8). Leo contemptuously replied that 'your persuasiveness is in no way whatever assisted by the subscription of certain bishops given, as you claim, sixty years ago, and never brought to the knowledge of the apostolic see by your predecessors' (Leo, Letter to Anatolius, Documents after the Council 10).

Nevertheless, the main body of bishops at Chalcedon did eventually recognize the Niceno-Constantinopolitan Creed of 381 as a necessary supplement to Nicaea, particularly to clarify the doctrine of the Holy Spirit, and this recognition helped to pave the way for the Chalcedonian Definition (Acts V. 31–4). The ongoing controversies of the preceding decades had already demonstrated that appeal to Nicaea was not in itself sufficient to secure unity in the Church. Yet the initial request of the imperial commissioners for a new statement of faith in 451 faced considerable hostility, founded to a significant degree on a rigorous insistence upon canon 7 of 431. The assertion that the teachings of the 150 fathers in 381 represented not an independent creed but rather a 'seal' (V. 31) on the faith of Nicaea offered a precedent to overcome this strong opposition.[26] The creeds of 325 (V. 32) and 381 (V. 33) were included in the Definition proclaimed at Chalcedon,[27] which is thus placed within the gradual unfolding of the Christian orthodox tradition:

24 For a thorough analysis of this decree and its relationship to the third canon of 381 which was invoked as its precedent, see de Halleux (1988, 1989) and L'Huillier (1996), 267–96.
25 Price and Gaddis, III, 67–73.
26 As Pelikan (2003), 14 has observed, although the Definition quotes the creeds of both 325 and 381, the bishops then refer to 'this wise and saving symbol' (Acts V. 34) in the singular as sufficient for all.
27 For the textual difficulties raised by the versions of the two creeds included in the Definition, which differ between the various Greek and Latin manuscripts of the acts, see Price and Gaddis, II, 191–4. Interestingly, it is Eusebius of Caesarea's version of the Nicene Creed that appears to have been followed at Chalcedon and not that of Athanasius of Alexandria, whose text of the creed contains an additional anathema against those who teach that the Son was 'created' (Wiles 1993).

The creed of the 318 holy fathers is to remain inviolate. Furthermore, it confirms the teaching on the essence of the Holy Spirit that was handed down at a later date by the 150 fathers who assembled in the imperial city because of those who were making war on the Holy Spirit; this teaching they made known to all, not as though they were inserting something omitted by their predecessors, but rather making clear by written testimony their conception of the Holy Spirit against those who were trying to deny his sovereignty.

(V. 34)

Cyril's Second Letter to Nestorius, his Letter to John of Antioch concerning the Formula of Reunion and the Tome of Leo are likewise received as authoritative interpretations, 'for the instruction of those who with pious zeal seek the meaning of the saving creed' (V. 34). Finally the new Definition is brought forward as the conclusive expression of the traditional faith which these creeds and Fathers uphold. 'Now that these matters have been formulated by us with all possible care and precision, the holy and ecumenical council has decreed that no one is allowed to produce or compose or construct another creed or to think or teach otherwise' (V. 34).

This is not the place for a detailed discussion of the Chalcedonian Settlement. In the context of the present argument, however, it should once again be emphasized that the same gradual evolution in the definition of Christian tradition that I have traced here down to 451, particularly with regard to the status of the letters of Cyril and of the creed of 381, can of course also be seen in the contrasting attitudes of later generations towards the Council of Chalcedon itself.[28] The question of whether Chalcedon was true to the legacy of Cyril remained intensely divisive, as those who rejected Chalcedon denounced the Definition's formula of 'in two natures' as 'Nestorian' and a betrayal of Cyril's teachings.[29] In reaction to and opposition against such miaphysite accusations emerged the position often described as 'Neo-Chalcedonianism' but better understood as 'Cyrilline Chalcedonianism', insisting on Chalcedon as fully in accordance with Cyril and upholding the Twelve Anathemas. This was the position affirmed by the emperor Justinian at the Fifth Ecumenical Council of Constantinople in 553.

28 Modern studies of the reception of Chalcedon and the controversies of the following centuries include Frend (1972), Gray (1979), Meyendorff (1989), Grillmeier (1987, 1995, 1996), and Oort and Roldanus (1997).

29 The ambiguity of Cyril's numerous writings which made possible appeals to him from all sides in the subsequent centuries is brought out very well by Russell (2003).

Yet the initial question in the years following 451 did not concern the correct interpretation of Chalcedon but rather whether Chalcedon should be accepted at all within the tradition that it had sought to define. This is reflected in the Henotikon issued by the emperor Zeno and Patriarch Acacius of Constantinople on 28 July 482. Motivated by the desire to secure eastern unity, the Henotikon sidelined Chalcedon and approved only the first three ecumenical councils of Nicaea, Constantinople and Ephesus I together with the Twelve Anathemas of Cyril that had been omitted in 451.

> We know that the origin and composition, the power and irresistible shield of our empire is the sole correct and truthful faith, which through divine guidance the 318 holy fathers gathered at Nicaea expounded, while the 150 similarly holy fathers assembled at Constantinople confirmed it ... This too was followed also by all the holy fathers who gathered at the city of the Ephesians, who also deposed the impious Nestorius and those who subsequently shared his views. This Nestorius, together with Eutyches, men whose opinions are the opposite to the aforesaid, we too anathematize, accepting also the Twelve Chapters which were pronounced by Cyril of pious memory, archbishop of the holy and universal church of the Alexandrians ... But we anathematize anyone who has thought, or thinks, any other opinion, either now or at any time, whether at Chalcedon or at any synod whatsoever. (The Henotikon of Zeno, quoted in Evagrius, *Ecclesiastical History* III. 14)

By the time of the Henotikon, it would seem, the ecumenical status of the Council of Constantinople in 381 had achieved widespread acceptance. Indeed, when the 'Nicene Creed' was incorporated into the liturgy of the eastern churches in the late fifth and sixth centuries, it was the Constantinopolitan form that was adopted, perhaps due to its more liturgical character.[30] But Chalcedon and its place within Christian tradition remained very much open to debate. The definition of Christian tradition was far from complete in 451, while Chalcedon in turn created new divisions within Christianity and new and conflicting interpretations of how Christian tradition should be understood.

---

30 For the incorporation of the creed into the liturgy, first associated with the miaphysite Peter the Fuller, see Kelly (1972), 348–51.

Conclusion

The period surrounding Chalcedon that I have surveyed so briefly here marked a crucial phase in the definition of a conception of Christian tradition that rested not only on Scripture but on conciliar creeds and their correct patristic interpretation. This emphasis on an established canon of approved authority would strengthen further in subsequent centuries, with both positive and negative implications for the history of the Church. The construction by different Christian groups of their own monolithic conceptions of the 'orthodox' past narrowed the parameters of possible debate, excluding alternative traditions and distorting our understanding of the development of Christian doctrine and practices across time.[31] The 'Select Fathers' were idealized and de-historicized,[32] and the need to appeal to the authoritative past led inexorably to the rise of forgeries and false patristic attributions in subsequent centuries.[33] When the bishops at Chalcedon exclaim that 'no one makes a new exposition ... for it was the Fathers who taught, what they expounded is preserved in writing, and we cannot go beyond it' (Acts II. 3), one can almost hear the voice of Edward Gibbon mourning the sterility of fallen Byzantium. 'They held in their lifeless hands the riches of their fathers, without inheriting the spirit which had created and improved that sacred

---

31 The implications of rival conceptions of tradition for the modern ecumenical movement are brought out very clearly by Zizioulas in the dialogue between the Eastern Orthodox and Oriental Orthodox Churches over Chalcedon: 'The whole problem of Tradition emerges in the discussion as perhaps the ecclesiological issue par excellence. One could say that the difficulties we are here facing on the ecclesiological level are precisely due to the fact that both sides in our dialogue take Tradition seriously, and neither side is willing to sacrifice anything from what constitutes Tradition in their eyes. Do we not need a clarification of this issue? To what extent are we prepared to re-receive our Tradition in the context of our present day situation? Without such a re-reception the ecclesiological issues we are facing will remain insurmountable. If we intend to unite different Traditions we shall have an artificial unity. True unity of the Church requires one common Tradition as its basis' (1981, 154).
32 Gray (1989). See further the introduction to Gray (2006), 25–8 and his discussion of the famous declaration of Leontius of Jerusalem that 'none of the Select Fathers is at variance with himself or with his peers with respect to the intended sense of the faith' (Leontius, *Testimonies of the Saints* 1849D).
33 On the ever-increasing role of forgery in Christian controversies in this period see Grant (1960), Gray (1988) and (with a somewhat more positive emphasis) Wessel (2001).

patrimony. They read, they praised, they compiled, but their languid souls seemed alike incapable of thought and action. In the revolution of ten centuries, not a single discovery was made to exalt the dignity or promote the happiness of mankind.'[34]

Yet Christian tradition has never been truly static and the concept of tradition remains to this day of immense importance to the identity of the different Christian Churches and their foundation in the original historical revelation on which the Christian faith rests. Tradition is Christianity's memory, maintaining the continuity of modern Christians with the worlds of the scriptures and the ecumenical councils, and to remain relevant that traditional memory must remain a living dynamic force, constantly reinterpreted and proclaimed to a changing world. As John Henry Newman wrote in a famous essay in 1845, 'in a higher world it is otherwise; but here below to live is to change, and to be perfect is to have changed often.'[35] The purpose of the bishops who gathered at the Council of Chalcedon was to safeguard the essential continuity of Christian tradition while adapting and interpreting that tradition to meet the needs of their own times. This to a remarkable degree they achieved and the same challenge now faces Christians today and in the future. 'For each age the task of proclaiming the traditional picture of Christ within the framework of the current ideas and language still remains.'[36]

BIBLIOGRAPHY

Aprem, Mar (1978), *The Council of Ephesus* (Trichur, Kerala).

Ayres, Lewis (2004), *Nicaea and its Legacy: An Approach to Fourth-Century Trinitarian Theology* (Oxford).

Aubineau, Michel (1966), 'Les 318 serviteurs d'Abraham (Gen. XIV, 14) et le nombre des pères au concile de Nicée (325)', *RHE* 61: 5–43.

Behr, John (2004), *The Formation of Christian Theology*, vol. 2: *The Nicene Faith*, Pt 1 (Crestwood, NY).

Brock, Sebastian (1985), 'The Christology of the Church of the East in the Synods of the Fifth to Early Seventh Centuries: Preliminary Considerations and Materials', in G.D. Dragas, ed., *Aksum-Thyateira: A Festschrift for Archbishop Methodius* (London and Athens), 125–42 = id., *Studies in Syriac*

---

34 Gibbon (1912), VI, 112.

35 Newman (1845), 39. Newman applies this principle somewhat polemically to the controversies of the 'Nestorians' and the 'monophysites' in the same work at 281–317.

36 Grillmeier (1975), 556.

Christianity: History, Literature and Theology (Aldershot, 1992), XII.

Bruns, Peter (2000), 'Bemerkungen zur Rezeption des Nicaenums in der ostsyrischen Kirche', *AHC* 32: 1–22.

Chadwick, Henry (1972), 'The Origin of the Title "Ecumenical Council"', *JTS* n.s. 23: 132–5 = id., *History and Thought of the Early Church* (London, 1982), XI.

De Halleux, André (1976), 'La définition christologique à Chalcédoine', *RThL* 7: 3–23, 155–70 = id. (1990), 445–80.

—— (1982), 'Le IIe concile oecuménique: Une évaluation dogmatique et ecclésiologique', *Cristianesimo nella storia* 3: 297–327 = id. (1990), 269–99.

—— (1985), 'La réception du symbole oecuménique, de Nicée à Chalcédoine', *EThL* 61: 5–47 = id. (1990), 25–67.

—— (1988), 'Le décret chalcédonien sur les prérogatives de la Nouvelle Rome', *EThL* 64: 288–323 = id. (1990), 520–55.

—— (1989), 'Le vingt-huitième canon de Chalcédoine', *StP* 19: 28–36.

—— (1990), *Patrologie et oecuménisme. Recueil d'études* (Leuven).

Frend, W.H.C. (1972), *The Rise of the Monophysite Movement: Chapters in the History of the Church in the Fifth and Sixth Centuries* (Cambridge).

Gibbon, Edward (1912), *Decline and Fall of the Roman Empire*, ed. J.B. Bury, 7 vols (London).

Grant, R.M. (1960), 'The Appeal to the Early Fathers', *JTS* n.s. 11: 13–24.

Graumann, Thomas (2002), *Die Kirche der Väter: Vätertheologie und Väterbeweis in den Kirchen des Ostens bis zum Konzil von Ephesus (431)* (Tübingen).

Gray, P.T.R. (1979), *The Defense of Chalcedon in the East (451–553)* (Leiden).

—— (1988), 'Forgery as an Instrument of Progress: Reconstructing the Theological Tradition in the Sixth Century', *ByzZ* 81: 284–9.

—— (1989), '"The Select Fathers": Canonizing the Patristic Past', *StP*: 21–36.

—— (2006). *Leontius of Jerusalem, Against the Monophysites: Testimonies of the Saints and Aporiae*, ed. and trans. P.T.R. Gray (Oxford).

Gregorios, Paulos, Lazareth, W.H., and Nissiotis, N.A., eds. (1981), *Does Chalcedon Divide or Unite? Towards Convergence in Orthodox Christology* (Geneva).

Grillmeier, Aloys (1975), *Christ in Christian Tradition*, vol. 1, *From the Apostolic Age to Chalcedon (AD 451)*, 2nd edition (London).

—— (1979), *Jesus der Christus im Glauben der Kirche*, Band 1: *Von der Apostolischen Zeit bis zum Konzil von Chalcedon (451)*, 3rd edition (Freiburg).

—— (1987), *Christ in Christian Tradition*, vol. 2, *From the Council of Chalcedon (451) to Gregory the Great (590–604)*, Pt 1, *Reception and Contradiction: The development of the discussion about Chalcedon from 451 to the beginning of the reign of Justinian* (London).

—— (1995), *Christ in Christian Tradition*, vol. 2, *From the Council of Chalcedon*

(451) to Gregory the Great (590–604), Pt 2, *The Church in Constantinople in the Sixth Century* (London).

—— (1996), *Christ in Christian Tradition*, vol. 2, *From the Council of Chalcedon (451) to Gregory the Great (590–604)*, Pt 4, *The Church of Alexandria with Nubia and Ethiopia after 451* (London).

Hanson, R.P.C. (1988), *The Search for the Christian Doctrine of God: The Arian Controversy 318–381* (Edinburgh).

Honigmann, Ernest (1939), 'La liste originale des pères de Nicée', *Byz* 14: 17–76.

Kelly, J.N.D. (1972), *Early Christian Creeds*, 3rd edition (London).

L'Huillier, Peter (1996), *The Church of the Ancient Councils: The Disciplinary Work of the First Four Ecumenical Councils* (Crestwood, NY).

McGuckin, John (2004), *Saint Cyril of Alexandria and the Christological Controversy* (Crestwood, NY).

Meyendorff, John (1969), *Christ in Eastern Christian Thought* (Washington).

—— (1989), *Imperial Unity and Christian Divisions: The Church 450–680 AD* (Crestwood, NY).

Newman, J.H. (1845), *An Essay on the Development of Christian Doctrine* (London).

Norris, R.A. (1996), 'Chalcedon Revisited: A Historical and Theological Reflection', in Bradley Nassif, ed., *New Perspectives on Historical Theology: Essays in Memory of John Meyendorff* (Grand Rapids), 140–58.

Oort, J. van, and J. Roldanus, eds. (1997), *Chalkedon: Geschichte und Aktualität. Studien zur Rezeption der Christologischen Formel von Chalkedon* (Leuven).

Pelikan, Jaroslav (1971), *The Christian Tradition: A History of the Development of Doctrine*, vol. 1, *The Emergence of the Catholic Tradition (100–600)* (Chicago).

—— (2003), *Credo: Historical and Theological Guide to Creeds and Confessions of Faith in the Christian Tradition* (New Haven).

Person, R.E. (1978), *The Mode of Theological Decision Making at the Early Ecumenical Councils: An Inquiry into the Function of Scripture and Tradition at the Councils of Nicaea and Ephesus* (Basle).

Price, Richard and Gaddis, Michael (2005), *The Acts of Chalcedon*, 3 volumes, TTH 45 (Liverpool).

Ritter, A.M. (1965), *Das Konzil von Konstantinopel und sein Symbol* (Göttingen).

Russell, Norman (2003), '"Apostolic Man" and "Luminary of the Church": The Enduring Influence of Cyril of Alexandria', in T.G. Weinandy and D.A. Keating, eds., *The Theology of St Cyril of Alexandria: A Critical Appreciation* (London and New York), 237–57.

Samuel, V.C. (1977), *The Council of Chalcedon Re-examined: A Historical and Theological Survey* (Madras).

Sarkissian, Karekin (1965), *The Council of Chalcedon and the Armenian Church* (London).

Uthemann, K.-H. (2005), 'Zur Rezeption des Tomus Leonis in und nach Chalkedon' = id., *Christus, Kosmos, Diatribe: Themen der frühen Kirche als Beiträge zu einer historischen Theologie* (Berlin and New York), 1–36.

Wessel, Susan (2001), 'Literary Forgery and the Monothelete Controversy: Some Scrupulous Uses of Deception', *GRBS* 42: 201–20.

—— (2004), *Cyril of Alexandria and the Nestorian Controversy: The Making of a Saint and of a Heretic* (Oxford).

Wiles, Maurice (1993), 'A Textual Variant in the Creed of the Council of Nicaea', *StP* 26: 428–33.

Zizioulas, J.D. (1981), 'Ecclesiological Issues Inherent in the Relations between Eastern Chalcedonian and Oriental non-Chalcedonian Churches', in Gregorios and others (1981), 138–56.

'READING' THE FIRST COUNCIL OF EPHESUS (431)

Thomas Graumann

Acta conciliorum non leguntur – Nobody reads council acts. Eduard Schwartz's famous dictum[1] is slowly being overtaken by recent scholarly interest, no longer only of theologians and historians of the Church, but also of historians of late antiquity.[2] The fact that the first English translation of the Acts of Chalcedon appears in a series for historians is testimony to this development; it will surely spark many more studies into the riches of this material. With a distinctly historical rather than theological interest, new questions and scholarly perspectives open up. Yet, every examination must confront a number of difficulties of principle and of methodological and hermeneutical challenges arising from the character and the transmission of the body of conciliar records and documentation. In the case of the First Council of Ephesus and the acts associated with it, the complexity of the textual tradition, even more than the sheer volume of information, compounds this difficulty – so much so that their editor considered them to be more challenging in this respect than those of the Council of Chalcedon.[3] Council acts are highly complex, elaborate products. In the *Acta Conciliorum Oecumenicorum* seven (sub-) volumes of various Greek records and five of Latin translations and collections are concerned with the First Council of Ephesus.[4]

1 Schwartz (1927), 212.
2 André de Halleux (1993), 49–50, could still justifiably claim that the acts of the Council of Ephesus had not been scrutinized to any significant degree. The books of two eminent historians of antiquity may illustrate the new-found interest: Millar (2006); MacMullen (2006), for which see my review in *Zeitschrift für Antikes Christentum* 12 (2008), 172–4.
3 Schwartz (1956), 20.
4 It is important to note that E. Schwartz's edition counts all Acts of Ephesus as a single *Tomus*; consisting of a Greek and a Latin 'Volume'. The Greek 'Volume' is subdivided further into seven parts, the Latin into five; they total some 1800 pages. Further smaller collections outside the *ACO* and in other ancient languages could be listed; see Rücker (1935) and Kraatz (1904). A useful catalogue of the material is now available in Millar (2006), Appendix A; see also my brief sketch in Graumann (2002), 352–7. In general, Schwartz's prefaces, spread over the volumes of *ACO* and combined with several separate publications on the textual transmission of the collections, remain the indispensable basis for all further study (cf. amongst others Schwartz 1920 and 1934).

Their editor Eduard Schwartz's principal insight was that the collections in which we find them are what he called *publizistische Sammlungen*, that is to say collections with a propagandistic purpose, a 'spin' we might say in an age of modern media manipulation.[5] The historical context of any one collection and its intended usage determine and explain to a significant extent the choice and arrangement of documents, and in the case of Ephesus in particular helps to explain the growth of material around an original kernel of documentation. The most extensive, the *Collectio Vaticana*, in its final shape, comprises 172 items, including major works and many letters by Cyril and texts by several of his main allies. The collection's starting point was the original protocol of the first meeting of Cyril's council, created within ten days of the meeting. The already strongly pro-Cyrillian emphasis of this original protocol was further enhanced by the subsequent growth of the collection to include many more documents, mainly by Cyril. Only eventually, when the original confrontation was no longer of a practical concern, was some material in connection with the rival meetings of the Orientals added to it. Other collections tried to bring their own perspective to bear in similar ways, principally by adding documents and rearranging what they found. Hence, the collections of council acts and documents must not be mistaken for dispassionately presented information. This fundamental insight, to my mind, has not been applied sufficiently clearly to those initial kernels of records of the assembly in session, around which the ever-growing collections crystallised. In this connection the question also arises whether the documentation of council meetings presents us with an unbiased record of proceedings, with something akin to straightforward minutes, or whether these protocols follow a distinct agenda and propagandistic purpose of their own in a way similar to that of the later collections which Eduard Schwartz analysed. The question is of far-reaching consequence for our understanding of the historical events, and it may explain the patterns of their reception, which shaped the way in which the councils were remembered in later generations.

---

5 The insight is the basis for the entire edition and spelled out in many details in all the publications mentioned (see previous note). It is most concisely expressed in his 'Lebenslauf', which deserves to be quoted here: 'Man kann, muß sogar alle handschriftlichen Sammlungen von Konzilsakten als Publizistik auffassen. Das deutlichste Beispiel sind die ephesinischen Akten...' ['One can, indeed one must, regard all the manuscript collections of council acts as propaganda. The clearest example is that of the Acts of Ephesus...'] (Schwartz 1956, 13). See also Chrysos (1990).

For our analysis it is of course necessary to remember that the 'council' of Ephesus was effectively split in two: on the one hand the allies of Cyril of Alexandria, with whom the papal delegates later associated themselves, and on the other hand another group of bishops, essentially composed of prelates from the civil diocese of Oriens (hence usually the 'Orientals') who arrived belatedly and vehemently opposed the decisions presented by Cyril's side as a *fait accompli*. Over several weeks, Cyril's side convened formally at least six times, the Orientals in separate sessions at least twice. This split, and the acrimony between the opposing camps, provides the background against which the acts must be interpreted. Both sides also needed to present their case before the emperor. Cyril's first meeting in particular had to demonstrate how it could be considered a legitimate council despite convening before the arrival of the Orientals, and how the proceedings had met the requirements of a fair hearing set out in the imperial *sacra*, the letter of convocation. The latter aspect in particular informs the self-presentation of the 'Cyrillian council' in the acts. Accordingly, most attention will be devoted here to the meeting of bishops in association with Cyril of Alexandria on 22 June 431 that condemned Nestorius, then bishop of Constantinople, for heresy, and to those aspects of later meetings of the same group that shed light on the way they wanted this meeting to be understood.[6]

As a first approach to the complex problems of the records of these meetings, the following examination concentrates on 'reading' – reading *of* council acts and reading *in* council acts. These dimensions will turn out to be intimately linked.

The reading of council acts did not start with later collectors, let alone with modern scholarship, but commenced at the very councils we are concerned with. The Council of Chalcedon spent the entire first session

---

6   The meetings of Cyril's side are conventionally counted as at least six sessions (two (?) further meetings might be counted as sessions seven and eight; cf. CPG 8744, 8745). Following this reckoning, the meeting of 22 June is the first, that of 22 July the sixth session of the council. During this time the Orientals met in formal council on 26 and 29 June, and in all likelihood on a number of further occasions, from which no protocols survive. Traditional accounts of the history of the council – to which the cautionary notes of de Halleux 1993 (note 2) apply – can be found in Hefele/Leclerq (1908), 219–422; Kidd (1922), 218–53 (critical of the irregularities of Cyril's proceedings, but uncritical of the acts), and Camelot 1962. More recent but fairly condensed accounts are those of Fraisse-Coué (1995), esp. 517–42 and Perrone (1993), esp. 91–102.

reading and re-reading the protocols of earlier councils, namely that of the Second Council of Ephesus in 449 and indirectly also of the Home Synod of Constantinople in 448 and some of the acts of the First Council of Ephesus in 431 as read out at Ephesus in 449.[7] Richard Price's translation lucidly documents the complex layering of the various texts and readings and helps to distinguish the interjections and reactions of those attending. It is evident from the interjections that the reading of acts from earlier councils did not simply seek information about those occasions, but were deftly used to construct a case. They are our first indications of the modifying effects of 'reading' on the body of text thus scrutinised, and at the same time of the persuasiveness of such reading and its utility for the active, if subtle, manipulation of the course of the meeting in order to attain its desired result.

Some who had taken part in those meetings whose minutes were read feel misrepresented and claim to have been coerced into signing incomplete records or even blank sheets.[8] While some of their protests may simply reveal their anxiety to distance themselves from their involvement and responsibility in the face of a changed climate of ecclesiastical politics, the discussions nevertheless bring to the fore the question of the accuracy and reliability of the 'minuting'. In 449 two entire hearings at Constantinople sought to confirm or challenge the accuracy of the minuting of the trial of Eutyches before Bishop Flavian.[9] Much depended upon it as judicial consequences were severe. Reading the same texts afresh at the Second Council of Ephesus (449) was part of Eutyches' appeal against the verdict of the Home Synod which had condemned and deposed him. Accordingly much of the attention focused on possible evidence of misconduct and procedural flaws. At the same time the participants in the council of 449 looked for potentially heterodox opinions voiced in the context and applied, falsely, as standards against which Eutyches could be judged. The reading at Chalcedon, in turn, of the Acts of Ephesus II examined the legitimacy of that council, its proceedings and decisions. It seems inevitable that the distinct purpose of reading on any one occasion directed attention

7 See also the table in Price and Gaddis (2005), I, 113–14.
8 Take for example the debates at Chalcedon over alleged falsification of the minutes of the Home Synod, *Sessio prima* 865–73 and 877, Price and Gaddis, I, 272–3. The layering of readings, interjections, and interjections and readings within readings, can be traced throughout the first session, ibid., passim.
9 *ACO* II 1.1, pp. 148–76. Price and Gaddis, I, 28–9, 116–17 gives a brief account of the challenges to, and the examination of, the documentary record on this occasion.

towards some elements and in contrast more or less disregarded others.

Rather more technical problems related to this kind of 'reading', and the concomitant problem of note-taking and editorial managing of *acta* may also be instanced here, and applied to the task of interpreting occasions of 'reading' at Ephesus. The records presented as read in the first session of Chalcedon are so extensive that it seems implausible to assume a complete reading, even if the session was extraordinarily long.[10] Evidently, we have to expect editorial reworking of the minutes, in this case the insertion of the fuller records of earlier meetings at an editorial stage of the preparation of the *acta*. At the same time, some protocols of later meetings are so laconic that they can only be understood as abbreviated records, strictly limited to a summary of the outcome of the occasion and at times giving a few indications of the major contributory arguments or steps taken to arrive at it.[11] One deliberate and notable omission from the documents of Chalcedon is the first draft of the definition later promulgated in an altered form.[12] Here, evidently, the suppression of the earlier draft is not just a technical matter, but can only be interpreted as an effort to erase any trace of disputed notions, perhaps for fear of renewed future squabbling. The re-reading of council acts and related documents observed in the Acts of Chalcedon attests the complex genesis of such acts in general, and serves as a heuristic marker of the need to take seriously the purpose of their creation – and of any subsequent reading.

'Reading' and the initial acts of the session of 22 June

In looking more closely now at the *acta* of the so-called first session of the First Council of Ephesus, we can reconstruct the framework for the

---

10 *Acta* I. 942a refers to the lighting of the lamps; Price and Gaddis, I, 112 with n. 2, doubt the improbable length of the records and suggest several sections were possibly read in abbreviated form and later inserted in full during the editorial process. They consider parts of the Acts of Ephesus I a prime candidate for later addition.

11 Examples of this kind of abbreviated record in Ephesus I are the hearings of the case of Cypriot bishops, Coll. Ath. 81 (*ACO* 1.1.7; CPG 8744), and another of bishops of the province of Europa – that is the surroundings of Constantinople – Coll. Ath. 82 (CPG 8745; *ACO* 1.1.7, pp. 122–3); even shorter is the mere recording of a definition about Messalians, Coll. Ath. 80 (*ACO* 1.1.7, pp. 117–18). See in general Chrysos (1983).

12 Fifth Session 7–8, Price and Gaddis, II, 197, with the introductory remarks at 184–91.

original production of the basic record, and illuminate the central role of references to 'reading' in the composition of these *acta*.

From the correspondence of the council we know that the acts were probably sent to the emperor Theodosius by the end of June 431.[13] This leaves a span of approximately ten days for their preparation. One might consider this a relatively short period, given that the shorthand notations needed to be transcribed, while a copy for the emperor was usually carefully written on parchment and expensively fitted out. Nevertheless, ten days left many opportunities for editing and revising, and there was reason for it. As the synod of the Orientals had already met during the period, Cyril and his aides can have been in no doubt that they needed to convince the emperor of the legitimacy of their meeting in the face of severe protests. It is no surprise, then, that there is clear evidence for editorial 'improvement' of the acts. For example, it has been convincingly argued that some signed up to the deposition only during the following days. Not unusually, their signatures form part of the final edited version sent to Theodosius, added to those taken on the day as if recorded then.[14] This addition of further signatories, while politically important, does not impinge immediately upon the reliability of the records, but is a first indication that the direct record of the day was not necessarily considered the final expression of the 'real' achievement of the council. There are further indications of tampering not just with such lists, but also within the protocol of the day's events; these, crucially, underline the central importance of 'reading'. Claims in the acts that documents were read might have been the way in which editorial additions were camouflaged.

Yet reading was clearly a major part of the council's activity on the day. Nestorius' refusal to take part in what he saw as an illegitimate tribunal necessitated an inquiry by proxy of documents. So the reading and approval or rejection of documents was at the heart of the proceedings. The acts as we have them present us with the following sequence. The tumultuous opening of the session with the challenges to its legitimacy by the emperor's representative Count Candidianus and several bishops[15] is omitted – another obvious example of editorial trimming,

13 *Collectio Vaticana* 81,6 (*ACO* 1.1.3, p. 5, 21–2).
14 Crabbe (1981), with the criticism and additions in de Halleux (1993), 67–8.
15 Candidianus, *Contestatio*, and *Contestatio altera*: Collectio Casinensis 84–5 (*ACO* 1.4, pp. 31–3); cf. his account before the synod of the Orientals, Coll.Cas. 87 (*ACO* 1.4, pp. 86–7).

but one that is entirely to be expected. After the reports of the various delegations attempting to summon Nestorius, the bishops embarked on the agenda, conducting for the most part a tribunal *in absentia*. The Nicene Creed is read, followed by Cyril's Second Letter to Nestorius. The assembly is asked to adjudicate its orthodoxy measured against the Creed. The letter is endorsed by the votes of the bishops, 125 of which are quoted in the acts; then the protocol summarily claims the assent of the rest. The process is repeated with Nestorius' letter written in response to Cyril. It is read and rejected as heretical. This time far fewer individual votes are taken down, and the assembly resorts to the shouting of repeated anathemas against the abominations of his teachings.[16] Interestingly the final acclamation recorded leads back into an orderly procedure. It demands "Let the letter of the most holy bishop of Rome be read!"[17] The suggestion is immediately picked up by the council's leadership, and the proceedings move on with the reading of this and further documents. There can be little doubt that the bridging 'acclamation' was either carefully instrumented by the cheer-leaders on behest of the council's presidency, or – more likely – represents an editorial hinge, joining the first part of the proceedings, which comes to a conclusion with the condemnation of Nestorius' letter, to the second, which formalises this sentiment in view of the Roman decision of the previous year.

Except for the very end of the session, this is the last time that any reactions to events by participants are recorded. Partly for this reason interpreting what follows is very difficult. After this point the acts present us with the following sequence of documents and readings. First Pope Celestine's letter of summer 430 is read; it expresses a conditional condemnation of Nestorius, subject to his failing to recant within ten days of receiving the verdict. After that Cyril's Third Letter to Nestorius is read – no reaction is taken down. It is followed by the testimony of the bishops who delivered it to Nestorius in Constantinople in late November 430. Further witness statements from conversations in

---

16 *Gesta Ephesena*, Collectio Vaticana 33–48. For further proceedings after this point see n. 19. The protocol gives 35 individual *sententiae*, and sixteen acclamations afterwards. These acclamations can be understood as collective expressions of the views of the synod, providing essentially the remaining 'votes' by different means. For acclamations at synods and in public assemblies more widely, see MacMullen (2006), 12–23.

17 *ACO* 1.1.2, p. 36, 5–6.

Ephesus follow. Then extracts from orthodox fathers are read,[18] followed by extracts from various sermons and treatises by Nestorius – again without recorded reaction. Finally a letter from the bishop of Carthage is read, and only then is the verdict drafted, agreed and signed.[19]

If we start our inquiry into the reading of these texts with the last letter, we are immediately confronted with the problem of its purpose and the plausibility of its reading in the place indicated by the acts. Its placing seems extremely odd. In the letter, Bishop Capreolus of Carthage sends apologies for his inability to attend the council. He reports the situation in North Africa, which did not even allow him to convene a regional synod, let alone send an embassy to Ephesus: the Vandal occupation made any such enterprise hazardous.[20]

André de Halleux in his examination of the acts has argued that this letter must originally have featured at the beginning of the session, or even before it, when the presidency was trying to establish the range of attendance.[21] So the insertion of the letter at this late stage seems a clear example of editorial intervention – albeit (in his assessment) a rather

---

18 For this part of the protocol in particular, see Graumann (2002), 387–90, 398–400. I am convinced that these 'readings' represent editorial additions. The earliest reports by the council, to the emperor and the Pope, make no mention of such a reading (see Coll. Vat. 67, 81, 82, with the interpretation in Graumann 2002, 393–8). To establish their purpose the 'patristic' excerpts must be interpreted in conjunction with the following extracts from Nestorius. The arrangement carefully reproduces the similar juxtaposition of Cyril's and Nestorius' letters earlier, placing, in particular, textual evidence of 'orthodoxy' before heterodox statements. The supposed use of patristic texts in the meeting thus hinges on the plausibility of using Nestorian statements at this late stage (after his heterodoxy had been established in the sentences on his letter and after the applicability of Celestine's verdict has also been confirmed) as further accusations against him – which is their declared function according to the summary given after the 'reading' by the chief notary Peter and Bishop Flavian of Philippi, *Gesta* 60 (*ACO* 1.1.2, p. 52, 11). At this juncture, however, such accusations are out of place and have nothing to contribute to the trial of Nestorius. The insertion of patristic and contrasting Nestorian extracts, in my view, is an effort to show compliance with the imperial mandate for an open, substantial theological debate. The acts 'establish' the holding of a vicarious debate through the reading of contrasting extracts, necessitated by Nestorius' failure to attend the meeting.

19 *Gesta Ephesena*, Collectio Vaticana 49–62.

20 Capreolus of Carthage, Letter to the Synod = *Gesta* 61, *ACO* 1.1.2, pp. 52–3.

21 De Halleux (1993), 79, following Amann (1931), 114. Cf. Scipioni (1974), 219 and Festugière (1982), 244 n. 50. The same opinion is expressed, without discussion, in Millar (2006), 19.

mechanical and not very successful one. De Halleux has further noticed that at several junctures the reading of additional documents or proceeding to new agenda items is introduced by the same two people – Peter the chief-notary of the Alexandrian episcopal offices and Bishop Flavian of Philippi.[22] They alternate in proposing and seconding the reading of certain texts, and they attempt to summarise their import for the inquiry before moving on. It is of course possible that they acted in this way on the occasion,[23] but de Halleux's conjecture which finds in their interlinking remarks the work – and even the identities – of an editorial team is attractive.[24]

This, of course, is not to say that the documents introduced in this way were never read at all. The many hours of waiting for an answer from Nestorius, before his formal trial *in absentia* even began, left much time for it. Nevertheless, the sequence of documents in our acts owes much to the editorial skill of a team of redactors, and does not simply reflect the events of the day, however carefully they were choreographed by the Alexandrian presidency. In the ten days between the meeting and the sending of the acts to Theodosius, the supposedly mechanical process of producing the acts invited a perfecting of the council's achievement by means of a careful editing of the minutes. The redaction of the records could emphasise and clarify what the choreography of the day may already have tried to accomplish, or it could rework such choreography with the benefit of hindsight.

As a consequence, the acts need to be examined as the products of a deliberate editing process aimed at persuading a readership and contributing to the self-justification of the council, just as Eduard Schwartz has demonstrated in the case of the later collections.

The extent to which such a process could reshape the actual proceedings depended on the particular circumstances of any one council. At Ephesus the organisation of the meeting was firmly in the hands of the Alexandrian presidency, with Cyril's staff and aides. There was no significant opposition and no outside control by state officials or opponents; even the minuting we may safely assume to have been done exclusively by Alexandrian stenographers. What does this mean for the reading of documents on the occasion, and for our reading of the acts? Once we

22 De Halleux (1993), 78.
23 Similar roles can be identified at the Council of Chalcedon, see Price and Gaddis, I, 77.
24 De Halleux (1993), 78.

accept that the needs of self-promotion and apologetics inform the character of council records even at the initial stage of compilation, we have to analyse with care the sequence in which texts and documents occur, irrespective of whether we want to locate its origin in the design of the meeting or in the editorial process.

The reading of documents in their conciliar contexts

The most notorious problem with the use of documents on this occasion is, of course, the reading (if indeed it took place) of Cyril's famous Third Letter to Nestorius, concluding with the Twelve Chapters or Anathemas. Much ink has been spent on the question whether it was endorsed officially by the council as its Christological teaching.[25] If it was, did this endorsement include the anathemas as the most uncompromising expression of Cyril's position? As we noticed earlier, no reaction of the assembly to the purported reading of the letter is noted. From this alone it seems impossible to decide whether it was discussed or even read. The way in which the collections of the Acts of Ephesus are organised does not help with our problem. All relevant documents are placed at the head of the collection, before the proceedings. The minutes of proceedings, in turn, usually only quote the opening line by which to identify the document in question.[26] So, even if we take the information of the acts at face value as recording the actual proceedings, we cannot determine whether the anathemas were read with the letter. Nor do we know, here or in similar cases, exactly which version of the text of a document was

---

25 Best discussion by de Halleux (1992); he rejects the notion that the letter was even read.

26 For example *Gesta* 49 (*ACO* 1.1.2, p. 36, 22–5), Cyril's and the Alexandrian synod's letter to Nestorius: Τῶι εὐλαβεστάτωι καὶ θεοσεβεστάτωι συλλειτουργῶι Νεστορίωι Κύριλλος καὶ ἡ συνελθοῦσα σύνοδος ἐν Ἀλεξανδρείαι ἐκ τῆς Αἰγυπτιακῆς διοικήσεως ἐν κυρίωι χαίρειν. Τοῦ σωτῆρος ἡμῶν λέγοντος ἐναργῶς ὁ φιλῶν πατέρα ἢ μητέρα ὑπὲρ ἐμὲ οὐκ ἔστι μου ἄξιος καὶ τὰ λοιπά. [my emphasis]. The two recensions of the Collectio Seguierana (Codex Parisinus Coislinianus 32 and Codices Monacensis 115 and 116) reveal this arrangement even more clearly: καὶ ἀνεγνώσθη καθὼς προτέτακται, as do the codices of the Collectio Vaticana (Codex Vaticanus 830 and Codex Ambrosianus M 88, Codex Parisinus 416 and Monacensis 43) which read: ... καὶ τὰ λοιπά ὥσπερ προλάμπει; cf. Schwartz, p. 36, *apparatus ad loc.* The same formulas are used to indicate the reading of Celestine's letter to Nestorius, *Gesta* 49 (*ACO* 1.1.2, p. 36, 12–15 with *apparatus ad loc.*).

read. The separate placing of documents made it all too easy for later collectors and scribes to substitute a copy of a version of the document found elsewhere and considered preferable. So was the version of Cyril's letter read that of our critical editions, was it read in its entirety, and did this include the anathemas? We cannot be certain.

We can be certain, however, that this letter and those other documents played an important part in the self-presentation of the Cyrillian party before the emperor, and before a wider ecclesiastical audience. In other words, the rationale and the objectives of the edition of the published acts can be reconstructed with at least a measure of plausibility. And this task brings us back to the effects of the 'reading' of council acts and documents. The Council of Chalcedon demonstrates how the re-reading of earlier conciliar documents provides them with a new context and in so doing subtly modifies their original message. The same is true for the reading of documents at these councils. The context of the meeting provides a lens that focuses attention on some elements and obscures others. The principle is illustrated most easily from the undoubted readings in the first part of the day's proceedings.

At the meeting of 22 June 431 the effort to condemn Nestorius starts from the measuring of Cyril's and Nestorius' teaching against the Nicene Creed as the yardstick of orthodoxy. Recited immediately before Cyril's letter, the creed is still in the ears of those listening to the reading of the letter. In this perspective, and with the creed's wording fresh in the mind, Cyril's letter is perceived differently from its original context in the epistolary exchanges with Nestorius the year before. Cyril's letter is made to answer a specific question and takes on a new dimension.

Cyril quoted the creed near the opening of the letter; this would have been picked up immediately and gained added significance; for this fact on its own could now seem to be sufficient evidence for his adherence to the creed. The votes cast affirm just that without any substantive engagement with the disputed matters in hand or any detail of Cyril's exposition. The effect of this re-focussing of attention, brought about by the context of the reading, is even more pronounced in the case of Nestorius' letter. He too quotes the Nicene Creed, and his letter is as much an exposition of it as Cyril's. Yet after Cyril's orthodoxy had just been approved, his obvious opposition to, and contradiction of, Cyril's exposition put him immediately in the wrong, unless the bishops wanted to go back on their judgement about Cyril and revoke their agreement with him, solemnly professed only moments earlier. Again, there is no substantive engagement with Nestorius' teaching, and this should come as no surprise. The sequence of events had *de facto* changed the task of measuring Nestorius against the Nicene Creed into comparing his sentiments with Cyril's interpretation of it. Viewed through the prism of Cyril's approved orthodoxy, Nestorius' letter could only be rejected, and his interpretation of the Nicene Creed was not even considered seriously.

The historian of dogma, rightly, tends to examine the documents in question on their own merit, in order to assess the thinking of their authors. However, the historian of the councils needs to pay attention to the situational context determining their usage and reception, and wherever possible, to the change of audience that such a re-reading of texts entails.

Does this kind of reading of documents in the main trajectory, either of the council meeting or else of the publicised version of the acts, shed any light on the problem of Cyril's Third Letter or that of Capreolus? In Capreolus' case, the matter is surprisingly obvious. At the council it was not read out to make apology for the absence of the Carthaginian bishop at the early stage in the proceedings when the participants and the range of ecclesiastical representation were established. The reading of the letter at a much later time in the proceedings diverts the audience's attention away from this element and focuses it on an entirely different aspect of the letter. The subsequent statement of the president and the following reaction of the assembly demonstrate that the sequence of reading places the emphasis firmly on one central tenet, which the Carthaginian bishop had stated emphatically. Capreolus was evidently unaware of the substantive points of Christological teaching on the council's agenda; he therefore emphasised, in general terms and as a matter of principle – as people do if they do not know about the detail – the need to adhere fully and exclusively to tradition, and not to allow any novelty of teaching.[27] It is this sentiment that Cyril, the president, draws out in his brief summary of the letter[28] and that the acclamations of the assembly pick up: 'These are the words of us all! We all say this! This is the wish of us all!' they chant.[29] It is hardly a coincidence that this

27 *Gesta* 61 (*ACO* 1.1.2, p. 53, 12–21).
28 'Let the letter of the most-pious and most God-beloved Bishop of Carthage Capreolus also be inserted into the trust of the records, which has a clear meaning. For, he wants the old dogmas of the faith to be confirmed, but the new and inappropriate inventions and impious utterances to be rejected and thrown out' *Gesta* 61 (*ACO* 1.1.2, p. 54, 9–13).
29 *Gesta* 61 (*ACO* 1.1.2, p. 54, 14–15).

is the only time in the acts that we hear of the assembly's response to anything that has gone on before. The solemn emphasis on tradition chimes with Cyril's tactics to present himself as a humble follower in the footsteps of the fathers, thus 'walking on a royal road', and to portray Nestorius as the raging anti-traditionalist. Cyril's self-portrait and recourse to the fathers is present in both letters to Nestorius, and it is further emphasised by the quotation of patristic extracts in the council acts. The programmatic recourse to the Fathers and the self-styling in their image is another, largely concealed, thread linking together the various items of the agenda and of the documents employed to construct it.[30] By contrast, the collection of incriminating passages from Nestorius culminates in a brief statement in which he promises to remedy the deficiencies brought about by the teaching of his predecessors.[31] Cyril, and the council, take this to amount to a contemptuous repudiation of all tradition. The meeting's outrage over Nestorius' alleged anti-traditional stance, in itself an anti-heretical stereotype, is neatly summarised by Capreolus' stern warning. This, therefore, is the last word of the council before finalising the verdict of deposition. Rather than being misplaced, as de Halleux thought, the letter is at its most effective in provoking the desired reaction in the exact place where it was 'read'. Whether achieved through shrewd choreography at the meeting itself or astute editorial rearrangement, the sequence of documents fulfils its purpose perfectly.[32]

The knotty question of Cyril's Third Letter can, to my mind, at least

---

30 Cyril, *ep.* ad Nestorium II (= *ep.* 4), in particular *ep.* 4,2 (*ACO* 1.1.1, p. 26, 16–19) ; *ep.* ad Nestorium III (= *ep.* 17), the quotation at 17.3 (*ACO* 1.1.1, p. 35, 12–14); the 'patristic quotations' precede the extracts from Nestorius, *Gesta* 54 (*ACO* 1.1.2, pp. 39–45, with 26 quotations of 10 authors). For Cyril's strategy in evoking 'the fathers' see Graumann (2002), 278–419.

31 'I observe that our communities have got great devotion and most fervent piety but often slip up because of ignorance of the dogma about the knowledge of God. This is not a criticism of the people, but – how can I say it politely? – of the fact that your teachers do not have the time to provide you also with the more precise doctrines', *Gesta* 60, no. 25 (*ACO* 1.1.2, p. 52, 1–5). Peter, the chief notary, sums this statement up as follows: 'Look how openly he says in these [words] that of the teachers before him no-one said those things to the people which he said' *Gesta* 60 (*ACO* 1.1.2, p. 52, 6–8).

32 Vogt (1981), 94 also interprets the use of the letter in the place suggested by the acts as a certain sign of the careful arrangement of the agenda of the day. De Halleux accepts only Cyril's summarising remark as part of the meeting; in his interpretation, the editors of the acts used this remark to fit in the letter, which was read much earlier; see n. 22 above.

to some extent be resolved by a similar consideration. It follows the reading of Celestine's conditional condemnation, and is in turn followed by the testimony of the delegation of bishops delivering it to Nestorius. In their statements these clearly refer back to Celestine's letter, even grammatically; the observation led André de Halleux to claim that the decisive editorial intervention occurred precisely here with the insertion of this letter.[33] Strictly, the letter might indeed not be absolutely necessary in the context: its presence in the acts does improve, however, the stringency of the case against Nestorius. Celestine had left it to Cyril to enact the Roman verdict and the Egyptian synodal letter had an important role in the process; it spelled out what it was that Nestorius needed to recant to avoid the deposition threatened by Celestine. In November 430 the delegation sent to him from Egypt consequently delivered both letters, Celestine's and Cyril's Third Letter; the 'reading' in the acts reproduces this constellation. Any alleged editorial insertion only takes note of, and responds to, the implied argument in this sequence of events; it is therefore not entirely impossible, nor even implausible, that the letter should have been read for this purpose in the proceedings, even if the precise circumstances are obscured by evident editorial intervention. Crucially however, whether read or inserted editorially, in this sequence of documents and related procedural steps, its sole purpose is to testify to the correct passing on of Celestine's verdict to Nestorius, which starts the mechanism for his deposition.[34] Nestorius' failure to recant and, what is more, his repeated statement of incriminating ideas right up to the council, even during the weeks in Ephesus, is then established by the statements of witnesses.[35] These give sufficient grounds for Celestine's verdict to come into force. Juridically, this was of course not strictly accurate, since the convocation of the council explicitly suspended all previous decisions.[36] However, the council can portray its own verdict as merely acting upon the Roman decision, something Cyril was keen to emphasise in face of the foreseeable challenges to the legitimacy of his actions.

In this sense, the letter finds a convincing purpose in the meeting as

---

33 De Halleux (1992), 447–8. My reconstruction of the editorial agenda underlying this insertion differs from de Halleux; see Graumann (2002), 387–409.

34 In his introduction to the letter Wickham (1983), xxxvii, arrives at essentially the same solution.

35 *Gesta* 50–3 (*ACO* 1.1.2, pp. 37–8).

36 Theodosius, *sacra* (*ACO* 1.1.1, p. 115, 31–2)

well as in the published acts. Cyril may also have felt that the theology of the letter had been endorsed at the same time – or wanted to convey this perception in the days after the meeting. The Oriental bishops certainly took its insertion in the acts to amount to an endorsement. Their intention had been to challenge Cyril precisely over this document, so they were understandably suspicious of any apparently positive mention of it.[37] However, in the process leading to Nestorius' deposition, the acknowledgement of the theology of the letter or the anathemas was not even an issue. To this end, it was of no consequence.

Subsequent 'readings' of the initial protocol

The editorial composition of the protocol of this session of 22 June, by its references to real or pretended 'reading', anticipated the varied interests of potential readerships; it can be demonstrated to have achieved a fair degree of success.

Cyril's presentation of his case certainly had the desired effect upon the Roman legates. On their belated arrival, they requested to be informed of the council's activities and were presented, on 10 July, with the records of the meeting deposing Nestorius. They read them in private, and they were read again publicly and officially endorsed in session on the next day. Pope Celestine's envoys were manifestly relieved and satisfied with the way in which the council had followed and reinforced the Roman verdict – just what Cyril had wanted to demonstrate. Their reading of the acts, the first in a long series, singled out and underscored what was already one main emphasis in the composition of the earliest, Cyrillian version of the protocol, namely that the condemnation of Nestorius was completely consonant with the Roman decision.[38]

While the Roman embassy read the acts as the confirmation of

---

37 For the attacks on the anathemas by a number of theologians in the 'Antiochene' camp, see Mahé (1906). Their ongoing protestations at Ephesus are evident from Collectio Vaticana 151 (*ACO* 1.1.5, pp. 121–2), 153 (pp. 124–5), 154 (p. 125), 157 (p. 129).

38 *Acta* of July 10 and 11, Collectio Vaticana 106, *ACO* 1.1.3, pp. 53–63. This dimension of the acts of 22 June is also present in Capreolus' letter, who refers contentious questions to the 'authority of the Apostolic See', *Gesta* 61 (*ACO* 1.1.2, p. 53, 19–20; cf. 22–24), yet another link in the mesh of documents woven by the acts.

Rome's authority and theological judgement, the council, in a further meeting on 22 July, highlighted yet another dimension of their previous decision. It used the case brought by a presbyter who had complained that agents of Nestorius at Philadelphia had used an unauthorized creed in the reception of Quartodecimans, as a convenient opportunity to look back on the meeting of 22 June. The selective 'reading'[39] – or, in my view more probably, the editorial re-composition – of parts of the protocol of that occasion now supplied the explicit theological rationale for the argumentation against Nestorius which had been missing or was at best implicit in the earlier meeting. In the new presentation, the testimonies of fathers are repositioned to follow immediately the Nicene Creed. In consequence the doctrinal norms and authorities are spelled out with great conceptual clarity: the Nicene Creed is the irrevocable and sufficient expression of faith; as such it is the norm of doctrinal judgment; however, the patristic citations provide the necessary interpretation of the creed, protecting it against a merely formulaic acceptance without a real commitment to its 'proper' meaning. The case of the Quartodecimans then heard reveals Nestorius' breach of this standard, which the council eventually decides to condemn formally. In my contention these decisive moves are well-planned editorial interventions, rather than real cases of 'reading out'.[40] But in any case, the revisiting after four weeks of the acts of the earlier meeting reconstructs the sequence of documents and by this measure alters the perception of that meeting in such a way that the theological rather than the personal dimension of Nestorius' deposition is presented as the real achievement of the council. The Councils of Ephesus II and later Chalcedon read these passages alone rather than the original deposition of Nestorius. It shows how a specific interest in the construction of legitimate theological argument, and the concomitant demarcation of its limits, had become the dominant perspective on the council, and was as such a useful tool in building a case on those later occasions. Here the council's new self-presentation, achieved through reading and editing, proved effective with later readers; later reading, in turn, determined for the foreseeable future the dominant assessment of the council's outcome and importance.

---

39 So Price and Gaddis, I, p. 300, nn. 347 and 349, by analogy, one suspects, to the way in which such reading was conducted at Chalcedon and Ephesus II.

40 See Graumann (2002), 400–9. My hypothesis is now confirmed by the independent study of Abramowski (2004).

Conclusion

Reading has been shown to be a major activity of the councils of the time – both the reading of individual documents and the reading of entire sets of acts. The revisiting of texts in this way amounted to their re-contextualisation, in such a way as to shape distinct expectations in the readership, creating heightened attention to some elements in the documents and a corresponding neglect of others. The skilful presentation of documents in published acts purposely sought to create this effect for a secondary audience, an audience of the wider Church and – most importantly – the emperor and his court. It is here that we find expression of the ultimate objective of a council, which has to guide us in our criticism and interpretation. For the historian, attention to the thin thread of often skilfully concealed arguments, insinuated with the help of documents, is paramount in interpreting the dynamics of council meetings. In this way any modern 'reading' and interpretation of council acts and documents has to take seriously their production and use as instruments of propaganda and self-promotion.

BIBLIOGRAPHY

Abramowski, Luise (2004), 'Die Sitzung des Konzils von Ephesus am 22. Juli 431, „Über die Befestigung des Symbols von Nizäa und über den vom Presbyter Charisius übergebenen Libellus"', *ZKG* 115: 382–90.

Amann, Émile (1931), 'Nestorius', *DTC* 11: 76–156.

Camelot, P.-Th. (1962), *Histoire des conciles oecuméniques 2: Ephèse et Chalcédoine* (Paris).

Chrysos, Evangelos (1983), 'Konzilsakten und Konzilsprotokolle vom 4. bis 7. Jahrhundert', *AHC* 15: 30–40.

—— (1990), 'The Synodical Acts as Literary Products', in *L'icône dans la théologie et l'art*, Les études de Chambésy 9 (Chambésy), 85–93.

Crabbe, Anna (1981),'The Invitation List to the Council of Ephesus and Metropolitan Hierarchy in the Fifth Century', *JTS* 32: 369–400.

De Halleux, André (1992), 'Les douze chapitres cyrilliens au Concile d'Éphèse (430–433)', *RThL* 23: 425–58.

—— (1993) 'La première session du concile d' Éphèse (22 Juin 431)', *EThL* 69: 48–87.

Festugière, A.J. (1982). *Ephèse et Chalcédoine. Actes des Conciles,* trans. by A.J. Festugière (Paris).

Fraisse-Coué, Christiane (1995),'Le débat théologique au temps de Théodose

II: Nestorius', in Charles and Luce Pietri, eds, *Histoire du Christianisme des origines à nos jours*, vol. 2: *Naissance d'une chrétienté (250–430)* (Paris), 499–550.

Graumann, Thomas (2002), *Die Kirche der Väter. Vätertheologie und Väterbeweis in den Kirchen des Ostens bis zum Konzil von Ephesus (431)*, Beiträge zur Historischen Theologie, 118 (Tübingen).

Hefele, C.J. and Leclerq, H. (1908), *Histoire des Conciles d'après les documents originaux*, vol. II.1 (Paris)

Kidd, B. J. (1922), *A History of the Church to AD 461*, vol. III (Oxford).

Kraatz, Wilhelm (1904), *Koptische Akten zum ephesinischen Konzil vom Jahr 431* (TU 26.2), (Leipzig).

MacMullen, Ramsay (2006), *Voting about God in Early Church Councils* (New Haven & London).

Mahé, Joseph (1906), 'Les Anathématismes de S. Cyrille d'Alexandrie et les évêques orientaux du patriarchat d'Antioche', *RHE* 7: 505–43.

Millar, Fergus (2006), *A Greek Roman Empire: Power and Belief under Theodosius II (408–450)* (Berkeley).

Perrone, Lorenzo (1993), 'Da Nicea (325) a Calcedonia (451)', in G. Alberigo (ed.), *Storia dei concili ecumenici*, 2nd edition (Brescia), 11–118.

Price, Richard and Gaddis, Michael (2005), *The Acts of the Council of Chalcedon*, 3 vols, TTH 45 (Liverpool).

Rücker, Ignaz (1935) *Ephesinische Konzilsakten in syrischer Überlieferung* (Oxenbronn).

Schwartz, Eduard (1920), *Neue Aktenstücke zum ephesinischen Konzil von 431* (ABAW.PPH 30,8).

—— (1927), 'Die Kaiserin Pulcheria auf der Synode von Chalkedon', *Festgabe für A. Jülicher* (Tübingen), 203–212.

—— (1934), *Publizistische Sammlungen zum Acacianischen Schisma* ABAW.PH 10.

—— (1956), 'Wissenschaftlicher Lebenslauf', *Gesammelte Schriften*, vol. 2 (Berlin), 1–21.

Scipioni, L.I. (1974), *Nestorio e il concilio di Efeso, Storia dogma critica* (Milano).

Vogt, H. J. (1981), 'Das gespaltene Konzil von Ephesus und der Glaube an den einen Christus', *Trierer Theologische Zeitschrift* 90: 89–105.

Wickham, Lionel, ed. and trans. (1983), *Cyril of Alexandria, Select letters* (Oxford).

THE SYRIAC ACTS OF THE SECOND COUNCIL OF EPHESUS (449)

Fergus Millar

Introduction

The Second Council of Ephesus and the Council of Chalcedon, called two years later, are inextricably linked, by their historical context, in their theological conclusions (in that the one was called with the deliberate intention of annulling measures taken at the other, and of having a new definition of faith adopted), and in the manuscript tradition through which the record of most of their proceedings is preserved. The Council of Ephesus, called by Theodosius II when, as it turned out by accident, his reign had little more than a year to run, represented an emphatic victory for the 'miaphysite' (one-nature) tendency in the Greek Church. The presidency was given to Dioscorus, bishop of Alexandria; Theodoret, as the most prominent remaining proponent of a 'dyophysite' (two-nature) Christology not in exile, was excluded; and the first session, held on 8 August 449, rehearsed in immense detail the record of proceedings against the extreme-miaphysite archimandrite Eutyches in the autumn of 448, and of hearings called to hear disputes over that record earlier in 449, before absolving Eutyches, and declaring the deposition of Flavian, bishop of Constantinople.

It is the quotation in the acts of the first session at Chalcedon, called by the new emperor Marcian, of this part of the proceedings, incorporating verbatim re-quotations of the records of the hearings held between autumn 448 and spring 449, that preserves for us the record in Greek of the first session at Ephesus, ending with the written affirmations ('subscriptions' – ὑπογραφαί) of 140 participants. It may be worth noting here that there would now be no difficulty in extracting these quotations, in the original Greek from Schwartz' great edition (*ACO* II.1), and in English from the acts edited by Price and Gaddis, to produce an integrated edition, with facing English translation, of the whole surviving acts of the first session at Ephesus.

However, since this paper will essentially be concerned with the published Syriac text of subsequent proceedings at Ephesus, it should be noted that there is in fact a continuous text (i.e. one not quoted in sections in the proceedings of a later council) of the first session of Ephesus II, namely in a Syriac MS formerly in the British Museum and now in the British Library (*BM Add.* 12,156). According to the entry in the great catalogue by Wright 1871, no. DCCXXIX, these acts are included along with a large number of theological works in a sixth-century codex 'in a fine Edessene hand', written before CE 562. It appears to be a complete record of the proceedings, with quotation of relevant documents, but omitting the usual lists of participants at the beginning and of their 'subscriptions' at the end. It seems therefore to be approximately contemporary with the codex which is the main subject of this paper, and it is astonishing to find that it has never been printed (or still less commented on), and that the only published presentation of it is the English translation offered by Perry (1881), 401–36. A modern introduction, text, translation and commentary is surely overdue.

In the absence of any printed text, this paper can take the question of this early Syriac version no further, but will turn instead to another sixth-century version of proceedings at Ephesus II, which has a complex relationship to the record of some of the later sessions at Chalcedon. For, as we will see, some of these sessions at Chalcedon had the specific purpose of reviewing – and reversing – other decisions reached at Ephesus. In particular, Sessions VIII–X (following the Latin numbering; IX–XI in the Greek), held on 26–27 October 451, reviewed the cases of Theodoret of Cyrrhus, Sophronius of Tella, John of Germanicia, Amphilochius of Side and – most relevant of all – Ibas of Edessa, several of whom had been condemned at Ephesus (see below). But the acts of these sessions at Chalcedon, as recorded in Greek and subsequently in Latin translation, though they incorporate quotations of some earlier documents and records of proceedings, do not include any verbatim quotations of the proceedings at Ephesus two years earlier.

That is therefore the first of many different reasons why it is of exceptional importance that a record of the proceedings at Ephesus at a session subsequent to the first one is preserved in Syriac translation. The second is that the manuscript in question, a codex now held in the British Library (*BM Add.* 14, 530), was written at a monastery near Apamea in CE 535, less than a century after the events in question. Like the codex mentioned above, it is thus, first, centuries earlier than any of the other relevant MSS (i.e. those of Chalcedon), all of which belong (at best) to the high medieval period. As such, it therefore also has a place in a major historical question which will be no more than hinted at here, the evolution of Syriac as language of Christian culture, and its complex relation to Greek.[1] More specifically, it has a place in the chronological and spatial record of the public writing of Syriac (see below); and, more specifically still, it can be located within the truly remarkable series of Syriac codices dated from the beginning of the fifth century to the end of the sixth (see also below). The writing and copying of Syriac codices of course represents a continuous tradition lasting into the modern era. But for our purposes the known examples from the fifth–sixth centuries, all written in the 'rounded' Estrangela script, normal in the pre-Islamic period, will be sufficient.

The date at which this record of proceedings (or, to be more precise, this series of extracts from proceedings) was written in Syriac, CE 535, is also highly significant in itself, as it derives from the earlier period of Justinian's reign, in which the emperor was making every effort to reach agreement with the proponents of a miaphysite theology – only (as we will see below) to abandon this effort a year later, in 536, and to have the key figures condemned by a synod in Constantinople. The Syriac extracts represent two essential aspects of the miaphysite outlook of the 530s; a record of proceedings against some prominent dyophysite bishops from Syria and Osrhoene who had been condemned and deposed at Ephesus; and, with that, a recall of what had turned out to be a brief moment of triumph for the miaphysite side under Theodosius II, only for the cause to be betrayed, as they saw it, by Marcian.

Thus, though what the codex contains is strongly biased towards local issues and personalities, in Edessa above all, and though it is written in a Semitic language and script which had only quite recently acquired an established role in the Near Eastern Church, the proceedings of which it is a record had taken place in the heart of the Greek world, on the coast of the Aegean, and had originally been recorded in Greek.

This is not the place to discuss the very complex question of how and by whom a record, or a set of competing records, of the proceedings at Ephesus had first been generated in Greek, and then entered into circulation.[2] Suffice to say that there were disputes at Ephesus about the

---

1 For some recent approaches to this issue see Brock (1984), (1990), (1992); Millar (1998); (2006), 107–116; Taylor (2002).
2 For some discussion of the generation and character of the Acts of Ephesus, the subject of impassioned debate at Chalcedon, see Millar (2006), App. I–II.

validity of the records of earlier proceedings, and then at Chalcedon as to the record of Ephesus itself (which reveal that several rival records were being made simultaneously), showing that there never was a single agreed, or official, version. Even without allowing for the acutely controversial and partial character of the record-taking, the processes of generating written texts of oral exchanges which also involved quotation of earlier records, or of relevant theological texts, or of letters from emperors or officials, indicate that any such record was inevitably a construct, involving both editorial choices (When to abbreviate or summarize? What do to with interventions in languages – Latin, Syriac or Coptic – other than Greek?), and 'political' or theological structuring.

None the less, it is clear that very detailed records of the proceedings at fifth-century councils, including also the First Council of Ephesus of 431, were composed and circulated, and that the versions represented by high-medieval Greek MSS and by the equally high-medieval MSS containing Latin translations, of which the earliest are directly contemporary ones, while they do of course reveal significant variations (for instance in the numbering of sessions at Chalcedon), do actually produce, as the sterling work of Price and Gaddis shows, a record which is, if anything, surprisingly consistent and reliable. What is perhaps even more significant, a record of the Acts of Ephesus II which is consistent with what can be found in medieval MSS was available to Nestorius, in exile in the Great Oasis from late 431 to his death in the early 450s, and could be used by him for the composition of his acutely polemical work of self-justification, *The Book* (or *Bazaar) of Heraclides*, written in Greek, but known only from a Syriac translation (very probably with some editing, and also some addition of material), which also seems to have been made in the sixth century. Equally, at the end of the same century, Evagrius, in his *Ecclesiastical History*, was able to make very extensive and detailed use of the Greek Acts of Chalcedon.[3]

The vast and varied manuscript evidence, in which Latin versions play a very important part, would certainly allow for further detailed work on the composition of the original text – or rival texts – of the proceedings of Ephesus I and II and of Chalcedon, on the making of derivative copies, or partial copies, and then on circulation and availability. The manuscript tradition is also complicated by the fact that they incorpo-

3 See esp. the excellent introduction, translation and notes on Evagrius, by Michael Whitby (Liverpool, 2000). The most detailed use of the Acts of Chalcedon is made in the long epitome at the end of the second book (II. 18).

rate as well collections of relevant documents which are not in themselves reports of proceedings, but which were put together by contemporaries, and then attached to the acts proper.

As will be seen below, the Syriac codex of CE 535 is clearly a selection, designed to a particular end; but, for the reasons just stated, we have no means of knowing what Greek version lay behind it. Strictly speaking also, what the scribe who records his writing of the text claims is precisely that. His personal hand-written affirmation ('he has striven and produced this book'), which can be seen on the plate (overleaf), reproducing most of folio 108a of the codex, *may* imply that he was also responsible for the translation from Greek. But he does not say so, and it is perfectly possible that the Syriac translation was already in circulation. None the less this codex should be considered first in terms of its place in the history of public writing in Syriac.

The Syriac Codex and Writing in Syriac

In considering the remarkable rise of Syriac to the status of an established language of Christian culture, time and place are vital, above all if we are to avoid the confusion arising from thinking of the language and script which we call 'Syriac' as having been native to the Roman province of Syria. On the contrary, the evidence shows quite clearly that the area where Syriac had first come into use – on inscriptions, mosaic inscriptions and in official or legal documents – lay east of the Euphrates, in Mesopotamia and Osrhoene, a minor kingdom which became a Roman province in the third century.[4] It was here also that Bardesanes, the main speaker in (and probably author of) the early third-century Syriac work *The Book of the Laws of Countries*, had lived and written. Syriac is known to have been in use as a literary language also further east, in what became the Roman province of Mesopotamia with its main city (until its loss to the Persians in 363) Nisibis, where Ephraem, acknowledged as the greatest Syriac author, wrote before moving to Edessa. The language was used also further east still, in Sasanid Persian territory, where Aphraat wrote in the first half of the fourth century. There is, however, no documentary or manuscript evidence for the writing of Syriac in this area in this early period. But that is an accident of our evidence, and there is no reason to question the currency of Syriac

---

4 For a masterly introduction to the whole field see now Brock (2006).

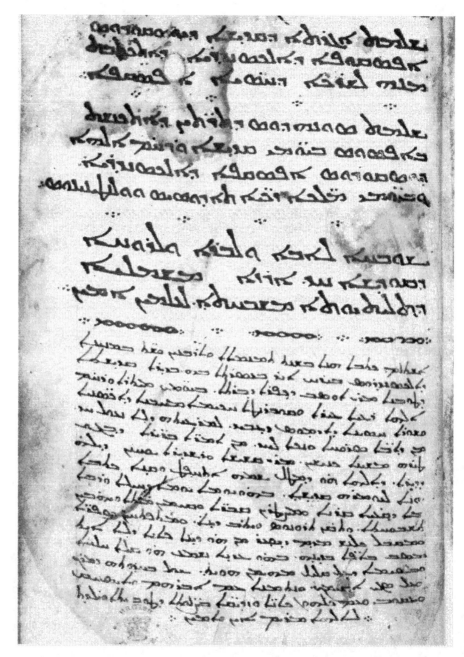

BM Add 14, 530, p. 108a. The formal conclusion of the Acts written in CE 535, with the first of two personal affirmations by the scribe. Reproduced by kind permission of the British Library. © *British Library Board. All Rights Reserved*

on either side of the Roman/Persian frontier. For a history of Syriac *writing*, however, we depend on material which comes, first, from Osrhoene and which then spreads west across the Euphrates to Syria proper: inscriptions (beginning in the first century and continuing), mosaic inscriptions, parchments (known only from the third century), and finally manuscripts, from the early fifth century onwards.

The available information is set out schematically here in two tables. The first traces the progressive appearance of Syriac in dated inscriptions on stone or mosaic known to come from west of the Euphrates, from the late fourth century to the end of the sixth.[5] Modest as the statistical basis is, the evidence makes clear that in this area the presence of written Syriac in public contexts developed only slowly, and was well established only in the sixth century.

(a) Dated Syriac inscriptions of the fourth to sixth centuries from west of the Euphrates

AAES = Littmann, Enno (1904), *Publications of an American Archaeological Expedition to Syria in 1899–1900. IV. Semitic Inscriptions,* Pt. I. *Syriac Inscriptions*
IGLS = *Inscriptions Grecques et Latines de la Syrie*
Pognon, *Inscriptions* = Pognon, Henri (1907), *Inscriptions sémitiques de la Syrie, de la Mésopotamie et de la région de Mossoul*
PUAES = Littmann, Enno (1934), *Publications of the Princeton University Archaeological Expeditions to Syria in 1904–5 and 1909. IV. Semitic Inscriptions,* Section B. *Syriac Inscriptions*

389	*IGLS* II.555	Babisqa. Bilingual. Names (one transliterated Greek name)
434	*PUAES* IV.B, 4	Dar Qita. Bilingual.
441/2	*PUAES* IV.B, 11	Qasr Iblisu. Construction of baptistery
456/7	*IGLS* II, 373 = *Ann. Isl.* 9, 1970, 190	Borj el Kas. Bilingual. Acclamations
473/4	*IGLS* II, 553	Khirbet el Khatib. Bilingual. Construction of church
491–6	*PUAES* IV.B, 50 = Pognon, *Inscriptions,* no. 21 (p. 60)	Basufan (near Qalaat Seman). Construction of church

5 Compare now the excellent paper by Sebastian Brock (2009), 'Edessene Syriac Inscriptions in Late Antique Syria', which also incorporates an integrated list of dated inscriptions and mss. Note that the list offered here relies on published texts, and is confined to the area west of the Euphrates.

500	P. Donceel–Voûte, *Les pavements des églises*, p. 192	Umm Hartain, near Hama. Church mosaic, with dated Greek inscription. Two Syriac words
501/2	*PUAES* IV.B, 57	Surqanya. Lintel of house
507/8	*AAES* IV, 6 = Pognon, *Inscriptions*, nos. 81–2 (p. 143)	Khirbet Khasan. Church
512	*IGLS* II, 310	Zebed. Trilingual. (Greek, Syriac, Arabic). Establishment of martyrion
513	*PUAES* IV.B, 23	Fidreh. Lintel of baptistery
515/16	*Orientalia* 64 (1995), p. 110	Ma ar-zayta. Church (?) mosaic
525/6	*PUAES* IV.B, 52	Kefr Nabu. Chapel
532	*PUAES* IV.B, 24	Fidreh. House
533	*PUAES* IV.B, 8	Khirbet el Khatib. Baptistery
539/40	*PUAES* IV.B, 58	Surqanya. Lintel of house
543/4 or 550/1	*PUAES* IV.B, 54	Kalota. House
545/6(?)	*PUAES* IV.B, 55	Kalota. House
546?	*AAES* IV, 10	Baqirha. Church
547	*AAES* IV, 14; 15	Babisqa. Stoa
547/8	*MUSJ* 16 (1932), p. 105	Harba'ara. Church
551/2?	*PUAES* IV.B, 2	Abu'l Kudur. House?
563/4	*IGLS* II, 317 = R. Mouterde, *Limes* (1945) 325, no. 10	Rasm al Hajal, Palmyrene. Construction of church
574/5	*MUSJ* 25 (1942/3), 81	Gebel Bil'as. Construction at monastery
577/8	*PUAES* IV.B, 26	Der Siman. Construction of house
578/9	*PUAES* IV.B, 27	Der Siman. Construction of house
579/80	Mouterde, 224, no. 7	Gneyd. Construction of church
593/4	*Syria* 10 (1929), p. 255	Bennaoui. Construction of church
593/4	Pognon, *Inscriptions*, no. 19 (p. 55)	Stablat, Jebel el Hass. Construction of church

(b) Dated Syriac manuscripts of the fifth to sixth centuries

The following table is based on slightly different principles, and for the most part simply summarizes the content of the magnificent *Album* produced by W.H.P. Hatch, and recently re-issued. It covers all those Syriac manuscripts which are explicitly dated within the fifth and sixth centuries, whether from east or west of the Euphrates. Obviously, experts will attribute many other manuscripts written in the Estrangela

script of the pre-Islamic period to these centuries, on the basis of script
or content. But the explicitly dated ones will serve as a framework, and
to quite a remarkable degree they confirm the pattern indicated by the
inscriptions: there are a few examples from the fifth century, but by far
the majority comes from the sixth. In many, but not all, cases the place
of writing is indicated, and these indications too illustrate a pattern by
which the 'homeland' of manuscript writing lies east of the Euphrates,
but by the sixth century production is also common in the Syrian area,
west of the Euphrates (I ignore here details of the late Roman subdivided provinces).

Wright, W. (1870–2), *Catalogue of the Syriac Manuscripts in the British Museum
acquired since 1838* I–III
Mango, M.M. (1982), 'Patrons and Scribes indicated in Syriac Manuscripts, 411
to 800 AD', *Jahrb. der Öst. Byzantinistik* 32.4, 3–12
—— (1991), 'The Production of Syriac Manuscripts 400–700 AD', in Gugliemo
Cavallo, Giuseppe De Gregorio, and Marilena Maniaci (eds.), *Scritture, libri
e testi nelle aree provinciali di Bisanzio* (Spoleto) I: 161–79 and Pl. I–IX.
Hatch, W.H.P. (1946; ²2002), *An Album of Dated Syriac Manuscripts* (1946;
reissued with Foreword by L. Van Rompay, Gorgias Press):

Number in Hatch, *Album*	Date	Place of writing (if indicated)	Contents
I	411	Edessa	Greek theological works in translation
II	459/60		Isaiah 16–17
III	462		Eusebius, *Ecclesiastical History*
IV	463/4	Amida	Genesis, Exodus
V	473	Dated by era of Antioch	*Life of Symeon Stylites*
VI	474	Edessa	Aphraat, *Hom.* I–X
VII	509	Pa'nun	Basil, *On the Holy Spirit*
VIII	510/11	Mabbug/ Hierapolis	Philoxenus of Mabbug, *Commentary on Matthew and Luke*
IX	512		Aphraat, *Hom.* XIII–XXII
X	518	Dated by era of Apamea	Ephraem, *Hymns*
XI	522		Ephraem, *Hymns*
XII	528	Edessa	Trans. of Greek theological works
XIII	528/9– 537/8		Gospels of Luke and John

XIV	532		Daniel
XV	532	Dated by era of Bostra	*Historia Monachorum*
XVI	533/4	Edessa	Pauline Epistles
XVII	534		Palladius, *Historia Lausiaca*
XVIII	535	KPR' DBRT' (near Apamea)	Acts of Council of Ephesus
XIX	540/1	Edessa	Ezekiel
BM Add. 14,431			Samuel I–II
= Wright (1870), no. XXII			
XX	548	Edessa	Four Gospels
XXI	550/1		Trans. of Greek theological works
XXII	552	Sarmin	Ephraem, *Hymns*
XXIII	553	Edessa	Cyril of Alexandria, *On Worship* IX–XII
XXIV	557		John Chrysostom, *Commentary on Matthew's Gospel*
XXV	563	Nairab	Severus of Antioch, *Homiliae Cathedrales*
XXVI	564		Philoxenus of Mabbug, *On the Trinity*
XXVII	564	Edessa?	Athanasius, *On the Incarnation*; Timothy, *Homily*
XXVIII	565	Edessa	Jacob of Sarug, *Metrical Discourses*
XXIX	569	Dated by era of Antioch	Severus of Antioch, *Homiliae Cathedrales*
XXX	569	Sarmin	Greek theological works
XXXI	581		John of Lycopolis, selected works
XXXII	581		Philoxenus of Mabbug, *Discourses*
XXXIII	584	Monastery of Gubba Barraya	John Chrysostom, *Commentary on 1 Corinthians*
XXXIV	586	Monastery of Beth-Zagba	Four Gospels [illuminated ms: facsimile ed. by C. Cechelli, I. Furlani and M. Salmi, *The Rabbula Gospels* (1959)]
XXXV	593		John Chrysostom, *Commentary on Thessalonians*
XXXVI	598/9		Joshua

As will be seen, the place of the codex of 535 has been highlighted, to indicate as clearly as possible the way in which it falls firmly within the period of established codex-composition in Syriac. Strictly speaking, the scribe, when he comes to mention the place of writing and to describe his own role and services, does not mention any city which would allow us to establish a location east or west of the Euphrates. But in fact KPR' DBRT' can be identified as a monastery near Apamea in Syria (now the metropolis of Syria Secunda), which establishes this codex as one of a minority of examples of 'western' scribal activity.[6]

It should be noted that in the page reproduced (designed to bring out the contrast between the large, formal script of the Acts and the smaller and more casual writing marking the scribe's own personal affirmation) he does not identify himself or his origins. But in the second affirmation on the next page (108b) he does so: 'I... Iohanan from the *chora* (KWR') of Antiochia, resident with Mar Eusebius of Kapra dBarta, wrote this text.' In the light of the lists of inscriptions and codices given above, the proof that a monk born in the territory of Antioch in the later fifth or early sixth century could write a long text in Syriac is quite significant.

We will come later to the content of the acts contained in the codex, but this is the place to set out a translation of the page (108a) reproduced in the Plate, in which the scribe first concludes the record of the proceedings with three brief and formal paragraphs before turning, in a smaller and less monumental script, to the first of his two rather moving personal affirmations. Of the three paragraphs, the first refers to a letter of Dioscorus, bishop of Alexandria, and the second to the conclusion of the council, while the third extols the Trinity. So far as possible, the text which follows reproduces the layout and letter-size of the original.

The translation is as literal as possible, in order to maintain the parallelism with the Syriac text as reproduced on the Plate (which should be clear enough for readers of Syriac).[7]

---

6 I am grateful to David Taylor for the information that this is a well-known monastery, of some significance situated near the modern villages of Kefr and Bara, north-west of Apamea. The archimandrite Ioannes, who is described by the scribe as an 'adamantine defensive rampart' against wolves (see below), commissioned the commentary on Psalms by Daniel of Salah, an expression of Severan miaphysite theology (see Taylor 2001), and is listed by Michael the Syrian, *Chron.* IX.14, among those condemned by Justinian for his opposition to Chalcedon.

7 I am very grateful for corrections of my draft translation to Alison Salvesen, and to David Taylor and the members of his Syriac reading class, who generously devoted a session in Summer 2007 to this text.

BM Add. 14,530, p. 108a. Conclusion and scribe's first affirmation

That concludes the letter of the holy Dioscorus,
bishop of Alexandria, which was written
by him to the remainder of the pious bishops.

That concludes the second Synod which met
at Ephesus in the days of the holy and God-loving
Dioscorus, bishop of Alexandria,
and in the days of the victorious kings Theodosius and Valentinianus.

Glory to the Father and to the Son and to the Spirit
of Holiness, one perfect mystery
of the glorious Trinity for ever. Amen.

1. This book was finished in the year eight hundred and forty-six by the reckoning
2. of Alexander, in the month Iyyar, on the tenth of it, in the holy monastery
3. of the blessed Mar Eusebius of Kapra dBarta, in the days of the excellent and
4. God-loving vigilant pastor and wise steersman, lover of strangers,
5. and adamantine defensive rampart made for his flock, so that none should enter
6. from among the ravenous wolves, and injure one from among the innocent lambs which within
7. his peaceful enclosure are gathered (namely), that of the Mar presbyter and archimandrite Iohanan of that
8. monastery. May God – He for whose name he [the scribe] has striven and produced this book
9. for his holy monastery – on that day, a terrible and great day,
10. when sounds the horn, and the graves are broken open, and the dead arise and give
11. praise, and the judgement-seat is set up, the judge takes his seat and the books are opened, and every man
12. receives (what he deserves for) what he has done from that upright judge in whose court there is no
13. regard for appearances – at that moment cause to be heard that voice sweet
14. and pleasing (saying) 'In a small thing have you been faithful, enter the joy of your Lord

¹⁵ and I will raise you to a great height.' And may he be counted with Abraham and Isaac

¹⁶ and Jacob, and all those who are just and righteous in the prayers of the Blessed One, and of Her (who) bore

¹⁷ God, Mary. Yea and Amen.

Nothing in this affirmation gives a clue to the theological bearing or current relevance of the acts whose writing is here concluded, not even the reference to Mary 'who bore God'. For, as we will see, the original Nestorian position that Mary could have born the *Christos*, but not God, was no longer maintained by anyone within the Roman Empire, and Justinian's own utterances of these years were filled with references to her as the Mother of God. What transpires from the affirmation is instead a strong expression of personal piety, combined with a hope of reward at the end of time, and a vivid sense of the monastery as a frontier against a dangerous world. It is time to turn to the contents of the codex, with a brief indication of its modern publication- and translation-history, and a tabulation of what it records.

Acts of Ephesus II, 449, Later Session. Syriac Translation

(a) *The Codex of CE 535, BM Add. 14,530*

Wright (1871), *Catalogue* II, 1027–30 (no. DCCCCV)
Hatch (1946), Plate XVIII

Vellum codex. 108 double-sided leaves (a/b). Single column, of 27–34 lines per page. Estrangela script. Writing completed in the 'year 846 by the reckoning of Alexander, on the 10th of the month of Iyyar [10 May 535], in the holy monastery of the blessed lord Eusebius of KPR' DBRT' ' (108a).

(b) *Syriac Text and German Translation and Notes*

Flemming, J.P.G. (1917), *Akten der ephesinischen Synode von Jahre 449, Syrisch* (*Abbhandlungen der Königlichen Gesellschaft der Wissenschaften zu Göttingen, Philologisch-historische Klasse*, N.F. XV.1). Printed in the Serta script which became normal for West Syrians after the beginning of the Islamic period, and also in modern printed texts

(c) *English and French Translations*

Martin, L'Abbé (1874), *Actes du brigandage d'Éphèse. Traduction faite sur le texte syriaque contenu dans le manuscrit 14530 du Musée Britannique*
Perry, S.G.F. (1881), *The Second Synod of Ephesus, together with Certain Extracts relating to it, from Syriac MSS. preserved in the British Museum...*
Doran, Robert (2006) *Stewards of the Poor. The Man of God, Rabbula and Hiba in Fifth-Century Edessa* (2006), 133f. (sections relating to Hiba/Ibas)

(d) *Content of Acts*
    (By page-nos. of codex)

Proceedings at Ephesus	Documents Quoted
	1b–2b. Theodosius and Valentinian III to Dioscorus of Alexandria, 30 Mar. 449 (Greek original in *ACO* II.1.1, para. 24 [pp. 68–9])
	2b–3b. Theodosius and Valentinian to Dioscorus about Theodoret, 6 Aug. 449 (Greek original in *ACO* II.1.1, para. 52 [p. 72])
	3b–4a. Theodosius and Valentinian to council calling for deposition of Ibas of Edessa (Greek original not preserved)
4a. Date and formal heading	
4b–8a. List of 113 participants	
8b. Verbatim report of interventions. Non-attendance of Roman representatives and of Domnus of Antioch. Beginning of proceedings against Ibas	
8b–10a. Proceedings relating to Ibas	
	10a–13b. Records (*hypomnemata*) of acclamations (*phonai*) at Edessa, April 449
	13b–23a. Report (*anaphora*) of Flavius Chaereas, *praeses* of Osrhoene, on events in Edessa, Apr. 449
	23a–38a. Further *anaphora* of Flavius Chaereas on events at Edessa, Apr. 449

	Note esp. 33b.	During proceedings at Edessa the *comes* Theodosius requests reading of Syriac letter ('GRT' SWRYYT') sent by Ibas to 'Mari the Persian'. Translation (PWŠQ') of letter read – text in 34a–36b [Greek translation of original in *ACO* II.1.3, para. 138, pp. 32–4 [391–3], from Session X/XI of Chalcedon]
38b–54a.	Proceedings. *Phonai.* Deposition of Ibas of Edessa, Daniel of Carrhae, Irenaeus of Tyre, Aquilinus of Byblus Note esp. Syriac *Acta* 43b: 'Uranius, bishop of Hemerium, said, with the deacon Libanius from Samosata translating for him [MPŠQ LH]…'. Similarly 48b	
54a–57a.	Proceedings against Sophronius of Tella	
		54a–57b. *Libellus* against Sophronius of Tella
57b onwards.	Proceedings against Theodoret of Cyrrhus	
		57b–61b. *Libellus* against Theodoret
		62a–72a. Letter of Theodoret to monks
		72b–75b. Extracts from Theodoret's *Defence of Diodore and Theodore*
75b–78a.	Verdicts of 10 bishops. Deposition (*kathairesis*)	
78b–79a.	Proceedings	
79b onwards.	Proceedings against Domnus of Antioch	
		79b–81b. *Libellus* against Domnus
		83a–85a. Letter of Domnus to Flavian of Constantinople
		85b–89a. *Libelli* against Domnus
		89b–90b. Testimony (*Exomosia*) of presbyter Pelagius
90b–91b.	Further proceedings	
		92b–96a. Letter of Dioscorus to Domnus
		96a–97a. Letter of Domnus to Dioscorus
		97a–99a. Letter of Dioscorus to Domnus

		99b–101b.	Letter of Domnus to Dioscorus
101b–104a.	Proceedings. Verdicts of 13 bishops on Domnus		
		104a–106b.	Two extracts from communication of Theodosius (to Dioscorus?) on decisions of council. (No Greek original preserved. Latin version in *ACO* II.3.2, para. 106, pp. 88–9 [347–8])
		106b	Extract from letter of Theodosius to Juvenal of Jerusalem (No Greek original preserved)
		106b–108a.	Circular letter of unidentified imperial official on procedures for enforced subscription to decisions of council (No Greek original)
108a.	Note of conclusion of council (as above)		
108a–b.	Two personal affirmations by the scribe		

It will be seen that, while the text as preserved begins by quoting the texts of the initial imperial instructions relating to the council, and equally ends with a series of official letters marking its conclusion, what is contained in the record is both extremely selective, and gives no hint of the proceedings at the first session of the council. In other words it focuses on the condemnation of a specific group of dyophysite bishops, all of them from the diocese of Oriens, who had been dealt with at a subsequent stage of the council.

As regards the formal character of these acts, note first that they preserve the style of the original Greek, to the extent of reproducing verbatim the two references to Syriac: in 33b, mentioning the Syriac letter ('GRT' SWRYYT') of Ibas of Edessa to Mari the Persian, and in 43b recording that Uranius of Hemerium in Osrhoene had a deacon to translate his spoken intervention for him. The original will also almost certainly have reproduced in Greek the two reports (*anaphorai*) of Flavius Chaereas, the *praeses* of Osrhoene (13b–38a), which will originally have been written in Latin. Since the reproduction of Latin documents in Latin is a very rare feature of fifth-century conciliar acts, at least as they have come down to us, and is found only on one MS of the Acts of Ephesus I,[8] we can assume that they had been circulating in Greek translation, before being now re-translated into Syriac.

The case of the 'Syriac Letter' of Ibas is an interesting example of how the interplay between languages functioned in the late antique Church. Ibas was bishop of Edessa from 435 onwards (see below), but evidently wrote this letter, in Syriac, to the unidentified 'Mari the Persian', earlier, while still a presbyter. It gave a strongly critical account of the Council of Ephesus of 431 and its aftermath, and must count as one of the most evocative of contemporary responses to the controversy. As we will see below, at session X/XI of the Council of Chalcedon a Greek translation of it was read out, and it is evident that at Ephesus II it had also been a Greek translation which was read – or at least referred to in the course of quoting earlier exchanges at Edessa (see above). The Syriac record in the codex of 535 faithfully records that this was a translation (PWŠQ') before producing the text in Syriac. Though we must allow for the possibility that the original text was still in circulation in the sixth century, and that a copy of it was inserted at this point, it is far more likely that whoever made the overall translation (whether the scribe himself or someone else) simply re-translated the text from the Greek of the acts. So it is very likely that, while we thus have a Syriac text of a letter written in Syriac, we do not have the original Syriac.

These acts follow the structure of the known Greek Acts of Ephesus I and II and Chalcedon in two important respects. First, they begin with three letters of Theodosius either summoning the council or giving directions concerning it, all written prior to the opening. In two cases the Greek original is available for comparison, and in the third not. Second, they conclude with two imperial letters, and one from an official, all written after the conclusion of proceedings (none of these three survives in Greek, but one is known in a Latin version). As always, precisely what other relevant material should be added to the text of a report of conciliar proceedings was a matter of editorial discretion, relating to the purpose of the record in question.

The proceedings as recorded here do not have the formal character of the record of Chalcedon, where each session is both numbered (even if

---

8 For the distinctive character of this codex of the 13th century, edited by Schwartz in *ACO* 1.1.7 see Millar (2004), esp. 117–119, and Millar (2006), 243. The acts of the synods held in Constantinople in 536, edited by Schwartz in *ACO* III (1940), incorporate a considerably higher proportion of Latin in the original: see Millar (2008).

differently in the Greek and the Latin) and given a date. A date is indeed provided (4a), namely the Egyptian month Mesore 29 (= 22 August). But whether all of the proceedings recorded here took place on that day is not clear. Secondly, as Hans Lietzmann pointed out in the introduction to Flemming's edition (p. v), with acknowledgement to notes by G. Hoffmann (reproduced ibid., p. 163), the proceedings (p. 6b) refer to an earlier session on a Sunday (hence 20 August) at which the Roman delegates and Domnus of Antioch had not been present. This is therefore, obviously enough, distinct from the initial session held on 8 August, and the upshot is that we do not know how many sessions there were at Ephesus II (any more than at Ephesus I), nor whether more than one are the subject of the Syriac proceedings.

Thirdly, what is immediately obvious from the tabulation above is that the form of the Syriac proceedings (like the Greek ones of both Ephesus II and Chalcedon) involves extensive quotation of pre-existing documents, including the records (*hypomnemata*) of acclamations (*phonai*) at Edessa (10a–13b), or the two reports (*anaphorai*) of Flavius Chaereas, the governor of Osrhoene, addressed to higher officials (13b–38a). These extensive secular documents apart, in the course of the rest of the proceedings we find the text of four *libelli* of complaint, one each against Sophronius of Tella and Theodoret of Cyrrhus, and two against Domnus of Antioch. There are also four letters between Domnus and Dioscorus of Alexandria, one from Domnus to Flavian of Constantinople, an affirmation (*exomosia*) by a presbyter, and extracts from a theological work by Theodoret. The proceedings themselves, tabulated in the left-hand column, lead to the condemnation of Ibas of Edessa, Daniel of Carrhae, Irenaeus of Tyre, Aquilinus of Byblus, Sophronius of Tella, Theodoret of Cyrrhus and Domnus of Antioch. The political and ecclesiastical context of these accusations and subsequent depositions is entirely Near Eastern, concerning the provinces of Osrhoene, Euphratesia, Syria and Phoenicia. But while reading the Syriac record of these heated exchanges, at certain points referring back to mass public demonstrations on the streets of Edessa, we have (as above) to remember that this Syriac record is in itself a secondary by-product of proceedings originally conducted in Greek in the heart of the late antique world, in Ephesus, and derive from a record in Greek of a council whose primary focus had been the acquittal of Eutyches and the condemnation of Flavian. But, as regards this group of strictly Near Eastern conflicts, fought out over one or more later sessions at Ephesus, what had been their background, and why was the record of them still relevant in 535? It will be sufficient, for the purpose of putting contents of the codex of 535 in context, to tabulate the key events of 431–451.[9]

The Historical Context: from Ephesus I to Chalcedon

431	Rabbula of Edessa supports Cyril of Alexandria at the time of the First Council of Ephesus. Theodoret supports Nestorius (who is deposed, and later exiled)
432	Rabbula of Edessa changes sides, to support Council
433?	Ibas, as presbyter, writes 'Letter to Mari the Persian' in Syriac, giving Nestorian viewpoint
435	Ibas succeeds Rabbula (many pro-Nestorian bishops deposed; Theodoret retains his see)
448	Four presbyters at Edessa accuse Ibas of Nestorianism, and financial malpractice, and appeal to Theodosius II. Theodosius orders setting-up of ecclesiastical court to examine charges; orders Theodoret not to leave Cyrrhus
Feb. 449	Court holds hearings in Tyre and Berytus (Greek Acts preserved in *ACO* II.1.3, pp. 19–37 [378–96], see below)
Apr. 449	Accusations and popular agitation against Ibas in Edessa (Syriac Acts, as above)
Aug. 449	*Second Council of Ephesus.* Condemnation of Ibas, Daniel of Carrhae, Irenaeus (already deposed as bishop of Tyre), Aquilinus of Byblus, Sophronius of Tella, Theodoret of Cyrrhus, Domnus of Antioch (Syriac Acts, as above)
July 450	Theodosius II dies
Aug. 450	Marcian becomes emperor
Oct. 451	*Council of Chalcedon* (*ACO* II.1.3; Price and Gaddis, vol. 2, pp. 250–7): Oct. 26. Session IX (Greek Acts)/VIII (Latin Acts). Theodoret, Sophronius of Tella, John of Germanicia and Amphilochius of Side reinstated on condition of anathematizing Nestorius and/or Eutyches as heretics), *ACO* II.1.3, pp. 7–11 [360–70] Oct. 26. Session X/IX. Case of Ibas of Edessa. Initial hearing (pp. 11–16 [370–5]) Oct. 26. Session XI/X. Ibas of Edessa. Hearing and readmission (extensive acts, pp. 16–42 [375–401]: with memorandum (*hypomnestikon*) of Theodosius II appointing ecclesiastical court

---

9 For the essentials see Frend (1972); Pietri (1998), ch. 1; Acerbi (2001); Price and Gaddis (2005), II, 265–70; Doran (2006).

in 448 (para. 27, see above), hearings at Tyre and Berytus in early 449 (paras. 28–137, see above). Greek version (ἑρμηνεῖα) of Ibas' 'Letter to Mari the Persian' (para. 138); petition in favour of Ibas from clergy of Edessa – 65 subscriptions, of which 18 are recorded as having been in Syriac *or* also in Syriac: καὶ ὑπογραφὴ Συριακή (para. 141); conclusion of proceedings and restoration of Ibas (paras. 142–81)

It will be seen at once that, in these cases as in others, the Council of Chalcedon functioned to produce a straightforward reversal of the decisions of Ephesus II, held only two years before. It did not as such reconsider the condemnation of Nestorius, who was still alive, in exile in the Great Oasis. But, in following the theological line set out in the famous Tome of Leo of Rome, addressed to Flavian of Constantinople in June 449, and in incorporating in the Definition of Faith adopted at Session VI the words 'in two natures', it gave rise to accusations of having adopted a Nestorian Christology, and, while gaining support in some areas of the Near East, also led to deeply-felt opposition on the part of those committed to a one-nature Christology, and to divisions in the Church which have never healed.

This is not the place to attempt an account of the theological divisions which marked the century following Chalcedon, even if the author were qualified to do so. But, to put the codex of 535 in context, it can be said that Nestorius himself ceased to be a prime subject of controversy, and his condemnation was never challenged. Instead, the focus came to be on the theological writers who were seen as the source of a two-nature Christology, Diodore of Tarsus and more particularly Theodore of Mopsuestia (who had died in 428, just when Nestorius began his brief period as bishop of Constantinople), along with Theodoret (and in particular his polemical writings against Cyril of Alexandria), and the Letter of Ibas to Mari the Persian. It was to be the work of these last three which was subsequently the subject of the 'Three Chapters' controversy under Justinian, culminating in the Council of Constantinople in 553.

Christological Disputes under Justinian, and the Background to the 'Three Chapters' Controversy (over Theodore of Mopsuestia, Theodoret and Ibas)

It may be allowable to pick out a few significant moments in the conflicts of the earlier sixth century between the followers of a one-nature Christology, led by the major figure of Severus, patriarch of Antioch in 512–18, and the Chalcedonians, before once again tabulating the sequence of events in the 530s which provide the immediate context for the production of the codex.[10]

The reign of Anastasius (491–518) had generally been favourable for the miaphysite side, and it was an important step when Severus, in his initial address (*prosphonesis*) in 512, chose to anathematize, as dyophysite, Diodore and Theodore 'the masters of Nestorius', along with Theodoret, Andrew (of Samosata), Ibas, Alexander (of Hierapolis) and others (*Patrologia Orientalis* II, 322–5, no. viii). To do so was precisely to focus on the issues and personalities of the 420s–450s. Under Justin (518–27), there came a strong pro-Chalcedonian reaction, in which Severus and others were deposed and went into hiding, followed however, under Justinian (527–65), first by a serious effort at compromise, in which the emperor as an individual was deeply involved, and then, in 536, by a determined imperial rejection of the miaphysite position and its advocates. Even after that, however, there followed a movement for the condemnation of the Three Chapters (the works of Theodore, Theodoret and Ibas), aimed at ridding the Chalcedonian, or 'neo-Chalcedonian', position of all theological taint of Nestorianism, but meeting strong resistance, not least in the recently reconquered Latin Africa; hence two significant contemporary polemical works in Latin, the *Breviarium Causae Nestorianorum et Eutychianorum* of Liberatus,[11] and the much more substantial *Pro defensione trium capitulorum* of Facundus of Hermiane.[12] However, this important debate, leading up to the Fifth Ecumenical Council of 553, need not concern us here, and we may return to the 530s, with its striking testimonies to the personal theological commitment of Justinian:

---

10 See esp. Frend (1972), ch. 7; Brock (1981); Maraval (1998); Grillmeier-Hainthaler (1995), esp. 344–55; Chadwick (2001), ch. 55; Gray (2005); Di Berardino (2006), 53–90; Price (2007).

11 Text printed by Schwartz in *ACO* 2.5, pp. 98–141.

12 Edited by I.-M. Clément and R.V. Plaetse, CCSL 90A (Turnhout, 1974).

532	Address of miaphysite monks to Justinian, see Ps-Zacharias, *HE*. IX, 15 (ed. Brooks, *CSCO* III.6, p. 80; partial trans. in Frend, *Rise*, pp. 362–6), with criticism of material drawn from Leo of Rome, Nestorius, Theodore, Diodore, Theodoret and the Acts of Chalcedon.
532	Meetings between miaphysite delegation from Syria and Chalcedonian bishops in Constantinople, with some participation by Justinian in person. Ps-Zacharias, *HE* IX.15; Innocentius of Maronea, *ACO* IV.2, pp. 169–84; two Syriac MSS, Harvard Syr. 22 and *BM Add*. 12155 (*PO* XIII, pp. 192–6), the former edited, and both translated, by Brock 1981.
15 March, 533	Profession of faith by Justinian, addressed to the people of Constantinople and twelve other cities, with denunciation of the heresies of Nestorius, Eutyches and Apollinarius, *CJ* I.1.6.
26 March, 533	Letter of Justinian to Epiphanius, archbishop and 'ecumenical patriarch' of Constantinople. Orthodoxy declared to be as laid down at Nicaea, and followed by the three further Councils, Constantinople, Ephesus I and Chalcedon, *CJ* I.1.7.
6 June, 533	Letter of Justinian to Iohannes, bishop of Rome (*CJ* I.1.8, 7–24), and Iohannes' reply, March, 534 (*CJ* I.1.8, 1–6; 25–39 = *Collectio Avellana*, *CSEL* XXXV, no. 84).
534/5	Severus of Antioch (in exile) persuaded to visit Constantinople; miaphysite Theodosius becomes patriarch of Alexandria; Anthimus becomes patriarch of Constantinople, and is then condemned, see Zacharias *HE* IX.19.
536	Anthimus leaves office or is deposed, and is regarded as having been influenced by Severus and Theodosius in moving to a miaphysite position. *Synodos endemousa* (Home Synod) meeting in five successive sessions in Constantinople in May–June. Acts quoted in those of subsequent synod of Jerusalem, 536, *ACO* III, para. 42 (pp. 123–89).
Aug. 6, 536	Letter of Justinian to Menas, archbishop and 'ecumenical patriarch' of Constantinople, confirming the deposition of Anthimus, the authority of the four ecumenical councils, anathema on Severus and the banning of his works; barred from Constantinople and all other cities. Condemnation of Peter of Apamea, with similar ban, also applied to monk Zoaras, see Justinian, *Novella* 42 = *ACO* III, para. 41 (pp. 119–23).

These bare details, accompanied by a listing of a few of the key documents, will be sufficient to make clear that the Syriac codex of the Acts of Ephesus II was written exactly at the moment when the miaphysite side had gained influence in both Constantinople and Alexandria, and at which Severus, as the long-deposed bishop of Antioch, had finally come to Constantinople and was enjoying a degree of imperial favour there, only for fortune to change drastically in the following year, with the anathema on Severus, and the banning of his works by a *Synodos endemousa* (Home Synod) at Constantinople being confirmed by Justinian.

Along with that of Severus came the condemnation and deposition of Peter of Apamea, deposed in 518, but clearly still influential, who had been one of the delegation of six miaphysites who came to Constantinople for the discussions of 532, and was evidently a leading figure in this cause. Whether that explains the miaphysite commitment of the monastery near Apamea where the Syriac codex was written is of course uncertain, since there could be conflicting, and changing, opinions within dioceses.

Paradoxically, as mentioned briefly above, Justinian's final commitment to the defence of Chalcedon and to the rejection of the miaphysite position did not end the relevance of the acts recalling the condemnation of Ibas, Theodoret and others at Ephesus in 449. For, as we have seen, the debate over the Three Chapters was an attempt by the now dominant Chalcedonians, or 'neo-Chalcedonians', to rid themselves of any taint of Nestorianism, and (unsuccessfully) to conciliate miaphysite opinion, by dissociating themselves from the figures concerned, and their most salient works – the Three Chapters of Ibas, Theodoret and Theodore. As it happens, we know more about the debate over these three theologians as it took place in Constantinople and Africa under Justinian than we do about any role which the beautifully written Syriac codex may have played in its bilingual, Greek and Syriac, local setting. But its potential value, as a moving personal expression of Christian faith, as a reflection of miaphysite commitment in the Syria of the 530s, and as the carefully-selected record of an earlier moment of miaphysite dominance, is perfectly clear. So also is its significance as testimony to the step-by-step establishment of Syriac as a recognized language of Christian culture along with Greek in the provinces west of the Euphrates.[13]

13 I am very grateful to the editors for corrections and guidance, as also to Alison Salvesen and David Taylor – and to Dr Williams' Library, Gordon Square, London, for the prolonged loan of the priceless (and very rare) work of Perry (1881).

BIBLIOGRAPHY

Acerbi, Silvia (2001), *Conflitti politico-ecclesiastici in oriente nella tarda antichità. Il II Concilio di Efeso (449)* (Madrid).

Brock, S.P. (1981), 'The Conversations with the Syrian Orthodox under Justinian (532)', *OCP* 47: 87–121 = Brock (1992), XIII.

—— (1984), *Syriac Perspectives on Late Antiquity* (London).

—— (1990), *From Ephrem to Romanos: Interactions between Syriac and Greek in Late Antiquity* (Aldershot).

—— (1992), *Studies in Syriac Christianity: History, Literature and Theology* (Aldershot).

—— (2006), *An Introduction to Syriac Studies* (New York).

—— (2009), 'Edessene Syriac Inscriptions in Late Antique Syria', in Cotton *et al.* (2009).

Chadwick, Henry (2001), *The Church in Ancient Society. From Galilee to Gregory the Great* (Oxford).

Cotton, H.M., Hoyland, R.G., Price, J.J. and Wasserstein, D.J. (eds.) (2008), *From Hellenism to Islam: Cultural and Linguistic Change in the Roman Near East* (Cambridge).

Di Berardino, Angelo (2006), *Patrology: the Eastern Fathers from the Council of Chalcedon to John of Damascus (†750)* (Cambridge).

Doran, Robert (2006), *Stewards of the Poor. The Man of God, Rabbula and Hiba in Fifth-Century Edessa* (Kalamazoo).

Flemming, Johannes (1917), *Akten der ephesinischen Synode vom Jahre 449, Syrisch* (*Abh. der kön. Gesellschaft der Wissenschaften zu Göttingen*, Philologisch-historische Klasse, NF 15.1).

Gray, P.T.R. (2005), 'The Legacy of Chalcedon: Christological Problems and their Significance' in Michael Maas, ed., *The Cambridge Companion to the Age of Justinian* (Cambridge), 215–38.

Grillmeier, Aloys and Hainthaler, Theresia (1995), *Christ in Christian Tradition* II. *From the Council of Chalcedon (451) to Gregory the Great (590–604)*. Pt. 2. *The Church of Constantinople in the Sixth Century* (London).

Frend, W.H.C. (1972), *The Rise of the Monophysite Movement* (Cambridge).

Hatch, W.H.P. (1946, repr. 2002), *An Album of Dated Syriac Manuscripts* (Boston; New York).

Littmann, Enno (1904), *Publications of an American Archaeological Expedition to Syria in 1899–1900*. IV. *Semitic Inscriptions*. Pt. I. *Syriac Inscriptions* (New York).

—— (1934), *Publications of the Princeton University Archaeological Expedition to Syria in 1904–5 and 1909*. IV. *Semitic Inscriptions*. Section B. *Syriac Inscriptions* (Leiden).

Mango, M.M. (1982), 'Patrons and Scribes indicated in Syriac Manuscripts, 411 to 800 AD', *Jahrb. d. Österreich. Byzantinistik* 32.4: 3–12.

—— (1991), 'The Production of Syriac Manuscripts 400–700 AD', in Gugliemo Cavallo, Giuseppe De Gregorio, and Marilena Maniaci (eds.), *Scritture, libri e testi nelle aree provinciali di Bisanzio* (Spoleto) I: 161–79.

Maraval, Pierre (1998), 'La politique religieuse de Justinien 3: La politique envers les opponants à Chalcédoine', in Pietri (1998), 399–426.

Martin, L'Abbé (1874), *Actes du brigandage d'Éphèse. Traduction faite sur le texte syriaque contenu dans le manuscript 14530 du Musée Britannique* (Paris).

Millar, Fergus (1998), 'Ethnic Identity in the Roman Near East, 325–450: Language, Religion and Culture', *Mediterranean Archaeology* 11: 159–76.

—— (2004), 'Repentant Heretics in Fifth-Century Lydia: Identity and Literacy', *Scripta Classica Israelica* 23: 111–30.

—— (2006), *A Greek Roman Empire: Power and Belief under Theodosius II (408–450)* (Berkeley).

—— (2008), 'Rome, Constantinople and the Near Eastern Church under Justinian: Two Synods of 536', *JRS* 98: 62–82.

Perry, S.G.F. (1881), *The Second Synod of Ephesus* (London).

Pietri, Luce (ed.), (1998), *Histoire du Christianisme* III. *Les Eglises d'Orient et d'Occident* (Paris).

Pognon, Henri (1907), *Inscriptions Sémitiques de la Syrie, de la Mésopotamie et de la région de Mossoul* (Paris).

Price, Richard and Gaddis, Michael (2005), *The Acts of the Council of Chalcedon*, 3 vols, TTH 45 (Liverpool).

Price, R.M. (2007), 'The Three Chapters Controversy and the Council of Chalcedon', in Chazelle, C., and Cubitt, C. (eds), *The Crisis of the* Oikoumene: *The Three Chapters and the Failed Quest for Unity in the Sixth-Century Mediterranean* (Turnhout), 17–37.

Taylor, D.G.T. (2001), 'The Christology of the Syriac Psalm Commentary (AD 541/2) of Daniel of Salah and the Phantasiast Controversy', in Wiles, M.F., and Yarnold, E.J. (eds), *StP* 35: 508–15.

—— (2002), 'Bilingualism and Diglossia in Late Antique Syria and Mesopotamia', in Adams, J.N., Janse, J., and Swain, S. (eds.), *Bilingualism in Ancient Society: language contact and the written word* (Oxford), 298–331.

Wright, William (1870–2), *Catalogue of the Syriac Manuscripts in the British Museum acquired since 1838* (London) I–III.

THE COUNCIL OF CHALCEDON (451):
A NARRATIVE

Richard Price

Before the Council

The conventional opening date for the Christological controversy of the fifth century of which the climax was the Council of Chalcedon is the arrival at Constantinople in 428 of its new archbishop, Nestorius, a Syrian monk, who publicly criticized the ascription to the Virgin Mary of the title *Theotokos* (Mother of God). The issue was not the status of the Virgin but the question who it was who was born of her – a human being, united to the Godhead but yet distinct from it (as Nestorius supposed), or God the Word himself, who, in the words of St Paul, 'being in the form of God, thought it not robbery to be equal with God, but emptied himself, taking the form of a servant, being born in the likeness of men.'[1] Opposition to Nestorius was led by Archbishop Cyril of Alexandria, who spotted the opportunity to humiliate the upstart see of Constantinople but was also genuinely shocked by Nestorius' stance – not out of any special devotion to the Virgin,[2] but because of his own emphasis on God the Word made flesh as the one personal subject in Christ and as the one to whom we are united in holy communion. The controversy led to the condemnation of Nestorius at the First Council of Ephesus (431), which was wildly popular in Ephesus itself (after the vote Cyril was escorted to his lodgings by women swinging thuribles)[3] but deeply resented in Syria. The rest of the decade saw the frustration of Cyril's further plans, as he was obliged by the emperor in 433 to accept the 'Formula of Reunion', an ambiguous profession of faith drawn up by Nestorius' allies, and in 439 to call off his campaign to secure the condemnation of the views of Theodore of Mopsuestia (d. 428), credited with having been Nestorius' teacher.[4]

1 Phil 2:6–7.
2 See Price (2007), esp. 64–5.
3 Cyril, *ep*. 24, *ACO* 1.1.1, p. 118, 8–9.
4 For the campaign by Cyril and Archbishop Proclus of Constantinople to force the Syrian bishops to disown Theodore see Chadwick (2001), 548–51 and Price, pp. 124–7 below.

Dioscorus, Cyril's successor in the see of Alexandria (444–51), determined to achieve the total victory that had eluded his predecessor. He got his chance when his opponents overplayed their hand. In 448 Flavian, the new archbishop of Constantinople (446–9), chaired a 'home synod' of available bishops at Constantinople, where Bishop Eusebius of Dorylaeum, a heresy-hunter who as a layman had opposed Nestorius twenty years before, brought an accusation of heresy against Eutyches, a senior and respected archimandrite in the city and an ally of Dioscorus; Eutyches was duly condemned and excommunicated for refusing to acknowledge two natures in Christ after the union. Eutyches was loyal to the tradition of Cyril of Alexandria, who, while acknowledging that Christ possessed the fullness of both Godhead and manhood, had always rejected a formal acknowledgement of two natures after the union, as suggesting the Nestorian heresy of splitting Christ into two distinct beings.[5] Flavian put on an act of impartial chairmanship and pastoral solicitude, saying of the absent Eutyches at one point, 'Let him come here: he will come to fathers and brothers, to people who are not ignorant of him and who even now persevere in friendship' (Acts I. 417). But once Eutyches appeared at the hearing, Flavian took off the mask, harassing the unfortunate archimandrite and pressing him to profess two natures after the union, the deed of condemnation already drawn up and in his pocket.[6]

A second Ecumenical Council of Ephesus was convened in August 449 to repair the scandal. Eutyches' condemnation was annulled. Flavian and Eusebius were condemned and deposed, not unreasonably, for imposing an improper doctrinal test.[7] Dioscorus acted as chairman, and took the opportunity to secure the total victory over Syrian sympathizers with Nestorius that had eluded Cyril in the 430s: Theodoret of Cyrrhus, Ibas of Edessa and other Syrian bishops sympathetic to Nestorius were all deposed, as well as their superior Bishop Domnus of Antioch, who had given them protection.[8] But the council was fatally undermined by

5 The charge of denying Christ's true humanity has been made against Eutyches ever since Leo's Tome of 449, but the evidence does not support it. See Draguet (1931).
6 All this was disguised in the minutes of the synod but revealed at an investigation in the following year. See Price and Gaddis, I, 116–7.
7 The acts of the first session, at which Eutyches was restored and Flavian and Eusebius condemned, were included in the minutes of the first session of Chalcedon, Acts I. 68–1067.
8 For this later stage of the council we are dependent on the Syriac Acts, for which see pp. 45–67 above.

Roman opposition. The Roman delegates at the council presented a letter from Pope Leo condemning Eutyches; the council received the document but ignored the request that it be read.[9] When the bishops proceeded to condemn Flavian, Deacon Hilary (one of the papal legates) attempted to exercise a veto, but was ignored.[10] Subsequently Theodosius II confirmed the decrees of the council, but Pope Leo and the western emperor, Valentinian III, refused to accept them. The result was schism between east and west; even without the sudden death from a riding accident of Theodosius II on 28 July 450 this could not have been tolerated indefinitely. With the accession of Marcian and his consort Pulcheria (a frequent correspondent of Leo's and a good friend of the Roman see), the court of Constantinople swung to a pro-Roman policy. The bishops deposed at Ephesus were instructed to return to their sees,[11] though their formal reinstatement had to wait for a new council. Imperial fiat, however, simply overrode Ephesus II's acquittal of Eutyches: he was again deposed, and vanishes from history.[12] Even Dioscorus abandoned him: he remained loyal to the faith of Ephesus II, and even (in autumn 451) declared Pope Leo excommunicate, but he was not ready to go to the stake in support of a mere presbyter.[13]

Archbishop Anatolius, Flavian's successor at Constantinople, and Bishop Maximus, Domnus' successor at Antioch, had both been agents of Dioscorus, but now, like weathercocks, followed the change of the wind; both pressed the bishops in their areas of authority to sign Leo's Tome, a letter written to Archbishop Flavian in June 449, condemning Eutyches with more eloquence than truth.[14] As Leo perceived, acceptance of the Tome throughout the east would be enough to end the schism and clarify the doctrine on Christ. Marcian, however, determined on a new ecumenical council, to settle any remaining doubts about the doctrinal issue. After his experience of Ephesus II Leo had no enthusiasm for councils, but yielded to the imperial will, agreeing to send

9 Acts of Chalcedon, I. 83–5, 958.
10 Acts I. 964.
11 See Leo, *ep.* 77 (a letter from Pulcheria), in Price and Gaddis, I, 93–4.
12 During Chalcedon he took refuge in Jerusalem, according to Pelagius, *In defensione*, pp. 2–3, and was still alive in 454, according to Leo, *ep.* 134.
13 Dioscorus said at Chalcedon, 'If Eutyches holds opinions contrary to the doctrines of the church, he deserves not only punishment but hell fire' (Acts I. 168). Cp. the statement of the Council of Antioch of 341 (accused of Arian sympathies), 'We have not become followers of Arius, for how shall we, who are bishops, follow a presbyter?' (Socrates, *Hist. Eccl.* II. 10.4).
14 See Leo, *ep.* 88, in Price and Gaddis, I, 102.

representatives – three clergy from Italy, headed by Bishop Paschasinus of Lilybaeum (in Sicily). Leo presumed that Paschasinus would chair the council; in fact, he chaired only the third session.[15]

The location chosen for the council was Nicaea,[16] with the intention that the new council would be seen as a second Nicaea, confirming and perfecting the work of the first and most revered of the ecumenical councils; here in September 451 the bishops assembled, numbering some 370,[17] which made this gathering the largest council in the history of the early Church. And there for a few weeks they waited, while Marcian was distracted by the troubles in the Balkans, devastated by Hunnic raids. We may presume that during this period more and more bishops signed Leo's Tome; it was perhaps in reaction to this that Dioscorus, who had bravely come from Alexandria with 19 other Egyptian bishops, declared Leo excommunicate. Letting, however, symbolism yield to practicality, Marcian changed the venue from Nicaea to Chalcedon, a small city within sight of Constantinople, on the Asiatic side of the Bosporus. The church of St Euphemia was large enough to accommodate the public sessions, which, if we include a rough estimate of the minor clergy who will have accompanied their bishops, may have added up to around a thousand persons.[18] Here on 8 October the council finally opened. Almost all its public sessions were chaired by a group of high government officials, and in practice by their leader, the patrician and general Anatolius. As *magister militum praesentalis* he was one of the two commanders of the central imperial armies, and (in the words of Ste. Croix) 'may have been second in the whole Eastern Empire only to the great Aspar', the power behind the throne. As Ste. Croix piously adds, his recent experience of negotiating with Attila (in 447 and 450) equipped him well for dealing with a council of bishops.[19]

15 See the letters of Leo in Price and Gaddis, I, 94–107.

16 See Marcian's letters to the council prior to its opening, Price and Gaddis, I, 107–10.

17 The attendance lists attached to the sessions are mainly bogus, and our essential evidence are the lists of signatories of the council's Definition of the Faith, which contain their own problems (see pp. 102–3 below). For details of the calculation of 'around 370' see Price and Gaddis, III, 193–6.

18 MacMullen (2006), 79 estimates that the proportion of accompanying clergy to bishops would regularly have been somewhat over two to one and sometimes higher still. It was only bishops, or clergy representing absent bishops, who had the right to speak and vote.

19 Ste. Croix (2006), 289–91. He justly complains that previous historians of Chalcedon have paid him far too little attention. He remains a colourless figure, but his role at the council was crucial.

The Early Sessions

At the first session on 8 October 451, as in a modern British parliament, the rival factions sat facing each other, with the supporters of Dioscorus on one side and his opponents on the other (Acts I. 4). The session was largely taken up by a reading of the minutes of the first session of Ephesus II, at which Eutyches had been reinstated and Bishops Flavian and Eusebius condemned. Dioscorus found himself cast as defendant with the acts of Ephesus II treated as evidence against him. 119 of the bishops present at Chalcedon had participated in Ephesus II and signed its decrees;[20] they now claimed that they had done so only under duress. But even they had to admit that they bore a share of responsibility, and were reduced to abject cries of repentance, 'We all sinned, we all beg forgiveness' (Acts I. 181–4). Dioscorus, however, maintained his courage and dignity; he alone, in the words of Otto Seeck, 'behaved like a man in this collection of howling old women.'[21] As the hours passed, the reading continued, interrupted by episcopal interjections (e.g., by Eusebius of Dorylaeum, 'He lied! There is no such decree; there is no canon that states this', Acts I. 158). After a time the interjections in the written record cease: were the bishops getting weary? Most probably, however, large barren tracts of the Acts of Ephesus II were simply taken as read, although given in full in the minutes published subsequently, to form a complete dossier to prove Dioscorus' guilt.[22] Early on in the session the great majority of his supporters deserted him, literally crossing the floor, including even four of his Egyptian suffragans, who were later to find themselves in a tiny and despised minority when they returned home (Acts I. 284–98). Finally, at the end of the session, without asking the bishops for their opinion, the lay chairman delivered his verdict: Dioscorus and the five other bishops who had played a leading role at Ephesus II were deposed, subject to imperial ratification of the verdict; meanwhile the bishops approved the decision by acclamation (I. 1068–71). The agenda for the following session were also set – an examination of the doctrinal issue.

Two days later, 10 October, the bishops duly reassembled. It is clear that they expected the doctrinal issue to be settled simply by a formal approval of Leo's Tome; a precedent was provided by Ephesus I (431)

20 So Honigmann (1942/3), 40.
21 I derive this quotation from Ste. Croix (2006), 314.
22 See Price and Gaddis, I, 112, n. 2.

and Ephesus II (449), which had settled doctrinal debate by the simple procedure of approving existing documents and deposing dissentients. To their alarm and amazement, however, the government now revealed its hand: the task it set the bishops was to draw up a new definition of the faith. The bishops protested vigorously: such a new definition was quite uncalled for, and was arguably contrary to Canon 7 of Ephesus I, which had forbidden the production and use of any creed apart from the Nicene Creed of 325.[23] There followed a reading of authoritative documents – the Nicene Creed, the Constantinopolitan Creed, two doctrinal letters of Cyril of Alexandria 'confirmed' at Ephesus I – his Second Letter to Nestorius and his *Laetentur caeli* letter to John of Antioch accepting the Formula of Reunion[24] –, and the Tome of Leo. The Constantinopolitan Creed was a free version of the Nicene, and was attributed to the Council of Constantinople of 381. This council had not hitherto been considered of ecumenical status, and few of the bishops will have been aware that a creed was attributed to it.[25] The production of this document at this particular juncture was probably intended to provide a precedent for supplementing the Nicene Creed. But this, wisely, was not said, and the bishops were happy to approve any orthodox document that might serve to define orthodoxy without requiring them to produce a new definition.

The readings went smoothly apart from that of the Tome of Leo, which was interrupted several times by bishops who had, till the middle of the first session, been supporting Dioscorus (Acts II. 24–6).[26] Objections against the orthodoxy of the document were countered by its supporters, who produced quotations from Cyril of Alexandria in line, they claimed, with the Tome. It was agreed that Archbishop Anatolius of Constantinople should hold a meeting of the bishops where the problems over the Tome could be thrashed out. One of the bishops urged

23 See Acts II. 3–7, and Acts I. 943 for Canon 7 of Ephesus.
24 This second letter was written many months after Ephesus I, but because it resolved the impasse that resulted from the council it came to be treated as one of the concil's decrees.
25 For a discussion of the origin of the so-called Creed of Constantinople see Kelly (1972), 296–331. It was but one of a family of creeds based on the original Nicene Creed and not regarded as new creeds; see Price and Gaddis, II, 191–4.
26 It is striking that Leo's critics included the bishops of Illyricum, who were subject to his authority, mediated through the papal vicar in the Balkans, the bishop of Thessalonica. Perhaps because of his invidious position, mediating between Rome and his obstreperous suffragans, Bishop Anastasius of Thessalonica did not attend the council.

that the Tome be compared to Cyril's Third Letter to Nestorius, containing the Twelve Chapters, an aggressive statement of his anti-Nestorian position and particularly dear to the uncompromising Cyrillians. His suggestion was recorded but ignored; throughout the council supreme authority after the creeds themselves was accorded to the two letters of Cyril mentioned above, 'confirmed' at Ephesus I, but the Third Letter was not deemed to be among them.[27] Further dissension was revealed when the same bishops who had been criticizing Leo's Tome clamoured for the reinstatement of the six bishops, including Dioscorus, who had been deposed at the previous session. The session ended with the chairman, in blithe disregard of the opposition he had encountered, declaring his proposals passed – which included the setting up of a committee to draft a new definition.

By the end of the session it was clear that the deposition of Dioscorus and his chief allies had seriously divided the council. Quite apart from the continued presence at the council of a small but vocal minority of bishops, largely from Illyricum and Palestine, who boldly opposed the ecclesiastical policy of the government, we may presume that not only the six bishops (all metropolitans) who had been deposed at the first session but virtually all their suffragans were now absenting themselves from the meetings.[28] Councils were supposed to make their decisions by general consensus, not by majority vote; so the effect of this was to cast doubt on the authority of whatever decrees the council might come to issue. The decision by the lay chairman to depose the six bishops at the end of the first session threatened to undermine the whole work of the council.

The next two sessions of the council succeeded, however, in putting it back on course. The chairman's hasty verdict was reinterpreted as a provisional verdict, requiring ratification by the bishops. Accordingly the third session was devoted to a formal trial of Dioscorus by the bishops, chaired not by the patrician Anatolius (this was the only full session of the council that he did not chair) but by the senior Roman delegate, Paschasinus of Lilybaeum, who always spoke in Latin but presumably understood enough Greek for the purpose.[29] The government wished to create the impression of a fair trial of Dioscorus by his peers; the pretence that the outcome was not pre-determined was

27 See pp. 117–19 below.
28 See pp. 103–4 below.
29 Note Acts III. 4, 'Paschasinus... said in Latin'. See Schwartz (1933).

pushed so far that at the following fourth session the lay chairman rebuked the bishops for deposing Dioscorus without reference to the imperial will (Acts IV. 12). The trial is fully recorded in the acts, which give a fuller account of this session than of any of the others (except the first), doubtless to prove that proper judicial procedures were followed. Dioscorus received the standard threefold summons, but he chose to absent himself, surely not out of cowardice, still less a guilty conscience, but to spare his supporters; his absence enabled them to approve his deposition on the ground that he had not responded to a threefold summons, without commenting on the rights of the case. Four witnesses from Alexandria were produced, who read out carefully prepared statements (all manifestly drafted by the same government secretary, who, it is clear, thoroughly enjoyed his work), accusing Dioscorus of persecuting the relatives and close associates of his predecessor Cyril (Acts III. 47–64); it appears that Dioscorus' 'offence' had been to make them disgorge wealth they had improperly purloined out of church funds, but the effect of these charges must have damaged Dioscorus' standing among the pro-Cyrillian majority at the council. No other charges were presented at this session (graver matters had been aired at the first session), and there was no discussion of the charges. Finally the bishops proceeded to pass sentence; 192 council fathers spoke in turn, condemning Dioscorus. What exactly did they condemn him for?[30] Most of the episcopal verdicts simply mention his non-attendance, but a few (very few) refer to specific offences, notably his treatment of Archbishop Flavian at Ephesus II. At the first session of the council Eusebius of Dorylaeum had accused him of heresy, and both during the council and subsequently his enemies were to speak of him as a heretic whose views as well as person stood condemned; but it could equally be claimed, as Archbishop Anatolius was to claim at the fifth session (Acts V. 14), that Dioscorus had been deposed for misconduct but not for heresy. In all, almost half the bishops at the council absented themselves from Dioscorus' trial, and those who did attend agreed to differ over what they were condemning him for. Count Candidianus, the emperor's representative at Ephesus I, declared at the time that Nestorius was condemned at that council 'without any trial, examination and investigation';[31] the condemnation of Dioscorus was equally a travesty of

30 See the full analysis in Price and Gaddis, II, 30–34.
31 *ACO* 1.1.5, p. 120, 30–2.

justice. The St Athanasius of his age, he deserves his place in the Coptic martyrology.[32]

Four days later (17 October) there followed the fourth session of the council. Its principal task was to pass judgement on the orthodoxy of the Tome of Leo. It was reported that since the acrimonious discussion at the second session a meeting had been held as agreed in the palace of Archbishop Anatolius, at which the Roman delegates had managed to reassure the Illyrian and Palestinian critics of the Tome. 161 bishops in turn, with monotonous repetition, expressed the view that the Tome was in accord with the creeds and with the proceedings at Ephesus I, by which they meant the Second Letter of Cyril to Nestorius, which had been formally approved at that council; the remaining bishops present expressed agreement by acclamation. It is striking that the Tome was approved because it agreed with Cyril's letter; throughout the council it was Cyril not Leo who was seen as the determinant voice of orthodoxy. As propaganda for the government line that Leo and Cyril were in perfect accord, the minutes of this session are less than compelling: the content of the Tome was not discussed, with the result that the proof of its orthodoxy was made to lie purely in the authority and sincerity of the bishops testifying in its favour; yet 119 of them had attended Ephesus II and acquiesced on that occasion in the suppression of a letter from Leo summarizing the Tome.

The rest of the session, however, was more lively. The five metropolitan bishops still under suspension since the first session, who had by now signed Leo's Tome, were reinstated, and immediately entered and took their seats, doubtless accompanied by their suffragans; episcopal consensus, seriously undermined by the suspension of these metropolitans, was re-established. The irreconcilable minority who were not ready to take part in the council was now reduced to the Egyptian bishops, who at this point put in a final appearance. The other bishops demanded their submission, and they responded, reasonably enough that, if they accepted the Tome of Leo (and by implication Dioscorus' deposition), it would not be safe for them to return to Egypt; the lay chairman sensibly ruled that they should not be forced to agree to anything until a new bishop of Alexandria had been appointed. Their appearance at

32 The account, however, in the Coptic Synaxarion of how the empress Pulcheria pulled at his beard and struck out his teeth when he refused to sign the Chalcedonian Definition, and thereby intimidated the other bishops into signing, errs on the side of fiction.

this session was followed by that of a group of pro-Eutychean Constantinopolitan archimandrites, who had been sent to the council by the emperor to present a petition; the petition was a demand (which one might judge either heroic or simply impudent) that Dioscorus be restored to the episcopate and the council. Why had the emperor assisted this group to present its demands? One may presume that his motive was to dent the bishops' new-found sense of unanimity and to impress on them that, even after the approval of Leo's Tome, more was needed to restore concord and order to the churches.

The Chalcedonian Definition

After a pair of unnumbered sessions held on 20 October to deal with some specific problems relating to persons there followed on 22 October the fifth and most momentous session of the council. It began with the presentation by Archbishop Anatolius' committee of a draft definition of the faith. The ground had been prepared, since the text had been shown to the bishops at an informal meeting on the day before, and (to quote from acclamations) 'The definition satisfied everyone... The definition has satisfied God' (Acts V. 8). But objections were raised immediately by some of the Syrian bishops and, more seriously, the papal representatives. It is not credible that Anatolius would have been so foolish as to present the draft without having secured Roman approval beforehand; we can but conclude that since the meeting of the day before they had been lobbied, presumably by the Syrians, and most probably by Bishop Theodoret of Cyrrhus, easily the leading representative of what we call the 'Antiochene School', meaning the Syrian clergy hostile to Cyril. Since Theodoret was a personal friend of the lay chairman, the patrician Anatolius,[33] the role the latter was to play in this session may also be attributed with plausibility to Theodoret's lobbying.[34] The minutes do not particularize the objections raised by the Romans, nor do they preserve the text of the draft definition. But it

---

33 For his period in Syria and Theodoret's letters to him see Martindale (1980), 84–6. Ste. Croix (2006), 291 describes him as 'the closest and most regular of Theodoret's secular correspondents'.

34 A non-Chalcedon source tells us that Theodoret was also in league with Aetius the archdeacon of Constantinople, who supplied him with a copy of the draft definition 'by night', clearly before the other bishops had seen it (Ps.-Zachariah, *Hist. Eccl.* III. 1, trans. Hamilton and Brooks, 46–7).

emerges from what is recorded of the subsequent debate that the formula expressive of the presence in Christ of both Godhead and manhood was '*from* two natures', an expression dear to Cyril, since it implied that Christ was compounded from two natures, with a stress on the unity that resulted. Fatally, however, Dioscorus had said at the first session, 'I accept *from two natures*, but I do not accept *two*' (Acts I. 332). The chairman insisted that this made 'from two natures' incompatible with Pope Leo's insistence on two natures in Christ. This was a distortion of the truth in several ways. First, as Archbishop Anatolius immediately pointed out, it was far from evident that Dioscorus had been condemned for heresy. Secondly the expression 'two natures' is not to be found in Leo's Tome; Leo was too good a theologian to attach prime importance to formulae. Thirdly, the most probable hypothesis is that the draft definition was very close to the confession of faith that Flavian of Constantinople had read out at the Home Synod of 448, which contained the phrase 'from two natures *after* the incarnation' (I. 271);[35] this was quite distinct from the position expressed by Eutyches at the same Home Synod, 'I acknowledge that our Lord came into being from two natures *before* the union, but after the union I acknowledge one nature' (I. 527). The bishops clearly realized that the chairman and the papal representatives were simply trying to pull the wool over their eyes, and refused to agree to a revision of the draft.[36]

At this the chairman suspended the session to give time for the emperor to be consulted. Marcian replied 'after a short time' (V. 21) to the effect that either the bishops should agree to amend the draft or he would consider referring the matter to a council to be held in the west, that is, at Rome and under papal chairmanship. It was one thing to resist the will of a chairman who was simply a senior court official; it was another to defy that of the emperor. Yet, amazingly, this is what the bishops continued for a time to do, until the chairman insisted on the setting up, and immediate activation, of a new committee to revise the draft. After deliberations whose length is not specified in the acts but cannot have been protracted, the archdeacon of Constantinople read

35 The presentation by Anatolius of Constantinople of a definition based on his predecessor's confession of faith may be seen as part of his campaign to boost the status of his see.

36 The account in the acts, taken at face value, can leave a very different impression, for which see p. 97 below. The later miaphysite champion Severus of Antioch (d. 538) argued, from selective citation of the minutes, that the bishops demonstrated their Nestorian sympathies by decrying 'from two natures' (Allen and Hayward 2004, 60).

out the amended definition, which was accepted by the bishops by acclamation; the fact that the new version was presented by twenty-three
council fathers, of whom the majority had solidly Cyrillian credentials
and none were dissentient Syrians, broke up the united front on which
opposition to the chairman had depended.[37]

Was the Definition in its final form faithful to Cyril, or accommo-
dating to Theodoret, or significantly Roman, or a mixture of all three?
Opinions have varied ever since. The historian will do best simply to
answer the question: how was the Definition understood by the Cyrillian majority on the committee that finalized its wording and by the
Cyrillian majority on the floor that accepted it by acclamation? It would
be absurd to suggest that either of these groups thought of themselves
as correcting Cyril; they must have given a Cyrillian interpretation to
what they approved, even if the Definition had to contain phrases that
would satisfy the Roman delegates. The final section of the Definition
states that 'one and the same Christ, Son, Lord, Only-begotten' – in
other words, the divine Son, God the Word, as defined in the Nicene
Creed – is 'acknowledged in two natures', while, however, 'the distinctive character of each nature is preserved and comes together into one
person and one hypostasis' (Acts V. 34). 'Acknowledged in two natures'
has been identified as a formula produced by the moderate Cyrillian
Basil of Seleucia on the basis of the description of Christ in a letter of
Cyril's as 'the same perfect in Godhead and the same perfect in
manhood'.[38] '*In* two natures' as a replacement of the original '*from* two
natures' was manifestly a surrender to the chairman's demands, but the
force of the latter formula was implied by the statement that the two
natures '*come together* into one person and one hypostasis'. In all, the
Definition attempted to take the sting out of its assertion of two natures
in Christ, as required by the lay chairman and the Roman delegates, by
expressing it in language derived from Cyril and placing it in the context
of a strong assertion of Christ's oneness. Unfortunately, any assertion of
'two natures' after the union was anathema to the Cyrillian purists, and
the Definition never had a hope of winning universal acceptance in the
eastern provinces.

37 For an analysis of the strongly Cyrillian make up of the committee see Price and
   Gaddis, II, 188–9. This is surely important evidence for what theological loyalties the
   Definition in its final form is likely to have expressed, but it has been overlooked in
   the long debate over the meaning of the Definition.
38 See de Halleux (1976), the most important discussion to date of the sources of the
   Definition.

Three days later (25 October) there followed the sixth session, attended by the emperor Marcian and his consort Pulcheria in person. Marcian made a self-congratulatory speech, in which he compared himself to his great predecessor Constantine, in securing the unity of the Church through unity of doctrine. His speech was followed by the inevitable acclamations and by a reading of the new definition. There follow in the acts the bishops' signatures, whose collection, however, had begun before the session and was to continue after it;[39] they come in this position in the acts as the result of an editorial decision to link them as closely as possible to the text of the Definition. In fact the reading of the text was followed immediately by further acclamations in praise of Marcian the new Constantine and Pulcheria the new Helena. Marcian betrayed awareness that the Definition was already proving divisive by proceeding to pronounce penalties on anyone who stirred up opposition to it in Constantinople. This he followed by a reading of the text of three miscellaneous church canons, which, he declared, should be approved by the bishops 'in council rather than enacted by our laws' (Acts VI. 16), and finally by the elevation of the city of Chalcedon to honorary metropolitan status.[40]

The Later Sessions

By now the council had held sessions spread out over eighteen days; it was to sit for a further week, meeting almost every day, to conduct the remainder of the business that fell to it, that was distinctly miscellaneous. The agenda either arose naturally from the earlier sessions or were set by the emperor. It was therefore unfair, as well as discourteous, when during the proceedings on 30 October the chairman complained, 'The attention to public business necessary for the state is being neglected as

39 Through the metropolitans adding the names of bishops who were not even present at the council the total number of signatories amounted to 452. Honigmann (1942–3) showed that, if we add double counting of bishops represented and their representatives, we reach the figure of 630 council fathers that appears in later sources.

40 This was immediately written into the opening of the Definition, which should be translated 'The holy, great and ecumenical council, assembled... in the metropolis of Chalcedon in the province of Bithynia', not (as so often) 'in Chalcedon the metropolis of the province of Bithynia', which is precisely the dignity that was *not* accorded to the city: Nicomedia remained the provincial capital.

a result of our having been ordered by the divine head to attend the council continually in this way for the sake of the faith' (Acts XII. 2).[41] It was true that much of the business could have despatched by a much smaller body, but it was by the emperor's choice that it received the attention of the whole council. The business consisted in the main of settling disputes over individuals (Theodoret of Cyrrhus, Ibas of Edessa, Domnus formerly bishop of Antioch) and between rival bishops or rival sees (the two claimants to the see of Ephesus, the two claimants to the see of Perrhe in Syria Euphratensis, the rival *metropoleis* of Nicomedia and Nicaea, the rival patriarchates of Antioch and Jerusalem).[42]

Most of the decisions taken were predictable. After the discrediting of the proceedings of Ephesus II it was inevitable that two of its victims, Theodoret and Ibas, would be reinstated. Domnus would also have been reinstated, but Pope Leo had already recognized his successor Maximus, and Domnus himself was happy to retire on a generous pension.[43] Undoing the work of Ephesus II also decided the dispute over the see of Perrhe. If this had been the only factor at play, it would also have settled the dispute between Antioch and Jerusalem (over patriarchal rights) to the advantage of the former, but Bishop Maximus of Antioch was in a weak position (Domnus' rights to his see had still to be discussed) and the two sees worked out a compromise that the council was happy to approve; in the words of a modern historian the two agreed that 'a bad peace was better than a good quarrel'.[44]

This meant that out of all this business the only genuinely contentious item was the dispute over the see of Ephesus, where neither of the rival bishops were edifying candidates for the post and the council fathers were divided.[45] Not surprisingly, in view of the dominant role that was played throughout the council by the imperial representatives, it was the chairman who pressed and secured agreement to a decision that both candidates should be excluded and a new bishop appointed. In the course of the debate there emerged, as a more important issue than the rival claims of the two bishops, the question whether the bishop of Ephesus should be consecrated at Ephesus itself by the bishops of

41 The implication that church affairs, in the view of a highly placed layman of indubitable piety, formed a minor category of government business is worth pondering.

42 See the table of the various sessions in Price and Gaddis, I, xiv (and II and III, viii).

43 See the unnumbered session on Domnus, II, 310–12.

44 Bolotov (1917), 302. The matter was despatched in Session VII of the council.

45 See Price and Gaddis, III, 1–3.

Asiana or at Constantinople by the archbishop of the imperial city;[46] there had been similar contention over the consecration of the metropolitan bishops of the Pontic and Thracian dioceses. The matter was not settled until the final session of the council, on 1 November, when Archbishop Anatolius of Constantinople presented a canon (later known as Canon 28) which laid down that the metropolitans of Thrace, Asiana and Pontica should all be consecrated at Constantinople; it justified the grant of these new privileges on the ground that the see of Constantinople, in view of its status as the imperial city, should enjoy in the eastern provinces rights comparable to those of Rome in Italy (Acts XVI. 8). This final session of the council ended on a sour note when the Roman legates, who had been singularly slow to wake up to the importance of the issue, attempted to impose a veto. The precise nature of their objection is not clear from the acts, but when Pope Leo subsequently took up the matter he contested not the privileges of Constantinople in its immediate hinterland but the bestowal on the city of a status superior to that of the ancient and apostolic sees of Alexandria and Antioch. These, like Rome, were Petrine sees (Mark of Alexandria was Peter's disciple, while Peter had, supposedly, been the first bishop of Antioch before proceeding to Rome), and Rome foresaw that a consequence of the canon would be a weakening of its own influence in Syria and Egypt. The issue was not, as has often been supposed, the relative status of Constantinople and Rome, since no one disputed Roman primacy; what was achieved was the formal erection of the patriarchate of Constantinople.[47]

The numeration 'Canon 28' arose from its later addition to a group of 27 canons that were subsequently issued in the name of the council, and which included the canons that Marcian had entrusted to the bishops at the end of the sixth session. These canons appear as the 'seventh act' of the council in the Greek Acts and as the fifteenth in the final Latin version, but there are no minutes of a conciliar session at which they were discussed. It is possible that they were simply drawn up by Archbishop Anatolius of Constantinople after the council and issued in its name, but in view of the emperor's directions that they were to be

---

46 Acts XI. 52–62. The Asian bishops exclaimed, 'If someone is consecrated here [at Constantinople], our children will perish and the city will be ruined' (53), referring to the extortionate consecration fees charged by the archbishop of Constantinople.

47 See the discussion in Price and Gaddis, III, 70–2, and the articles by A. de Halleux referred to there.

'decreed in council' it is more probable that they were approved at yet another semi-formal session chaired by the archbishop. These canons were principally concerned to secure episcopal control over priests and monks; they are sloppily drafted, and show scant concern for natural justice, but they certainly strengthened the hand of Anatolius, his colleagues and their successors against independent-minded spirits on the lower levels of the church hierarchy.[48] Two canons (9 and 17) are notable for establishing a wide appellate jurisdiction for Constantinople: one is again impressed by the skill of Anatolius is using the council to promote the interests of his own see.

The most important of these later sessions for subsequent church history were the eighth and tenth at which (respectively) Bishop Theodoret of Cyrrhus and Bishop Ibas of Edessa were restored to their sees. Anti-Chalcedonians were to claim repeatedly that these decisions betrayed Nestorian leanings that discredited the council.[49] It is true that Theodoret and Ibas were only restored after they had anathematized Nestorius in the presence of the council fathers, but Theodoret did so with obvious reluctance, and neither bishop was required to withdraw the writings in which a decade or two ago he had fiercely criticized Cyril of Alexandria. This omission was understandable in the context of 451, since they had specifically attacked the Twelve Chapters contained in Cyril's Third Letter to Nestorius, whose authority was not recognized at Chalcedon. By the middle of the sixth century, however, when this Third Letter was presumed to be one of the 'conciliar' letters connected to Ephesus I and acclaimed by Chalcedon, it had come to appear that the council had treated Theodoret and Ibas too leniently.

Particularly intriguing, and vastly debated during the Three Chapters controversy of the time of Justinian,[50] was the Letter of Ibas to Mari the Persian. This letter, written in 433, criticized Cyril and the pro-Cyrillian sessions of Ephesus I with wit and acerbity. It was read out at Chalcedon accidentally, because of its presence in the minutes of a hearing at Berytus in 449 that Ibas' accusers forced on the attention of the council

---

48 For an annotated text of the canons see Price and Gaddis, III, 92–103. For Marcian's directions see Acts VI. 16. Canon 18, forbidding clergy from 'plotting against bishops', has been used in Moscow in post-Soviet times to suppress priests who had the temerity to resist patriarchal injustice.

49 See the minutes of the dialogue between Chalcedonian and anti-Chalcedonian bishops at Constantinople in 532, in Brock (1981).

50 For an analysis of the sixth-century debate see Price (2009), I, 88–98.

fathers. The bishops were not sitting in judgement specifically on the letter, but in the verdicts in which they proceeded to restore Ibas to his see two of them referred to it: the Roman legate Paschasinus declared that 'the most devout Ibas has been proved innocent and from the reading of his letter we have found him to be orthodox' (Acts X. 161), and Maximus of Antioch stated that 'from the reading of the transcript of the letter produced by his adversary his writing has been seen to be orthodox' (X. 163). In view of the letter's disrespectful treatment of Cyril and Ephesus I, and curiously muted criticisms of Nestorius, these compliments seem oddly injudicious. One wonders whether Paschasinus had really taken in the full contents of the letter; he was not a native Greek-speaker, and one may suspect that by the end of the reading of the Acts of Berytus he was not listening very carefully; and as a westerner he may in any case have been less than sensitive to the way in which the letter was acutely embarrassing to the eastern bishops, who recognized that Ibas had to be restored to his see but were hugely respectful of Cyril and Ephesus I. But once Paschasinus as the senior bishop present had uttered his verdict, it was contrary to conciliar etiquette for anyone to question it. Maximus of Antioch, like the other bishops, could simply have ignored the letter when it came to his turn to speak, but his tenure of the see of Antioch (to which Domnus' superior rights had not yet been discounted) depended on Roman support, and he chose to echo Paschasinus. Even Juvenal of Jerusalem, a fierce enemy of all suspected Nestorians and the speaker immediately after Maximus, could go no further than to say, 'Divine Scripture orders the receiving back of those who repent, which is why we also receive people from heresy. I therefore resolve that the most devout Ibas should receive clemency, also because he is elderly, so as to retain episcopal dignity, being orthodox' (X. 164).[51]

Paschasinus also erred in acquitting Ibas without attaching any conditions. The main proof of his orthodoxy presented to the council had been a promise he had made to Photius of Tyre at a hearing back in February 449, recorded in a document that had been read out at the previous session (Acts IX. 7):

The aforesaid most God-beloved man undertook, even beyond the call of duty, to address the church in his own city and publicly anathematize Nesto-

---

51 Michael Whitby comments (p. 190 below), 'A judgement of orthodoxy could scarcely be more damning.'

rius, the fomenter of wicked impiety, and those who shared his beliefs and cited his words or writings; he also undertook to profess belief in what is contained in the letter of accord between the most God-beloved and sacred in memory bishops John of the very great city of Antioch and Cyril of the very great city of Alexandria (a letter whose agent was Paul of blessed memory, bishop of the city of Emesa, and which established universal harmony), to assent to all the recent transactions of the holy synod that met in imperial and Christ-loving Constantinople, and to embrace everything that was decreed in the metropolis of Ephesus, as stemming from a council guided by the Holy Spirit, and to consider it equal to the one convoked at Nicaea, acknowledging no difference between them.[52]

But no one at Chalcedon thought to ask whether Ibas had in fact kept his promise; the minutes of the hearing at Edessa shortly afterwards suggest that hostility towards him was so intense that he had not even been able to return to the city, except possibly on the most fleeting of visits.[53] Yet after Paschasinus' unconditional acquittal of Ibas none of the bishops who spoke individually dared to state unambiguously that Ibas needed to prove his orthodoxy in the presence of the council. Only when it came to the subsequent acclamations did the bishops make the demand, 'Let him now anathematize Nestorius' (Acts X. 179). The council only narrowly escaped the disaster of restoring Ibas without his repudiating Nestorius.

Conciliar Fundamentalism

The question of the judgement of the fathers of Chalcedon on the Letter to Mari the Persian was to prove the most contentious issue in the Three Chapters controversy of the reign of Justinian. The truth was that the council had seen no call to issue a verdict on the matter; but, as we have seen, the letter was referred to with approval by two of the most senior bishops present. Justinian tried to play this down by asserting:

---

52 Reference is to Cyril's *Laetentur caeli* letter in which in 433 he made peace with John of Antioch and the Syrian bishops, the Home Synod of 448 which condemned Eutyches, and the decrees of Ephesus I.
53 These minutes are contained in the Syriac Acts of Ephesus II and translated in Doran (2006), 139–75.

> Often at councils some things are said by some of those found at them out of
> partiality or disagreement or ignorance, but no one attends to what is said
> individually by a few, but only to what is decreed by all by common consent;
> for if one were to choose to attend to such disagreement in the way they do,
> each council will be found refuting itself.[54]

For the reasons I have given it was not really possible to dismiss the
verdict of the senior bishop in so cavalier a fashion, but why could
Justinian not simply have said that the bishops were not judging the
letter and that the favourable references to it were no more than *obiter
dicta*? It is revealing that he felt it necessary to argue that contradictory
statements by different bishops could be discounted; the implication is
that authority attached not simply to conciliar decrees but to whatever
had been said at councils. Even odder is another of his arguments:

> They [Ibas' defenders] claim that the impious letter ought not to be subjected
> to criticism because it is included in some documents. But if one were to
> accept this according to their folly, it would be necessary to accept Nestorius
> and Eutyches, since much about them as well is included in conciliar proceed-
> ings. But no one right-minded will attend to these claims of theirs. For
> information about heretics that is cited at councils and becomes part of the
> minutes is accepted not to absolve them but to convict them and for the
> stronger condemnation both of them and of those who hold the same tenets
> as they do.[55]

The implication is that a document possessed *prima facie* authority
simply because it was to be found in conciliar acts, and Justinian felt it
necessary to make the crassly obvious point that acts contain heretical
documents purely in order to condemn with greater clarity the heresies
they contain.

This tendency to what we call conciliar fundamentalism had not yet
developed by the time of Chalcedon; if it had, the acts would have been
more reticent in revealing dissent and disagreement. We may also note
the attitude of the fathers of Chalcedon to the First Council of Ephesus
of 431. When they referred to the 'proceedings' or 'decrees' of Ephesus
I,[56] they were thinking of Nestorius' condemnation, of Cyril's 'conciliar'

54 Justinian, *De recta fide* (*On the orthodox faith*), Price (2009), I, 150–1.
55 Ibid. p. 150.
56 Note especially the reiterated references to Ephesus I in the judgements passed on
   Leo's Tome at Acts IV. 9.

letters associated with the council, and of the canon forbidding the composition of new creeds.[57] Yet at the same time they felt free to ignore Cyril's Twelve Chapters, despite their citation in the first session of the council.[58]

This new conciliar fundamentalism, where all the acts and not just the decrees were treated with exaggerated respect, not only developed after Chalcedon, but was closely connected to the dissemination of its acts, since no such acts survived from the ecumenical councils of Nicaea and Constantinople I, and only partial acts from Ephesus I. It found eloquent expression in a letter written by Deacon Ferrandus of Carthage in the mid-540s in protest at Justinian's First Edict against the Three Chapters (which seemed to reverse some of the decisions of Chalcedon):

> If there is disapproval of any part of the Council of Chalcedon, the approval of the whole is in danger of becoming disapproval... But the whole Council of Chalcedon, since the whole of it is the Council of Chalcedon, is true; no part of it is open to criticism. Whatever we know to have been uttered, transacted, decreed and confirmed there was worked by the ineffable and secret power of the Holy Spirit.[59]

Whence came this failure to make appropriate distinction between the decrees of the councils and their debates? The explanation lies, I would suggest, in the likening of conciliar acts to the books of Holy Scripture. As Ferrandus wrote in the same letter, 'General councils, particularly those that have gained the assent of the Roman church, hold a place of authority second only to the canonical books.'[60] Of course not everything in conciliar acts was accorded equal weight, and they manifestly contained utterances by heretics, such as Nestorius and Eutyches;[61] but after all not everything in Scripture was of equal weight, and Scripture likewise contained the utterances of the ungodly, such as Jezebel and Caiaphas. Perhaps a still more apt comparison would be with the writings of the Church Fathers: not all of the Fathers were equally venerated, and some of the writings of each one were more

57 The canon on creeds (given at I. 943) was appealed to at the second session (II. 7) and incorporated at the end of the Definition.
58 *ACO* 1.1.2, p. 36, with 1.1.1, pp. 33–42. See de Halleux (1992), 445–54.
59 Ferrandus, *ep.* 6.3 (in Price 2009, I, 114–15)..
60 Ibid. 926A.
61 Acts of Chalcedon I. 470–545 (*passim*) and 944.

central in the tradition than others, but all of them had to be treated with respect and had *prima facie* authority.

The Council of Chalcedon was the first ecumenical council of which complete and full acts were published, and the emperor Marcian in authorizing their publication must have calculated that their honest disclosure of tensions and disagreements would prove the thoroughness and the freedom of the council's work. For a modern reader they show the human side of what was brought about 'by the ineffable and secret power of the Holy Spirit'. But by the sixth century the Acts of Chalcedon had come to be read by Chalcedonians as an authoritative text, and the story of the Council of Chalcedon, as revealed in the acts, was viewed as akin to sacred history.

BIBLIOGRAPHY

Acta Conciliorum Oecumenicorum, ed. Eduard Schwartz and others (Berlin, 1914–).

Allen, Pauline and C.T.R. Hayward (2004), *Severus of Antioch* (London).

Bolotov, V.V. (1917), *Lektsii po istorii drevnei tserkvi*, Vol. 4 (St Petersburg).

Brock, Sebastian (1981), 'The Conversations with the Syrian Orthodox under Justinian (532)', *Orientalia Christiana Peridoica* 47: 87–121 = id., *Studies in Syriac Christianity* (Variorum, 1992), XIII.

Chadwick, Henry (2001), *The Church in Ancient Society: From Galilee to Gregory the Great* (Oxford).

De Halleux, André (1976), 'La définition christologique à Chalcédoine', *RThL* 7: 3–23, 155–70 = id., *Patrologie et oecuménisme* (Leuven, 1990), 445–80.

—— (1992), 'Les douze chapitres cyrilliens au concile d'Ephèse (430–433)', *RThL* 23: 425–58.

Doran, Robert (2006), *Stewards of the Poor: The Man of God, Rabbula, and Hiba in Fifth-Century Edessa* (Kalamazoo).

Draguet, R. (1931), 'La christologie d'Eutychès d'après les Actes du synode de Flavien', *Byz* 6: 441–57.

Honigmann, Ernest (1942–3), 'The Original Lists of the Members of the Council of Nicaea, the Robber Synod and the Council of Chalcedon', *Byz* 16: 20–80.

Kelly, J.N.D. (1972), *Early Christian Creeds*, 3rd edition (London).

MacMullen, Ramsay (2006), *Voting for God in Early Church Councils* (New Haven & London).

Martindale, J. R. (1980), *The Prosopography of the Later Roman Empire*, vol. 2: A.D. 395–527 (Cambridge).

Pelagius [Pope Pelagius I], *In defensione trium capitulorum*, ed. Robert

Devreesse, Studi e Testi 57 (Vatican City, 1932), and PL, Suppl. 4, 1313–69 (Paris, 1967).

Price, Richard and Gaddis, Michael (2005), *The Acts of the Council of Chalcedon*, 3 vols, TTH 45 (Liverpool).

Price, R.M. (2007), 'Theotokos: The Title and its Significance in Doctrine and Devotion', in S.J. Boss, ed., *Mary: The Complete Resource* (London), 56–73.

—— (2009). *Acts of the Council of Constantinople of 553*, trans. with introduction and notes, 2 vols, TTH 51 (Liverpool).

Ps.-Zachariah of Mitylene, *Historia Ecclesiastica*. Trans. F.J. Hamilton and E.W. Brooks, *The Syriac Chronicle known as that of Zachariah of Mitylene* (London, 1899; New York, 1979).

Ste. Croix, G.E.M. de (2006), 'The Council of Chalcedon' (with additions by Michael Whitby), in *Christian Persecution, Martyrdom, and Orthodoxy* (Oxford), 259–319.

Schwartz, Eduard (1933), 'Zweisprachigkeit in den Konzilsakten', *Philologus* 88: 245–53.

TRUTH, OMISSION, AND FICTION
IN THE ACTS OF CHALCEDON

Richard Price

Truth

Who in the early church published conciliar acts and why? Without attempting a generalization, I shall simply say that the Acts of Chalcedon were manifestly produced and published by the imperial government, shortly after the council.[1] What was the purpose of publishing the minutes, and not just the decrees? The minutes inevitably showed up disagreements: how was this of any advantage to the winning side?

It is to be noted that conciliar decisions had to be unanimous. All the bishops at Chalcedon, save the Egyptians (allowed to drop out after their patriarch's deposition), had to sign the Definition of Faith. Anti-Chalcedonian sources inform us of bishops who only signed the Definition under compulsion or whose signatures had to be provided by colleagues.[2] Regularly throughout the council when a formal decision had to be reached, a period of open discussion (where the minutes are more likely to be selective than complete) would be closed by the senior bishop present delivering his judgement; this would be followed by similar pronouncements by other bishops, delivered in rough order of seniority. The total number of individual verdicts varied – 192 (almost all the bishops present) in the condemnation of Dioscorus in Session III, 161 in the approval of Leo's Tome in Session IV, a mere 18 in the reinstatement of Bishop Ibas of Edessa in Session X.[3] The remaining bishops would then express their view by acclamation, after an invitation (not always recorded) by the chairman. There was no scope for contrary voices: this imposed a duty on the senior bishop to express the common consensus, but once he had spoken the other bishops had no option but

---

1 A date of 455 for the publication of the Acts of Chalcedon can be deduced from dates of the documents in the attached documentary collections (Price and Gaddis, III, 180).
2 See Price and Gaddis, II, 207 and 234 (n. 47).
3 Acts of Chalcedon III. 94–6; IV. 9; X. 161–78.

to confirm his decision.[4] Indeed, the verdict of the senior bishop took immediate effect, even before the other bishops had spoken. This is clear from the trial of Dioscorus at the third session, where the first bishop to pronounce a verdict was the papal legate Paschasinus, who declared Dioscorus deposed: once he had done so, all the bishops who subsequently delivered verdicts referred to Dioscorus as 'formerly' bishop of Alexandria (Acts III. 94–6). This is in stark contrast to the proceedings of the Roman Senate, where senators also spoke in order of seniority but enjoyed a freedom, absent from ecumenical councils, to express contrary opinions or to make counter-proposals when their turn to speak came round.

This unanimity, credible in the case of judicial verdicts on individuals, was, of course, artificial in the case of debates over doctrine, for if a particular doctrine was really held unanimously there would have been no need for a conciliar debate at all. When the emperor Constantine arrived in the eastern provinces in 324 as victor over Licinius, he was shocked to discover bitter contention over the niceties of how to describe the relation between the First and Second Persons of the Trinity, and wrote to a council of bishops at Antioch,

> You surely know how even the philosophers themselves all agree in one set of principles, and often when they disagree in some part of their statements, although they are separated by their learned skill, yet they agree together again in unity when it comes to basic principle... Let us reconsider what was said with more thought and greater understanding, to see whether it is right that, through a few futile verbal quarrels between you, brothers are set against brothers and the honourable synod divided in ungodly variance through us, when we quarrel with each other over such small and utterly unimportant matters.[5]

Constantine's perception that the essence of Christianity lies in the united worship of God rather than in a futile demand for intellectual precision was not shared by the dominant figures in the late antique episcopate in the eastern provinces. For them it was the truth that was at issue, and there could only be one truth. Whoever did not share the convictions of the majority was an enemy of the truth, a heretic; there

---

4 See my discussion of the verdicts on Ibas of Edessa, pp. 85–6 above.
5 Eusebius, *Life of Constantine* 2.70.2–3, trans. Cameron and Hall, 118. See note on p. 250.

was therefore no scope at councils for the toleration of dissident minorities. In retrospect, moreover, each council was perceived to have been guided by the Holy Spirit, and a fruit and sign of the presence of the Holy Spirit was 'one heart and soul' (Acts of the Apostles 4:32). As Deacon Ferrandus of Carthage was to write of the Council of Chalcedon in the mid-540s:

> Whatever we know to have been uttered, transacted, decreed and confirmed there was worked by the ineffable and secret power of the Holy Spirit... No one there condemned anyone against the will of others, no one acquitted anyone against the will of others; all agreed with one another and readily fulfilled the words of the teacher of the Gentiles, heeding his words, 'I beseech you, brethren, that you all say the same and that there be not divisions among you.'[6]

The presumption of unanimity imposed on the editors of the minutes a particular responsibility. The problems of writing up the minutes of councils are delightfully illustrated in the minutes, read out at the first session of Chalcedon, of a hearing held in April 449 to examine the Acts of the Home Synod of November 448 at which Eutyches had been condemned for refusing to recognize two natures in Christ.[7] Revealing is the evidence that at the synod Bishop Basil of Seleucia had tried to help Eutyches by suggesting a sound miaphysite (one-nature) formula and that this had led to an angry exchange with Eutyches' accuser, Eusebius of Dorylaeum, an uncompromising dyophysite.[8] None of this appears in the minutes, which represent the synod fathers as united in their support of Eusebius and their hounding of Eutyches. One of the notaries commented that some of the bishops' interventions were not intended for recording (Acts I. 792); at no less than three points in the examination of the minutes the patrician Florentius reacted to the inclusion of ill-judged interventions he had made by saying that they should not have been minuted (I. 772–8). Then as now minute-takers had the unenviable task of distinguishing between remarks whose omission would offend and remarks whose inclusion would be equally unwelcome.

Yet the acts are surprisingly honest about the degree of dissent, particularly the disagreement between the lay chairman and the bishops as a

---

6   Ferrandus, *ep.* 6. 3,5 (in Price 2009, I, 114–16), citing 1 Cor 1:10.
7   Acts I. 555–828.
8   See Acts I. 754, 791, 798.

whole that arose at a number of points in the council. At the beginning of the second session the chairman said to the bishops, 'Apply yourselves without fear, favour or enmity to produce a pure exposition of the faith' (II. 2). The bishops, however, had no wish to produce a new definition of the faith and responded, 'What has already been expounded is sufficient. It is not permissible to produce another exposition' (II. 5). This was a straight rejection of the chairman's proposal. The chairman got round it by ignoring it: he closed the session with the words, 'The proposals will be put into effect' (II. 45).

Particularly striking is the dramatic confrontation between the lay chairman and the bishops that took place at the fifth session, which began with the presentation of a draft definition of the faith, produced by a committee chaired by Archbishop Anatolius of Constantinople. The Roman delegates and a few of the Syrian bishops objected to the draft, at which the lay chairman said it would have to be amended. The bishops responded, 'Let the definition be signed now. Whoever will not sign is a heretic' (V. 12). The chairman proceeded to argue that the Definition had to be amended so as to make clear a real and continuing duality in Christ even after the union, in accord with the teaching of Pope Leo; the bishops responded, 'The definition contains everything... Exclude all chicanery from the letter' (V. 20). The matter was referred to the emperor, who told the bishops they had to give way. Amazingly, they still put up resistance, exclaiming, 'Let the definition be confirmed or we shall leave' (V. 23), and again, 'The dissenters are Nestorians. Let the dissenters go off to Rome' (V. 25). It needed further persuasion, or rather dictation, from the chairman before they agreed to amendment of the draft.

All this was highly useful information for subsequent critics of the council, who could claim that the bishops had produced the Definition only under coercion, and what was worse, under coercion by lay officials with Nestorian sympathies. As a non-Chalcedonian of the mid-sixth century, John Philoponus, was to write: 'He (Marcian) made the bishops sit as judges in appearance, but he joined to them as the true judges the notables and senators, among whom were to be found supporters of paganism, of Manichaeism and of other heresies, and the majority were friends of Nestorius.'[9]

9 Philoponus, *Four Tmêmata against Chalcedon*, as abridged in Michael the Syrian, *Chronicle*, trans. Chabot, II, 99. Several of the officials who presided over the council had corresponded with Theodoret, and the chairman Anatolius was Theodoret's friend. See Price and Gaddis, I, 122–3, notes.

So how are we to account for the truthfulness of the acts about dissension at the council? In the first session the minutes of the first session of the so-called 'Robber Council' of Ephesus of 449 were read out; of the bishops who had attended that council and supported Dioscorus 119 were present at Chalcedon (out of a total attendance at Chalcedon of around 370). They attempted to excuse their behaviour at Ephesus by claiming that they had acted under duress and that the minutes of Ephesus gave a false impression of unanimity.[10] The emperor Marcian was therefore concerned that at Chalcedon there should be free debate and faithful minutes that recorded disagreement[11] – within, however, certain limits, that must now be discussed.

Omission

At the fifth session (as I have already said) the draft definition was read out, discussed, and eventually amended; it was the most significant and the most dramatic of all the sessions of the council. There are striking omissions in the minutes: they leave out the draft definition, as also the objections raised to it by the Roman delegates and by some of the Syrian bishops. The sheer brevity of the record is proof of extensive omissions. At the end of the session, after the reading out of the revised definition, the bishops are recorded as approving it by universal acclamation: 'This is the faith of the fathers. Let the metropolitans sign at once... To this we all assent. We all believe accordingly' (Acts V. 35). Whence suddenly this happy consensus? Did the mere reading of the Definition in its final form silence all dissent and leave scope for nothing but applause? Even if, as we have seen, the main sequence of the session was recorded with surprising honesty, it is clear that the editors of the acts used plenty of red pencil: although the existence of disagreement over the drafting of the Definition was to be admitted as evidence of honest debate, the details of the discussion were to be excised, since they would have revealed real theological disagreement, and that would have been scandalous. The work of the council had been to suppress innovation in

10 E.g., Acts I. 134 and 121–2.
11 Note the alternative explanation advanced by Michael Whitby (p. 183 below): the honesty of the acts as to the degree of episcopal dissension was intended to bring out the need for firm imperial direction of church affairs. It is certainly true that the acts, and the documentary collections that accompanied them (for which see Price and Gaddis, III, 157–92), stress rather than minimize imperial involvement.

doctrine and respond to the guidance of the Holy Spirit;[12] there may have been disagreement on how exactly to word the common belief shared by all, but nothing was to be left in the minutes that would undermine the impression of unity in belief and witness, and a genuine unanimity in approving the Definition in its final form.

The result has sometimes deceived historians as to what was really going on. It emerges from the acts that the draft definition stated that Christ is 'from two natures'. The Roman delegates and the chairman wanted this formula to be replaced by a wholly unambiguous statement of a continued distinction between the two natures even after the union; the majority of bishops present resisted this, since it smacked to them of Nestorianism. In the minutes as they stand, however, 'from two natures' features as the favoured expression of the recently condemned Dioscorus, while the stronger expression that the chairman demanded is presented as the teaching of Pope Leo that all the bishops had approved without reservation at the fourth session (Acts V. 13–17). The bishops, according to this account, had no solid reason to raise difficulties, and the chairman's task was not to compel them to accept something against their will, but simply to explain to them, as to slow-witted schoolchildren, the clear logic of the question before them; and this he did, one modern historian has naively remarked, 'with exemplary patience'.[13]

One may likewise suspect omission in the closing paragraphs of the acts of the eighth session. The minutes give a frank account of the testy discussion that preceded the bishops' approval of the reinstatement of Theodoret to his see of Cyrrhus, after he had reluctantly anathematized Nestorius, and then record the uttering of similar anathemas by three further bishops suspected of heresy (Sophronius of Constantia, John of Germanicia, and Amphilochius of Side) in response to demands from 'the most devout bishops' (Acts VIII. 26–31).[14] But there must have been discussion of each of these bishops in turn, and the lay chairman must have played a part. Yet none of this appears in the acts; what we have is manifestly the barest summary.

The most obvious cases of omission in the acts are, of course, the

12 See Marcian's edicts confirming the decrees of the council, Price and Gaddis, III, 128–36.

13 Kidd (1922), III, 325.

14 The preceding sections (VIII. 4–25) treat the case of Theodoret at length; the only unclarity is the comparative sizes of the episcopal party that declared him a 'heretic' (12) and of the party that hailed him as an 'orthodox teacher' (15).

sessions of which there are simply no minutes, notably those held separately under the chairmanship of Archbishop Anatolius of Constantinople. The public sessions were held in the church of St Euphemia, and were chaired by a bench of high state officials (in practice by their leader, the patrician Anatolius), except for the third session, when the senior Roman legate presided. But in addition to these we hear of meetings of large numbers of bishops under the chairmanship of Archbishop Anatolius of Constantinople, some in the same church and some in his palace on the other side of the Bosporus.[15] The acts contain references to four of these: first, to a meeting aimed at ironing out disagreement over Leo's Tome before the matter was brought to a public session of the council (Acts II. 31).[16] When it was brought to the formal fourth session two groups of bishops testified to assurances on the meaning of the Tome that had been given at this earlier session by the Roman delegates, who clearly went out of their way to assure the doubters that the Tome's insistence on the distinction between the natures was in no way intended to teach their separation.[17] But otherwise the minutes of the fourth session consist of nothing more than the bishops declaring briefly and repetitively that the Tome was orthodox. Since many of the same bishops had acquiesced in the suppression at Ephesus II of a letter from Leo summarizing the Tome, just two years previously, their testimony at Chalcedon was all too obviously mere conformism. Minutes of the earlier meeting, where in contrast there was serious and frank discussion, would have provided more convincing testimony to the Tome's orthodoxy; the lack of such minutes in the acts weakened their effectiveness as propaganda.

Secondly, there are references at the fifth session to a meeting of the bishops on the previous day where the draft definition 'satisfied everyone' (Acts V. 7, 8, 12). Thirdly, we read in the minutes of the sixteenth session of a previous meeting of the bishops, again under the chairmanship of Archbishop Anatolius, where Canon 28 on the status and privileges of the see of Constantinople was approved and signed by

---

15 The initial meeting that approved Canon 28 was held in St Euphemia's after the officials had departed (Acts XVI. 4), while another of these meetings was held 'in the residence of the most holy Archbishop Anatolius' (II. 31).

16 This meeting was intended primarily for those in doubt over the Tome and some carefully selected bishops able to reassure them (Acts II. 33), but other bishops are likely to have attended out of interest.

17 Acts IV.9, after §§98 and 114.

182 bishops (XVI. 4–9).[18] Fourthly, there may also have been a session to approve the other 27 canons; there is no reference to such a session, but the emperor had asked for one when he himself attended the session at which the Definition was formally proclaimed (VI. 16).[19] We can also detect some omissions in the extant acts resulting from revision of the text subsequent to its initial publication under Marcian. The minutes of the tenth session contain, within the minutes of a previous hearing at Berytus that were read out at this session, the notorious Letter of Bishop Ibas of Edessa to Mari the Persian, presented very barely without any introduction or comment (X. 137–8). Yet the inclusion in the acts just before the reading of the letter of a formula of verification ('I have read, we have read, he had read') that regularly follows statements by the chairman at Chalcedon proves that a statement by him at this point was originally given in the minutes. The Berytus minutes must likewise have contained a statement by the chairman at Berytus authorizing the reading, and there would surely have followed discussion of the letter, both at Berytus and at Chalcedon. Why and when was all this suppressed? The natural presumption is that this was done during the Three Chapters controversy in the time of Justinian: Justinian claimed that the bishops of Chalcedon regarded the letter as a forgery, and the suppressed part of the minutes may well have contained evidence that disproved this claim. Should the suppression be attributed to Justinian himself? However, he himself asserted that there was no trace of this particular session among the original conciliar documents;[20] can we really believe him to have been so duplicitous as to make this claim while knowing that he himself had secreted the original minutes? Moreover, if they had survived till Justinian's time, they would surely have been unearthed by those defenders of Ibas' letter, notably Rusticus and Facundus, who searched the archives of Constantinople.[21] It remains

18 Attendance was in no way restricted to the bishops (of the Thracian, Asian and Pontic dioceses) who were directly affected: the signatories include many bishops from Syria and Palestine.

19 Price and Gaddis, III, 92–3 suggest that no such session took place, and that the canons were simply issued by Anatolius in the council's name; but I think now that I failed to give sufficient weight to Marcian's instructions and that there must have been some meeting of bishops to rubber-stamp the canons.

20 Justinian, *Letter on the Three Chapters* (Schwartz 1939, p. 66, 15–18) and *On the orthodox faith* (ibid., p. 100, 4–6).

21 Note that the *Codex Acumitanus*, an early manuscript used by Rusticus, contained the minutes of the tenth session (Schwartz 1923, 16–17). Eduard Schwartz first suspected that Justinian had suppressed the record, but later changed his mind; I now withdraw my earlier preference (Price and Gaddis, II, 271–2) for his original opinion.

plausible to suppose that the tampering with the record was due to embarrassment over the Letter to Ibas, but at an earlier date than the reign of Justinian.

Fiction and Falsification

The acts have reached us in two editions: the original edition produced in the 450s is lost, but we have a fairly complete Latin edition dating from the 550s, and a less complete Greek edition dating perhaps to the early seventh century.[22] There is some variation in contents. It would appear that the unnumbered acts (whether surviving in Greek or Latin) were not part of the original edition.[23] Both of the two surviving editions, though particularly the Greek edition, go in for a certain amount of sensible abbreviation – of minor sessions,[24] of documents read out,[25] of some of the more repetitive verdicts,[26] and of some of the lists of bishops.[27] There are occasionally interesting variations in the wording of statements made. In the eighth session, after the reinstatement of Theodoret of Cyrrhus, we have the acclamation, 'May the church be restored to the orthodox teacher Theodoret' (Acts VIII. 15). By 600, after the condemnation of a number of Theodoret's writings at the council of 553, this was an embarrassment, and in the Greek Acts the words 'the orthodox teacher' are omitted.

There are significant variations between the Greek and Latin versions in the minutes of Session XVI (XVII in the Greek edition), at which the Roman delegates protested unavailingly against Canon 28, which assigned new powers to the see of Constantinople. In support of this canon the archdeacon of Constantinople produced the canons of the Council of Constantinople of 381, which had accorded Constantinople

---

22 See Price and Gaddis, I, 78–85.

23 These are the Acts on Carosus and Dorotheus (Price and Gaddis, II, 164–8), on Photius and Eustathius (ibid., 169–82), and on Domnus of Antioch (ibid., 310–12).

24 Of the three just listed, the first two survive only in Greek, the third only in Latin.

25 For example, the Greek edition omits the acts of the session of the Council of Ephesus of 22 July 431, which were read out at Ephesus II and consequently found their way into the Acts of Chalcedon (I. 911–45).

26 For example, the Greek edition gives at III. 96 the bare names of the bishops who condemned Dioscorus but omits their verdicts.

27 For example, the Latin edition omits or abbreviates the attendance lists of Sessions II, III and IV.

honorary primacy in the east. The Roman delegates rejected them as lacking authority – they were indeed absent from the standard collection of conciliar canons that was used throughout the council.[28] These Romans objections are frankly recorded in the Latin Acts, but the Greek edition waters them down, reducing the Roman rejection of all these canons to an expression of unease; it likewise toned down the words with which at the end of the session the Roman delegates attempted to veto the new canon.[29] Likewise, in the third session, when the Roman delegates pronounced sentence against Dioscorus, they referred to the pope as 'the head of the universal church', as we know from the text preserved in a letter of Pope Leo's; but in the conciliar acts, in both the Greek and Latin editions, this high claim for Roman authority is omitted.[30]

Both the Latin and Greek editions of the acts omit one curiosity in the original list of episcopal verdicts delivered against Dioscorus of Alexandria in Session III. The Roman deacon Rusticus in his edition of the Latin version gives a number to each of these verdicts, starting with that of Anatolius of Constantinople, as no 9. He informs us that in the original list (now lost) the three Roman delegates (who counted as the senior bishops at Chalcedon) were numbered 6–8 and preceded by five still more august judges who had pronounced sentence against Dioscorus, no 5 being Pope Leo himself, no 4 St Peter, and 1–3 the three Persons of the Most Holy Trinity.[31] It was clearly an embarrassment to the government that the list of bishops who pronounced sentence against Dioscorus was on the short side, only 192 out of the 370 bishops who attended the council; so to boost the number the Persons of the Trinity were dragooned into service.[32]

---

28 The existence of a collected edition of canons is revealed by the citation of canons with a consecutive numbering (e.g. at Session on Carosus and Dorotheus 8). The absence of the canons of 381 from this collection was pointed out by the Roman delegate Lucentius (XVI. 12) and is confirmed by the fact that the archdeacon of Constantinople had to read them from a separate document (see Price and Gaddis, III, 86, n. 39).

29 See Price and Gaddis, III, 84 with nn. 30 and 32, and p. 91 with n. 51.

30 Price and Gaddis, II, 69–70, with nn. 96 and 100. For signs of a similar bias in the editing of the documentary collections see I, 80–1.

31 *ACO* 2.3, p. 305.

32 The variety of efforts to produce an impressive list of bishops who condemned Dioscorus is also evidenced by the survival of two quite independent subscription lists, one in the Greek and one in the Latin edition of the Acts; see Price and Gaddis, II, 36–7, 93–110.

But there are problems about virtually all the bishops' lists. We have supposedly complete attendance lists for the first four and the sixth sessions, and a list of metropolitans present for most of the other sessions. In addition we have subscription lists (that is, lists of signatories) for Dioscorus' condemnation, for the Definition, and for Canon 28. Schwartz demonstrated that all the attendance lists, save that for the third session, are based on the version of the subscription list to the Definition that is included in the acts. There are a number of bizarre features here, of which I can only offer a tentative and partial explanation.[33]

The subscription list for the Definition that we find in the acts was carefully compiled: it is full and accurate on the cases where absent bishops were represented by other bishops or their clergy. Yet it is not complete: it omits 28 names that we happen to know of from another edition of the list (otherwise less complete) that survives in Latin and Syriac canonical sources.[34]

All but one of the full attendance lists are based on this subscription list to the Definition contained in the acts: this is clear from the fact that they present essentially the same names in the same (inevitably arbitrary) order and that all the omissions in the subscription list recur in all the attendance lists (save, as I have said, for the list for Session III, which is wholly independent and sets its own problems). These attendance lists include the odd name of someone we happen to know was absent – for example, Meliphthongus of Juliopolis, who said when signing Dioscorus' condemnation that he had only just arrived, but is listed as having attended all the earlier sessions.[35] It is true that some of the omissions can be confirmed as accurate from data in the minutes, and it might appear that some corrections were made in these lists on the basis of the original, authentic attendance lists. But there are two problems with this. Firstly, if the lists were revised through comparison with the original attendance lists, why do they not include some at least of the 28 names omitted by accident from the subscription list to the Definition? Secondly, it is highly likely that attendance fell significantly in Sessions II–IV because of the suspension at the end of the first session, and restoration only in the course of the fourth session, of five metropolitan

---

33 Schwartz (1937). Honigmann (1942–3) refined on Schwartz's data and offered his own solution. My own discussion is in Price and Gaddis, III, 196–201.

34 This is Dionysius Exiguus, *Collectio Dionysiana* (*ACO* 2.2, pp. 157–69), translated in Price and Gaddis, II, 232–9, as emended by Honigmann (1942–3).

35 Acts I. 3.164, II. 1.128, III. 97.235 (Greek version, Price and Gaddis, II, 98).

bishops who had collaborated with Dioscorus at Ephesus II.[36] Yet the attendance lists show only a modest fall in attendance in Sessions II and IV.

The council was uniquely well attended; it was indeed the ecumenical council with the highest attendance until the First Vatican Council of 1869–70. It was clearly important to prove this by full and impressive attendance and subscription lists. Why then were the lists so imperfect? The sheer number of bishops present – around 370[37] – seems to have led to confusion, compounded by the presence in attendance on the bishops of numerous lower clergy, some of whom make it into the lists through representing absent bishops.[38] One must presume that the original signed lists, whether subscription lists or attendance lists, were a complete mess, and that the notaries took the easy way out of taking one single list – a *fairly* complete subscription list to the Definition – and concocting on its basis neat but bogus attendance lists.

If this explanation be accepted, we may then recognize in the independent attendance list for the third session a survival of the original, authentic attendance lists: it is indeed a most unsatisfactory document, marred by a number of omissions detectable from the minutes that follow, and often inaccurate as to which bishops were present in person and which were represented by others.[39] Why was this list not tidied up like the rest? It may be relevant that this was the only session that was not chaired by a lay official but by a bishop (namely, Paschasinus of Lilybaeum, the senior Roman delegate). Somehow this led to the employment, at some key stage of editing, of less competent, but more honest, scribes.

To what extent do these bogus lists mislead the reader as to the course of the council? They do not disguise the poor attendance at Dioscorus' trial in Session III (at which scarcely over 200 bishops were present), since the authentic attendance list for this session was preserved. What they do disguise, however, is the poor attendance at Sessions II and IV. The virtually identical attendance lists for Sessions II and IV give 305

36 See Acts I. 1068 and IV. 14–18.
37 For this calculation see Price and Gaddis, III, 193–6.
38 MacMullen (2006), 79 estimates the number of clergy in attendance on their bishops at councils (but not counting as active participants) at anything up to twice the number of bishops.
39 See Price and Gaddis, II, 35–6, with footnotes on pp. 38–41. In the minutes that follow speeches are attributed to six bishops who were not personally present at the council (see footnotes on pp. 75–91).

names. This may be compared to the 343 listed attendances for Session I and to the 324 for Session VI,[40] the fall from Session I being accounted for by the absence, from all the sessions after the first, of the 20 Egyptian bishops. At the end of Session I not only Dioscorus but also five other leading metropolitans were deposed, and were not restored till a midway point in Session IV. This will have led to the non-participation in the council for a whole week not only of these bishops but also of the great majority of the 60 suffragans who had accompanied them to the council; we may also surmise that some other bishops will have absented themselves from Sessions II and IV out of solidarity.[41] This was a sufficiently large number to dent the ability of the council to claim to be the voice of the whole Church. What saved the council was a decision to cancel the sentence of deposition pronounced by the lay chairman at the end of Session I. Instead, Dioscorus was put on trial and deposed at Session III, while the other five deposed metropolitans were all reinstated in the course of the following session, after they had expressed their adherence to the majority by signing Leo's Tome (Acts IV. 16).

Once the suspended metropolitans and all their suffragans returned to full participation in the council, the only group of abstainers were the Egyptian bishops; at the fourth session the other bishops pressed for them to be forced to accept the council's decrees, but the lay chairman accepted their plea that, while there was no bishop of Alexandria to give a lead, they could not speak for the Egyptian Church. Apart from them, all the bishops attending the council were obliged to sign the Definition,[42] and an appearance of unanimity was achieved.

40 Since these two lists were based on a less than complete subscription list to the Definition, as already mentioned, these figures are actually too low. We may presume that all the 370 bishops (or bishops' representatives) who came to the council attended the first session (barring the odd late arrival) and that all the bishops, save the Egyptians, attended the sixth. Attendance at the latter was made compulsory by the presence of the emperor himself.

41 However, the inclusion of Palestinian bishops in the minority that interrupted the reading of Leo's Tome at Session II (Acts II. 24–6) shows that not all of them chose to share the absence from the council of the suspended Juvenal of Jerusalem; moreover the Illyrian bishops, who largely absented themselves from Session III, were also prominent at Session II (Acts II. 24–6, 37–44). Attendance at Sessions II and IV will have been significantly higher than that at Session III (the trial of Dioscorus), where attendance was diminished yet further by the unpopularity of the victimizing of Dioscorus.

42 See Price and Gaddis, II, 207.

Conclusion

Of my three categories of truth, omission and fiction, the first, fortunately, greatly outweighs the third. We have no reason to suppose that the Acts of Chalcedon are seriously misleading as to the proceedings of the council. Compared to the acts of other councils, they are extraordinarily frank about the degree of disagreement and dissent, even if we can from time to time detect some degree of toning down.

The category of omission is much more significant than that of fiction. We must not read the Acts of Chalcedon as if they were a complete record. If the acts of the first session are so long that not all the documents they contain can actually have been read out, the acts of some of the later sessions, most obviously the crucial fifth session, are suspiciously brief. As we read the acts, we must allow for the omission of *obiter dicta* that it was in no one's interest to record for posterity. Above all, we must remember the crucial importance of the unminuted meetings chaired by Archbishop Anatolius. Nor shall we forget the work of committees (notably those that drafted and revised the Definition) or the role of private lobbying and confabulation. The historian of Chalcedon has before him the longest single document that survives from the early Church; but he needs to supplement it through two gifts essential for any historian – common sense and imagination.

BIBLIOGRAPHY

Acta Conciliorum Oecumenicorum, ed. Eduard Schwartz and others (Berlin, 1914–).

Eusebius, *Life of Constantine*, trans. with introduction and commentary by Averil Cameron and S.G. Hall (Oxford, 1999).

Honigmann, Ernest (1942–3), 'The Original Lists of the Members of the Council of Nicaea, the Robber Synod and the Council of Chalcedon', *Byz* 16: 20–80.

Kidd, B.J. (1922), *A History of the Church to A.D. 461*, 3 vols (Oxford).

MacMullen, Ramsay (2006), *Voting for God in Early Church Councils* (New Haven & London).

Michael the Syrian, *Chronicle. Chronique de Michel le Syrien Patriarche Jacobite d'Antioche (1166–99)*, ed. and trans. J.-B. Chabot, vol. 2 [trans. of VII–XI] (Paris, 1901).

Price, Richard and Gaddis, Michael (2005), *The Acts of the Council of Chalcedon*, 3 vols, TTH 45 (Liverpool).

Price, R.M. (2009). *Acts of the Council of Constantinople of 553*, trans. with introduction and notes, 2 vols, TTH 51 (Liverpool).

Schwartz, Eduard (1923), 'Aus den Akten des Concils von Chalkedon', ABAW.PPH 32.2.

—— (1937), *Über die Bischofslisten der Synoden von Chalkedon, Nicaea und Konstantinopel,* ABAW.PH NF 13 (Munich).

—— (1939), *Drei dogmatische Schriften Justinians.* ABAW.PH NF 18 (Munich).

WHY DID THE SYRIANS REJECT
THE COUNCIL OF CHALCEDON?[1]

Andrew Louth

After the deposition of Dioscorus of Alexandria at the Synod of Chalcedon, the 'Oriental bishops and those with them' are represented as exclaiming: 'Many years to the senate! Holy God, Holy Strong, Holy Immortal, have mercy on us. Many years to the emperors! The impious are always routed; Christ has deposed Dioscorus.'[2] This is the earliest record of the Thrice-Holy Hymn, the *Trisagion*. It is not clear why the bishops of the diocese of Oriens thought it appropriate to exclaim it on this occasion. It is striking, however, that barely a quarter of a century later, the thrice-holy hymn, with the theopaschite addition ('Holy God, Holy Strong, Holy Immortal, who was crucified for us, have mercy on us') became popular in Antioch, as a chant encapsulating the rejection of the Chalcedonian Definition. For even though the controversy over the *Trisagion* was really a misunderstanding between a Trinitarian understanding of the hymn, found in Constantinople, in which the theopaschite addition implied the possibility of the divine nature, rejected on all sides, and a Christological understanding of the hymn, which affirmed that Christ suffered on the Cross, for the Syrians the theopaschite version of the *Trisagion* underlined what they believed to be the defect of Chalcedon, namely its failure to affirm with uncompromising clarity that through the Incarnation, God himself, the second person of the Trinity, assumed human nature and human experience, and in particular the human experience of death, in order to redeem humanity from the curse of death unleashed by the Fall of Adam. It is this Syrian rejection of Chalcedon that this paper seeks to reflect on. Not so much the question as to why the non-Chalcedonians, dubbed by their opponents 'monophysite' (or by modern scholars 'miaphysite', despite the barbarity of such a Greek construction), rejected Chalcedon, which

---

1 This paper has been vastly improved by the comments and suggestions of Mary Whitby and Richard Price, to whom I want to record my gratitude.
2 Acts of Chalcedon I. 1071, Price and Gaddis (2005), I, 364 (changing 'Almighty' to 'Strong', surely a more natural translation of ἰσχυρός).

is a fairly straightforward matter, but specifically the 'Syrians', symbolized in the contrast I have just made between the Oriental bishops chanting the *Trisagion* in its original unadorned form against Dioscorus and their successors making of the *Trisagion* with its theopaschite addition an emblem of their rejection of the very Chalcedon that had deposed Dioscorus. My question is not just why did the monophysites reject Chalcedon, but how did the Syrian bishops come to be amongst their number?

This question is rendered the more puzzling by the way in which the course of the fifth-century Christological controversy is generally presented (and this is true of the excellent introduction to the volumes we are celebrating today, though some of the footnotes suggest another story). It is presented as a clash between the Alexandrian tradition and the Antiochene tradition, or more precisely between the Alexandrian *school* and the Antiochene *school*. These two 'schools' are often represented as having a long history, reaching right back to the beginnings of Christianity, and coming to a collision over Christology in the late fourth and early fifth century – a collision that led to the synods of Ephesus I, Ephesus II (the 'Robber Synod', as Pope Leo called it), and Chalcedon. For the later dominant traditions of Eastern Orthodoxy and Latin Christianity, the issue was solved at Chalcedon, but in reality the result of these synods was a couple of schisms that last to the present day. Ephesus I produced a schism in which those who refused to accept the condemnation of Nestorius formed a separate church, very soon located over the imperial frontier in Persia, now called the 'Assyrian Church of the East'; Chalcedon produced a schism that divided the Christians in the eastern part of the Empire: in the course of the sixth century a separate hierarchy was established, while by the middle of the seventh virtually all these Christians who rejected Chalcedon found themselves under Islam, beyond the frontier of the Empire, where they have remained, and are today known as the 'Oriental Orthodox'. The strongholds of the Oriental Orthodox were, from the beginning, in Syria, where they were called 'Jacobites', after Jacob Baradaeus, who established the monophysite hierarchy, and in Egypt, where they were called 'Theodosians', after Theodosius, a contemporary of Jacob. It seems obvious why the non-Chalcedonians include the Egyptians. But why the Syrians, if the controversy was the culmination of a long-standing rivalry between the two opposing schools of Alexandria and Antioch?

The abandonment of Chalcedon by Antioch and Syria did not take place overnight. To begin with, the bishops of the Orient (which included Asia Minor and Thrace, as well as Syria) upheld Chalcedon: the Emperor Leo I's encyclical letter (*Encyclia* or *Codex Encyclius*) of 457, issued after the murder of the Alexandrian patriarch Proterius, received from the bishops of the Empire, including the Syrians, a response almost entirely favourable to Chalcedon, though this unanimity had more to do with desire for peace and genuine outrage at the murder of Proterius than any enthusiasm for the Chalcedonian Definition.[3] But in the wake of Emperor Zeno's *Henotikon* (482), Antioch became more determinedly anti-Chalcedonian; the three main names associated with Antioch in this period were Peter the Fuller, patriarch with interruptions from 470 until his death in 488, Philoxenus of Mabbog and Severus, patriarch from 512 to 518. It is true, nonetheless, that Antioch was later to swing behind the pro-Chalcedonian policies of Justinian, with Patriarch Ephraem (526–44) and his successors, but the Syrian hinterland by then had become strongly Jacobite, and by the seventh century the patriarchal see was in Jacobite hands. Nevertheless, as we recount this story, we find ourselves with a sense of having been here before. Antioch had a long history of controversy and divided loyalties: in the fourth century, Bishop Leontius, already presiding over a divided church in Antioch, is said to have stroked his white hairs and remarked, 'When this snow melts, there will be lots of mud'.[4] For Antioch was not a tightly organized see, and its control over the rest of the Oriens diocese was comparatively weak. There were many powerful metropolitan bishops; centres of learning like Edessa and Nisibis represented traditions quite independent of Antioch. The patriarch of Antioch had nothing like the power of the patriarch of Alexandria, who ruled a region in which Alexandria was supreme, and who had no metropolitan bishops to challenge his sovereign rule. Furthermore, Antioch was in other ways unstable. The frontier with Persia was not far away; several times in the sixth century the city was sacked by the Persians, or found itself the centre of military operations against them. Furthermore, its geological situation was unfortunate. It was prone to earthquakes; in the century and a half after Chalcedon there were nine earthquakes, some of them serious.[5] The monolithic entity conjured up by talk of the 'school' of Antioch does not correspond to any historical reality.

---

3 See the analysis of the content and reception of the *Codex Encyclius* in Grillmeier (1987), 195–235.
4 Sozomen, *Hist. Eccl.* III. 22. 9 (ed. Bidez–Hansen, p. 135, 16–17).
5 For this account of Antioch see Grillmeier (2002), 179–91.

In the case of Alexandria there is greater coherence – the patriarch, as we have seen, could exercise real control, and Alexandria had largely unchallenged dominance – nevertheless, even the picture that is often built up of the Christology of an 'Alexandrian school' is unconvincing in many respects. This 'school' is often assimilated to the 'Catechetical School', the history of which Eusebius traces back to Pantaenus, the teacher of Clement of Alexandria, but apart from the period of Origen and his immediate successors, it looks very much as if Eusebius is spinning a story out of very little evidence.[6] But whatever it is that we know, or don't know, about the history of the Catechetical School of Alexandria, nothing of it bears on the question of 'Alexandrian Christology', which is really the Christology of Athanasius and Cyril, neither of whom had anything directly to do with the Catechetical School, so far as we know, though if it existed during their patriarchates, then we may suppose they exercised some oversight. But we only suppose, and our suppositions are really very puzzling: if Didymus the Blind, the great Alexandrian exegete and theologian (c.313–98), was appointed head of the Catechetical School by Athanasius as Rufinus affirms,[7] it is hard to see what links there might be between their theologies.

I want to suggest another way of looking at the Christological controversies that culminated in Ephesus and Chalcedon, mainly by way of assisting our understanding of what took place in the aftermath of Chalcedon. To talk of a collision of two 'schools' suggests two more-or-less equivalent, broadly-based tendencies in fourth-century theology that at some point were bound to encounter one another and result in some sort of resolution that ultimately respected the deepest convictions of each: there is a distinct whiff of Hegelianism about such a scenario, and we shouldn't be surprised – nor should we necessarily be predisposed to accept such a model. I want to suggest that we deconstruct this language of schools, but in different ways. The 'Antiochene' school may well correspond to ideas passed on from master to disciple: from Diodore to Theodore to Nestorius, though it has been suggested that such a 'genealogical' representation of Antiochene theology may well be a

---

6   Eusebius, *Hist. Eccl.* V. 10. 1 (Pantaenus appointed head of 'a school of sacred learning' in Alexandria, which 'has lasted till our own time'); *Hist. Eccl.* VI presented episodically a succession of heads of this school. There is a good deal of scholarly doubt as to what lies behind Eusebius' account.
7   Rufinus, *Hist. Eccl.* 11. 7.

construction of Alexandrian polemic,[8] and when it moves beyond traditions of scriptural exegesis to Christology, then it becomes distinctly
ragged. John Chrysostom illustrates the sobriety of Antiochene
exegesis, but his Christology has much more in common with the so-
called 'Alexandrians'; he has, for instance, a 'one-subject' Christology,
in contrast to the 'two-subject' Christology of Theodore and Nestorius,
and sees the purpose of the Incarnation as human deification.[9] It might
be better to think of Antiochene Christology as amounting to the influential ideas of one or two theologians associated with Antioch, with
none of the sense of some sort of commanding movement that the notion
of a 'school' suggests.[10] So far as the 'Alexandrian' school of Christology
is concerned, I would argue in a counter direction. The vision of St
Athanasius, as represented in his amazing treatise *On the Incarnation*,
had enormous power amongst eastern theologians, both in his century
and for centuries to come. The manuscript tradition is vast. The treatise
was translated into Syriac maybe even in Athanasius' lifetime. The
thrust of Athanasius' vision can be found throughout Greek theology:
from the learned theology of the Cappadocians to the simple, though
profound, insights of the author of the homilies attributed to St
Macarius.[11] This is no merely 'Alexandrian' presentation of the central
significance of the Incarnation: it is something of nearly universal
appeal. The Christological controversy was not the clash of two more-
or-less equipollent 'schools', but rather a response to the dangers
represented by an eccentric, and rather scholarly approach to Christology, associated with Antioch, by the broad consensus of Christian
confession, of which Cyril projected himself as the spokesman. Cyril had
the good fortune to find in Nestorius an opponent who, as Lionel
Wickham has put it with customary elegance, 'lost the argument because
his picture of Christ was incredible; [...] and lost his throne because he

---

8 In an unpublished PhD dissertation by Helen Marie Sillett, referred to by Price and
   Gaddis, I, 23, n. 77.
9 See Lawrenz (1989) and Fairbairn (2003), 203–11.
10 Theresia Hainthaler seems to me to dissolve the notion of an influential Antiochene
   school in her discussion in the latest volume of Grillmeier, though I am not sure that
   this was her intention: see Grillmeier (2002), 227–61.
11 See, especially, *Hom.* 11, e.g. 'Now therefore the one who fashioned the body and soul
   himself comes and undoes all the disorder of the wicked one and the works that he
   had done in [human] thoughts, and renewed and formed the heavenly image and
   made a new soul, that once again Adam might be king of death and lord of the crea-
   tures' (*Hom.* 11. 7; ed. H. Dörries–E. Klostermann–M. Kroeger, p. 99, 78–82).

blundered'.[12] Lionel Wickham's pupil, Donald Fairbairn, has argued for such a view of the Christological controversy in his recent book, *Grace and Christology in the Early Church*, though the argument is, at times, confused by another set of agendas, notably the contrast he wishes to draw between what he calls a 'two-act' and 'three-act' pattern of salvation. A similar questioning of the traditional view is found in another recent book, by Paul Gavrilyuk,[13] as Richard Price notes in his introductory section to the *Acta*.[14]

Cyril, I am suggesting, was not standing for one of the 'options' in early Christology, but for the broad consensus, as represented in the compelling vision of Athanasius. Although Cyril does make use of technical philosophical language, neither he nor Athanasius is strong in their analysis of what happened in the Incarnation. Both, indeed, make it clear that any analytical understanding of the Incarnation is beyond human grasp. Both of them express by powerful and evocative imagery the sense that Christ is a unity of the divine and human so profound that it is impossible to separate them or to consider separately the activity of the divine and the human in the incarnate Christ. Any attempt to do this would frustrate the whole purpose of the Incarnation, in which the dying of the human must be experienced (or perhaps, 'owned' is a better word) by the divine, if human kind is to be redeemed (see, e.g., *De Incarnatione* 20. 5). In defending what he believed to be the common faith of Christendom, Cyril was determined to see Nestorius condemned (for reasons of both faith and rivalry), and made his demands of Nestorius more and more uncompromising. This was to have fateful consequences, for in his determination to have Nestorius condemned, Cyril ratcheted up his dogmatic demands of Nestorius, with the intention, it would seem, of making them completely unacceptable to Nestorius. And that he achieved in the 'Twelve Chapters' (or 'Anathemas'). The unwitting inclusion of terminology of Apollinarian descent,[15] notably the formula 'one incarnate hypostasis of God the Word' to characterize Christ – altogether too close to what was to become the clarion cry of the later 'Cyrillians', 'one incarnate nature of God the Word' – caused genuine anger amongst the Syrians who rallied to the support of Nestorius, their

---

12 Cyril of Alexandria, *Select Letters*, ed. and trans. by Wickham, p. xix.

13 Gavrilyuk (2004).

14 Price and Gaddis, I, 60, n. 209.

15 For a study of the Apollinarian (or apparently Apollinarian) elements in Cyril's Third Letter and the chapters, see Galtier (1956).

sense of injustice at Cyril's treatment of him now heightened by dogmatic indignation. The Twelve Chapters had been unnecessary for the condemnation of Nestorius, and concern for the *oikoumene* led to the Formula of Reunion of 433, brokered by John of Antioch and accepted by Cyril, which secured the fundamental demands of the ecumenical faith expressed in the title for the Virgin of *Theotokos* and Cyril's requirement of Nestorius' condemnation. The Syrians assumed that with the Formula of Reunion the Twelve Chapters had been quietly put to one side, something that Cyril could not concede. The ensuing controversy was to have repercussions for a century or more after Chalcedon. Nevertheless, Cyril secured Nestorius' condemnation; there were not many as reluctant as Theodoret to acquiesce in Nestorius' condemnation, and even he finally yielded. The lengths to which Cyril was prepared to go to make things impossible for Nestorius, combined with his own lack of analytical clarity, mean that Cyril's own position is difficult to characterize precisely. Richard Price suggests in his introductory section that there are two Cyrils, though Grillmeier's judgment may be yet nearer the truth, when he says that '[t]he historical development of Cyril was in fact so ambivalent that his works could become a common arsenal for contrary Christologies depending on what one sought in them'.[16] By the time of Chalcedon, as again Richard Price makes clear beyond a peradventure, Cyril of Alexandria was the authority in accordance with which the fathers of the Council reached their judgments. But which Cyril? Price argues that, either way, the Chalcedonian Definition can be judged genuinely Cyrilline, but he confesses that '[t]here is something defective in a conciliar document that requires such nicety of exegesis as we have attempted above':[17] referring to ten closely argued pages,[18] in which he demonstrates that even the 'theopaschism' so ringingly endorsed by the Twelve Chapters can be found in the Chalcedonian Definition.

However, the Chalcedonian Definition could not always expect such a carefully considered reflection.[19]

---

16 Grillmeier (1995), 23 (in the German original, 22).

17 Price and Gaddis, I, 74.

18 Ibid., 62–72.

19 There is a point that should perhaps be made here, not often raised in scholarly discussion. The interpretation of such ecclesial statements as the Chalcedonian Definition is not just a matter of scholarly acumen: it has an impact on relationships between Christians today. There is, it seems to me, something more ecclesially responsible

...the communication
Of the dead is tongued with fire beyond the language of the living.[20]

Whereas the voice (and mind) of Cyril while he still lived, was concerned with theological substance and could treat formulas as secondary, the voice of the dead Cyril, 'tongued with fire', came to be identified with the uncompromising clarity of the Twelve Chapters and summed up, as a sacrosanct formula, in the phrase he took from a quite innocent treatise by Apollinarius,[21] which he wrongly ascribed to his revered mentor, Athanasius: μία φύσις τοῦ Θεοῦ Λόγου σεσαρκωμένη – 'one incarnate nature of God the Word' – which he first seems to have used in the preface to the second book of *Against Nestorius*.[22] The so-called 'Neo-Chalcedonianism' of the sixth-century was concerned to reconcile the Chalcedonian Definition with this voice of the dead Cyril – a task just about possible, as Price argues – with the result that, by the middle of the sixth century Chalcedon was accepted or rejected according to whether it was thought to measure up to the more sharply expressed views of Cyril's later polemic.

But before? After the pressure of the imperial will was lifted with the death of Leo I in 474, acceptance of Chalcedon as faithful to the clarity of Cyril's dead voice would need some further reason. Rome and the West had such a reason: for them the council was Pope Leo's council and the measure of Christological orthodoxy his Tome. Constantinople, too, had a reason: Canon 28, which granted 'equal privileges [with Old Rome] to the most holy see of New Rome', stood or fell with Chalcedon, so Constantinople had very good reasons to endorse the council. But Antioch? The views of Theodore and Theodoret – and Nestorius – had probably, I have suggested, never been more than the view of a few learned scholars. As the voice of Cyril hardened in retrospect (and without Cyril himself there to interpret his views afresh, as Susan Wessel has suggested),[23] the choice seemed to be between the moderation of the

about an interpretation such as Price's that is alive to what has been read into doctrinal nuances, than an attempt (I name no names, but they exist) to narrow down the significance of such an ecumenical confession as the Chalcedonian Definition, without regard to the consequences of such a position.

20 T.S. Eliot, *Four Quartets*, Little Gidding, I.
21 E.g., *Ad Jovianum*, Lietzmann (1904), 250,7–251,1.
22 *ACO* 1.7, p. 33, 6–7.
23 Wessel (2004), 289.

Henotikon and a more strident rejection of Chalcedon. The *Henotikon* had affirmed the decrees of Ephesus, together with the Twelve Chapters, and anathematized anyone who 'has thought or thinks anything else, either now or any time, either in Chalcedon or in any synod whatever',[24] thus neither clearly condemning or accepting Chalcedon: this was the position accepted by Acacius, patriarch of Constantinople, and Peter the Fuller, patriarch of Antioch, thus provoking the 'Acacian' schism, which lasted until the accession of the emperor Justin I. The alternative in the east was an outright disavowal of Chalcedon, for which Philoxenus and Severus argued; none of the eastern patriarchs adopted this position, so its adherents were dubbed 'headless', *akephaloi*. The Syrians, led by Severus, later patriarch of Antioch (511–18), were numbered among the *akephaloi*.

So why did the Syrians reject the Council of Chalcedon? This is not at all the same question as the one that might be thought to hide behind it: why did the 'Antiochenes' reject Chalcedon? – which might well cause puzzlement. The Syrians rejected the council for the same reason as most of the east: because they judged Chalcedon to have betrayed the faith of Cyril, in which they saw the faith of the Church.

BIBLIOGRAPHY

Coleman-Norton, P.R. (1966), *Roman State and Christian Church: A Collection of Legal Documents to A.D. 535*, 3 vols (London, 1966).

Cyril of Alexandria, *Select Letters*, ed. and trans. L.R. Wickham (Oxford, 1983).

Fairbairn, Donald (2003), *Grace and Christology in the Early Church*, Oxford Early Christian Studies (Oxford).

Galtier, Paul (1956), 'Saint Cyrille et Apollinaire', *Gregorianum* 37: 584–609.

Gavrilyuk, Paul (2004), *The Suffering of the Impassible God*, Oxford Early Christian Studies (Oxford).

Grillmeier, Alois (1987), *Christ in Christian Tradition*, vol. 2, *From the Council of Chalcedon (451) to Gregory the Great (590–604)*, Pt 1: *Reception and Contradiction: The development of the discussion about Chalcedon from 451 to the beginning of the reign of Justinian* (London).

—— (1995), *Christ in Christian Tradition*, vol. 2: *From the Council of Chalcedon (451) to Gregory the Great (590–604)*, Pt 2: *The Church in Constantinople in the Sixth Century* (London).

---

24 Translation of the *Henotikon* in Coleman–Norton (1966), III, 927.

—— (2002), ed. Theresia Hainthaler, *Jesus der Christus im Glauben der Kirche*, Band 2/3: *Die Kirche von Jerusalem und Antiochien nach 451 bis 600* (Freiburg–Basel–Vienna).

Lawrenz, M.E. (1989), 'The Christology of John Chrysostom', *StP* 22: 148–53.

Lietzmann, Hans (1904), *Apollinaris und seine Schule* (Tübingen).

Macarius. *Die 50 Geistlichen Homilien des Makarios*, ed. H. Dörries, E. Klostermann, and M. Kroeger, Patristische Texte und Studien 4 (Berlin 1964).

Price, Richard and Gaddis, Michael (2005), *The Acts of the Council of Chalcedon*, 3 vols, TTH 45 (Liverpool).

Sozomen, *Hist. Eccl.* ed. Joseph Bidez and G.C. Hansen, GCS NF 4 (Berlin, 1995).

Wessel, Susan (2004), *Cyril of Alexandria and the Nestorian Controversy*, Oxford Early Christian Studies (Oxford).

THE SECOND COUNCIL OF CONSTANTINOPLE (553) AND THE MALLEABLE PAST

Richard Price

The past, we are told, is eternally fixed and immutable. Against this assertion, and the restriction on human freedom that it implies, the Russian philosopher Lev Shestov (1866–1938) uttered a powerful protest. A supposed fact, such as Socrates' death by poison, might just be tolerable if it was restricted to a single historical period. 'But', he continued,[1] –

> to promise it immortality, timeless existence, which no oblivion can obliterate – who has the audacity to take to himself the right to issue such a promise? Why should a philosopher, who knows that everything that has a beginning must have an end, forget this eternal truth and bestow everlasting existence on a 'fact' that did not even exist before 399 BC?

Shestov surely exaggerates the sheer givenness of historical events. A death is certainly a death, and the cause of Socrates' death is not open to dispute, but many 'facts' of history have a more ambiguous character, and it is impossible to recount any event without some degree of interpretation. It should also be noted that no objective events are directly part of human experience: while they occur, they must be observed, and after they have occurred they survive only in memory. Historical memory can be reshaped by the historian. It is the reshaping in the age of Justinian (and at the ecumenical council of 553) of episodes in the Christological controversy of the mid-fifth century that is the subject of this essay.

Cyril of Alexandria's Twelve Chapters

The first 'fact' whose reshaping I wish to discuss is the approval that the First Council of Ephesus (431) accorded – or did not accord – to Cyril of

1   Shestov (2001), 70.

Alexandria's aggressive exposition of his Christology in his Third Letter to Nestorius, with its accompanying Twelve Chapters (or Anathemas).[2] The letter comes in the acts of the first session of the council, but André de Halleux detected an oddity: it is manifestly intrusive where it occurs, since it interrupts a discussion of Pope Celestine's letter, which resumes at the end of it as if it had never been read. It does not follow, however, that it was not read out at some other stage of the session: it was included in the minutes that the bishops loyal to Cyril signed shortly after the session, and when the Syrian bishops arrived a week later they were in no doubt that the letter and the anathemas had been formally approved.[3] Was this a correct interpretation of the bishops' signing of the minutes? There was scope for disagreement then, as there is scope for disagreement today.

Twenty years later, the fathers of Chalcedon paid their respects to 'the decrees of Ephesus under Cyril of holy memory when Nestorius was deposed on account of his errors'.[4] What decrees did they mean? 'The teaching of the blessed Cyril at Ephesus' is used as an equivalent expression.[5] In the Chalcedonian Definition itself authority is accorded to 'the conciliar letters of the blessed Cyril, then shepherd of the church of Alexandria, to Nestorius and to those of the Orient, for the refutation of the madness of Nestorius and for the instruction of those who with pious zeal seek the meaning of the saving creed'.[6] This follows mention of the Creeds of Nicaea and Constantinople I and precedes mention of the Tome of Leo. If we turn to the second session of the council, we find a reading of the following documents in turn: the two creeds, Cyril's Second Letter to Nestorius, his *Laetentur caeli* letter to John of Antioch, and the Tome of Leo. This, plus the fact that the Third Letter to Nestorius was not read out at Chalcedon at any point, shows that the Third Letter was not included among the 'conciliar letters' accorded authority in the Definition.[7] There is but one place in the Acts of Chalcedon where

2 See the discussion by Thomas Graumann above, pp. 39–41.

3 See de Halleux (1992), 425–58.

4 Acts of Chalcedon IV. 9.2–4, one of a whole series of verdicts in favour of the orthodoxy of the Tome of Leo on the grounds that it was harmony with the Nicene Creed and the decrees of Ephesus I.

5 E.g. at Acts IV. 9.28.

6 Acts V. 34.

7 Note too how at the end of the first session the chairman referred to 'the *two* canonical letters of Cyril' (Acts I. 1072). Even though the two letters in question are said to have been approved and published at Ephesus it is clear from the choice of letters read out at the second session that this phrase includes the Letter to John of Antioch rather than the Third Letter to Nestorius.

the Third Letter is referred to, and that is in the second session, where Atticus of Nicopolis requests that in the projected examination of the Tome of Leo 'we should also be provided with the letter of the blessed Cyril written to Nestorius in which he urged him to assent to the Twelve Chapters'.[8] No response to this request is recorded, and in the examination of the Tome in the fourth session it is clear that it was the Second Letter to Nestorius that alone was treated as authoritative. Therefore, taking the Acts of Chalcedon as a single coherent text, there can be no doubt that the Definition is not to be understood as including the Third Letter among Cyril's 'conciliar letters'. But this does not wholly end the matter. It is striking that Atticus' request is recorded in the minutes, which are not a complete record of everything that was said. Moreover, the committee that produced the final version of the Definition was completely dominated by those in the Cyrillian tradition, most of whom will have had few or no difficulties over the Twelve Chapters:[9] there is no way of excluding the possibility that they, or at least some of their number, were well aware of a convenient ambiguity over which of Cyril's letters they were solemnly approving.

What do we find when we move on to the age of Justinian? The Acts as a whole became available to conscientious readers, and as such formed a topic of discussion at the conference between Chalcedonians and non-Chalcedonians held at Constantinople in 532. The miaphysite (one-nature) delegates brought up as an objection to Chalcedon that it had not received the Twelve Chapters. The leader of the Chalcedonian delegation, Hypatius of Ephesus, gave the ingenious reply that the reason for this was that the chapters referred to 'the hypostases' of Christ in the plural, meaning of course the two natures but still contrary to the correct formulation, which admitted only one hypostasis in Christ.[10] When, however, we move on to the 540s and 550s, the period of the Three Chapters controversy, we find general agreement, among both the supporters and the opponents of Justinian's ecclesiastical policy, that the Third Letter to Nestorius, together with the Twelve Chapters, was a text with the highest authority, formally approved at both Ephesus I and Chalcedon. Justinian added for good measure that Pope Leo himself had

8 Acts II. 29.
9 See Price and Gaddis, II, 188–9.
10 *ACO* 4.2, p. 173, 21–9. The reference is to the third of the chapters: 'If anyone in respect of the one Christ separates the hypostases after the union...'

approved the chapters.[11] Several of the distinctive themes of the letter duly appeared in Justinian's edict of 551 *On the orthodox faith* and in the canons of the ecumenical council of 553 – notably the formula 'one incarnate hypostasis of the Word' and the insistence that all Christ's experiences, including the passion of the cross, are to be assigned to God the Word as the sole subject of attribution.

The council of 553 asserted that this was the teaching approved at Chalcedon. The miaphysite philosopher John Philoponus claimed in opposition that this was what Chalcedon *ought* to have taught, but that it had actually approved the Tome of Leo, in which the one Christ is divided into two separate subjects of experience and operation.[12] This raises another question where there is no single right answer: certainly the fathers of Chalcedon had accepted the Tome of Leo as orthodox, but was this equivalent to approving every statement within it? They did so only after receiving assurances from the Roman delegates that, whatever the appearances, Leo intended no division between the Godhead and the flesh of Christ.[13]

In all, Justinian and his council insisted that in giving weight to the Twelve Chapters they were simply following the example and authority of Chalcedon. This claim was tendentious, but surely we cannot say that it was simply false. They were taking advantage of what was a genuine ambiguity in the Acts of Ephesus I and those of Chalcedon.

The judgements on Ibas and Theodoret of Cyrrhus

The elevation to canonical status of Cyril's Twelve Chapters had an unfortunate effect on the reputation of two bishops who, having been deposed for alleged Nestorianism at the Second Council of Ephesus (449), were reinstated at Chalcedon – Theodoret of Cyrrhus and Ibas of Edessa. Their reinstatement followed their demonstration of orthodoxy by publicly anathematizing Nestorius.[14] As miaphysite critics of the

11 Schwartz (1939), 62. Pope Leo, in fact, acclaimed the Second Letter to Nestorius but never mentions the Third.
12 See his *Four Tmêmata against Chalcedon*, in Michael the Syrian, *Chronicle*, II, 92–121.
13 See Acts III. 9, after '(98)' and after '(114)'.
14 To be precise, through an oversight it was only *after* the senior bishops had pronounced Ibas' reinstatement that a demand from their juniors led Ibas to anathematize Nestorius (Acts X. 180). But the exact moment when Ibas' restoration took effect was itself ambiguous.

council were later to point out, they were not required to withdraw the writings in which they had attacked Cyril of Alexandria. Theodoret in a whole sequence of texts and Ibas in his Letter to Mari the Persian had directed their fire principally at the Twelve Chapters. It is therefore not at all surprising that the fathers chose to ignore these texts, but once the chapters had received canonical status, Chalcedon was open to the charge of having let the two bishops off too lightly.

I have discussed the Letter to Mari the Persian and its reception in an earlier essay in this volume.[15] Suffice it to say here that the letter, written in the wake of the union of 433, was highly critical of both the Twelve Chapters and the Council of Ephesus. It was read out at Chalcedon and received apparently without comment.[16] When the bishops came to deliver their verdicts on Ibas, two of the most senior among them, the Roman legate Paschasinus and Bishop Maximus of Antioch, referred to the letter as evidence of Ibas' orthodoxy.[17] This apparent approval of a text attacking Cyril, plus the mildness of the language in which the same letter treated Nestorius, was used by miaphysites in the sixth century to cast doubt on the sincerity of Chalcedon's profession of respect for Cyril and rejection of Nestorius. The solution adopted by Justinian in the 540s and 550s, and endorsed by Pope Vigilius in his second *Constitutum* of 554, was to admit that the letter was unacceptable, indeed to argue that it was grossly heretical, and to conclude that the council cannot possibly have given it approval; the two bishops who referred to the 'letter' as orthodox must have been referring to another document, and if the bishops after hearing the letter still acquitted Ibas of heresy it can only be because Ibas himself repudiated the letter. These claims rewrote history with a will, and the defenders of the chapters dismissed them scornfully.[18] But there certainly is a puzzle about the reception of the letter at Chalcedon: the bishops must have been more offended by it than they felt able in the circumstances to express.

There are likewise intriguing ambiguities in the record of Session VIII, which dealt with the case of Theodoret. Theodoret had been deposed from his see at the Council of Ephesus of 449, but both Pope Leo and the emperor Marcian regarded his deposition as invalid, and he

---

15 See above, pp. 85–7. For the text of the letter see Price (2009), II, 6–10.

16 See p. 99 above: whatever comments there may have been were suppressed in subsequent editing.

17 Acts X. 161, 163.

18 For the sixth-century debate, which reached rare heights of sophistry, see Price (2009), I, 93–7.

played a full role at Chalcedon from the second session onwards.[19] It was at the eighth session that the council fathers got round to reviewing his case, in order to reinstate him formally. The result was a foregone conclusion, but Theodoret determined to exploit it to secure official approbation of his orthodoxy. He appeared in the council-chamber equipped with petitions he had written protesting his innocence and proving the soundness of his faith. But when he asked for them to be read out, the bishops refused permission and curtly told him to anathematize Nestorius, something that Theodoret had managed to avoid doing for twenty years. Theodoret retorted, 'If I may not expound what I believe, I shall not speak but simply believe.' The bishops (or some of them) responded, 'He is a heretic. He is a Nestorian. Drive out the heretic.' Theodoret capitulated and uttered an anathema against Nestorius in the form demanded of him, concluding irately, 'And after all this may you be preserved!' The chairman closed the discussion by declaring, 'All remaining doubts about the most God-beloved Theodoret have been resolved.' 'All the most devout bishops', as the acts put it, then approved his reinstatement in a series of acclamations, in which he was hailed as 'the orthodox teacher'.[20] But how many bishops, one wonders, actually took part in these acclamations: scarcely the same ones, surely, who a moment before had shouted him down as 'a heretic' and 'a Nestorian'! At an hearing at Constantinople in April 449 to examine the accuracy of the minutes of the Home Synod of November 448 one of the notaries observed, 'It often happens at these most holy gatherings that one of the most God-beloved bishops present says something, and what one man says is recorded and counted as if everyone alike had said it. This is what has happened from time immemorial: for instance, one person speaks, and we write, "The holy council said…".'[21]

In any case the acclamations were not the last word at this session of Chalcedon. They are followed in the acts by a series of verdicts by senior bishops, who agreed that Theodoret was orthodox, but stressed that he had proved this by anathematizing Nestorius.[22] This was a less fulsome tribute to Theodoret's orthodoxy than describing him as 'the orthodox teacher'.

---

19 At the first session he had the status of a plaintiff rather than a member of the council (Acts I. 35). From the second session, however, he appears as a full member (II. 26).
20 Acts VIII. 5–15.
21 Acts (of Chalcedon) I. 767.
22 Acts VIII. 16–23.

How, then, should we sum up the judgement of Chalcedon on Theodoret's orthodoxy? Manifestly, the council fathers were not all of one mind. Reading though the acts as a whole, it is clear that Theodoret's critics must greatly have outnumbered his admirers; apart from various incidental indications, this may be deduced from the universal respect paid throughout the council to Theodoret's old enemy, Cyril of Alexandria. But conciliar authority was accorded not to the majority voice but to the general consensus; where this consensus was lacking, one cannot attribute any particular judgement to 'the council'. What the fathers at Chalcedon were agreed upon was simply that, in view first of the invalidity of Theodoret's deposition at the Second Council of Ephesus and secondly of his public anathematization of Nestorius, there were no grounds for refusing to restore him to his see.

How, we must now ask, was all this viewed a century later, at the time of the controversy over the 'Three Chapters' – the person and works of Theodore of Mopsuestia, Theodoret's writings against Cyril, and the Letter to Mari the Persian, as condemned by the emperor Justinian? Defenders of Theodoret could point to the fact that Chalcedon had reinstated him, while his opponents could point to the evident lack of enthusiasm with which most of them did so. The miaphysite philosopher and controversialist John Philoponus castigated the Council of Chalcedon for declaring that Theodoret was an 'orthodox teacher', and argued that the Council of Constantinople of 553, by anathematizing 'the impious writings of Theodoret against the orthodox faith' (Canon 13), had thereby anathematized all those who accepted the decrees of Chalcedon.[23] In contrast, the emperor Justinian, responding a few years earlier to the same accusation, wrote as follows on Chalcedon's verdicts on Theodoret and Ibas:[24]

Both Ibas and Theodoret were accepted not as teachers and fathers but as penitents who anathematized the heresy of which they had been accused and had accepted the Definition of the Council of Chalcedon and signed it, since it is the custom of the catholic church that all heretics who abandon their own error and return to the orthodox faith are received into communion but are not numbered with the fathers as teachers.

23 Philoponus in Michael the Syrian, *Chronicle*, II, 121.
24 Justinian, *Letter on the Three Chapters*, Schwartz (1939), p. 66, 28–32.

It is likely that the great majority of the bishops at Chalcedon did indeed regard Theodoret and Ibas as repentant heretics rather than doctors of the Church, but Justinian betrays awareness of a weakness in his position when he talks of their being received into communion while making no mention of the fact that both were restored to their sees as bishops in good standing.[25]

The main embarrassment, however, remained the fact that Theodoret and Ibas, though required at Chalcedon to anathematize Nestorius, had not been required to withdraw their writings against Cyril. Their defenders in the sixth century argued that they should not now be condemned for offences that Chalcedon had thought best to pass over. And they added a telling argument: Cyril himself, when he made peace with the Syrian bishops in 433, declared himself satisfied with their abandonment of Nestorius and did not ask for the withdrawal of the criticisms they had directed at himself; Justinian in condemning the Three Chapters was therefore going against Cyril as well as Chalcedon.[26] What had Cyril's attitude been in the 430s? The council of 553 conducted a full investigation of his attitude during this decade to the remaining member of the Three Chapters, the person and writings of Theodore of Mopsuestia. To this we may now turn.

Cyril against Theodore, in reality and in retrospect

Under imperial pressure Cyril of Alexandria made peace with his Syrian opponents in 433. Those who accept the sincerity of the tones of delight in which he wrote to Bishop John of Antioch accepting the Formula of Union[27] may be surprised to hear that towards the end of the decade he took an eager part, in alliance with Archbishop Proclus of Constantinople, in attacking the memory of the greatest figure in the 'school' of Antioch, the not long deceased Theodore of Mopsuestia (d. 428). Justinian appealed to this attack as justifying his own condemnation of Theodore in his edicts of 544/5 and 551; Theodore's defenders

---

25 The same embarrassed silence is to be found in the acts of the council of 553 (VIII. 4.26; *ACO* 4.1, pp. 213,37–214,8).

26 See the proceedings of the conference of Constantinople of 532 in Brock (1981), 98–9; Facundus, *Pro defensione trium capitulorum* III. 5.3–7; Pope Vigilius, first *Constitutum* 225 (Price 2009, II, 192).

27 In his *Laetentur caeli* letter to John of Antioch, Price and Gaddis, I, 178–83.

responded by citing letters in which Cyril had apparently deplored the assault on Theodore's memory, arguing that the dead should be left in peace. Questions arose about the authenticity of certain documents as well as their interpretation. Since they were uniformly undated, it was not easy to place them in the correct sequence, and a lot depended on which of Cyril's various and varied utterances were taken to constitute his last word.[28]

Modern historians, notably Eduard Schwartz and Marcel Richard, have painstakingly reconstructed the chronology and sequence of events.[29] The trouble started in 435 when two priests from Persian Armenia came to see Proclus of Constantinople, claiming (falsely) to represent Armenian bishops puzzled by the claims for and against Theodore of Mopsuestia advanced by rival factions, but in fact desirous to stir up trouble. Proclus responded with his Tome to the Armenians, which included a florilegium of allegedly heretical excerpts, to which he attached no name but which he and everyone else knew came from Theodore. The excerpts were not found in the least shocking by Ibas, newly elected bishop of Edessa, who translated them into Syriac in order to win them wider circulation.

In 438 Proclus of Constantinople wrote to John of Antioch more than once, deploring Ibas' circulation of the heretical excerpts, and pressing John to make Ibas, and indeed all the Syrian bishops, sign the Tome to the Armenians and anathematize the excerpts. John replied deploring the attempt to anathematize a writer who in his lifetime had suffered no criticism from the orthodox (including Proclus himself). At the same time John appealed to Cyril of Alexandria, urging him to use his influence to restore peace to the churches. Cyril, meanwhile, had been approached by a number of clergy and high-ranking laymen in Antioch, who accused the Syrian bishops of using Theodore as a cloak to spread Nestorianism. He therefore replied to John in far from friendly terms, attacking Theodore and stressing the need to root out Nestorianism from the Syrian clergy. The representations from his friends in Syria also spurred him into literary activity: supplied with a new florilegium of numerous excerpts both from Theodore and from the earlier Anti-

---

28 For a fuller, and fully documented, account see my introduction to Session V of the Council of Constantinople of 553, Price (2009), I, 271–7.

29 See Schwartz (1914), 27–36, and Richard (1942), 303–31. More recent is Abramowski (1992), and the brief accounts in Pietri (1998), 26–32 and Chadwick (2001), 548–51.

ochene theologian Diodore of Tarsus, he rapidly compiled three books *Against Diodore and Theodore*. This work made its way to Syria, where Theodoret of Cyrrhus wrote a reply, *In defence of Diodore and Theodore*.

In the meantime all sides in the controversy appealed to the emperor Theodosius II. Cyril severely criticized the stance of the Syrian bishops and urged the emperor to steer well clear of the heresy of Diodore and Theodore, while the Syrians reminded the emperor that both he and his grandfather Theodosius I had expressed admiration for Theodore as a teacher. Theodosius' response was to insist on a restoration of peace to the churches. In a reply to the Syrians he added, 'What could be more useful than that you resolve together with the whole church that no one should presume in future to do anything of the kind against those who died in her peace?'[30]

An embarrassed Proclus now wrote to John of Antioch, protesting that, despite his concern over the 'anonymous' heretical excerpts, he had no wish to see Theodore or any other deceased person condemned by name. Cyril had no choice but to follow suit (we must now be in 439), and wrote accordingly to all concerned. In an extraordinarily tortuous letter addressed to the Syrian bishops he commended the caution that had been shown by the Council of Ephesus back in 431, when, while condemning an heretical creed attributed to Theodore, it avoided naming its author, 'lest perchance the easterners, respecting the reputation which the man enjoys, might separate themselves from the communion of the body of the universal church.' He also conceded that it would be better to leave the dead in peace, admitting that Theodore's enemies had been carried too far by their godly zeal:[31]

> Those who are responsible will justly hear, although they do not wish it, 'You forget yourselves when you draw bows against ashes; for the person you accuse is no longer alive.' And let no one blame me for being so explicit. I yield to those who think it a serious matter to revile the dead, even if they are laymen, and all the more if they departed from this life in the episcopacy.

Cyril had to some extent covered himself: he could point to the fact that he had not explicitly demanded Theodore's condemnation by name. But

---

30 Quoted in Facundus, *Pro defensione* VIII. 3.13.
31 Acts of 553, V. 66 (*ACO* 4.1, p. 106, 10–14). My first quotation is from p. 106, 5–7.

he had clearly given ground, and his more intransigent followers felt he had betrayed them, as they had back in 433 when he first made his peace with the Syrian bishops. The controversy now petered out. A decade later, the Council of Chalcedon maintained a discrete silence over Theodore.

If this is the tale that a modern historian can derive from the scattered evidence, it is not the story that Justinian wanted to hear, or which is recounted in the acts of the council of 553. A major part of the record of the fifth session (the longest section of these acts) consists of documents relating to this controversy. No attempt is made to place them in chronological order, but the leading spirit at the council, Bishop Theodore Ascidas of Caesarea in Cappadocia, provided a commentary that offered a very different picture of the sequence of documents and events from the one I have just given. Ascidas was much concerned to stress the contrast between the letter that I have quoted and other letters of Cyril in which he attacked Theodore without restraint: the conclusion he drew was that the peacemaking letter was manifestly a forgery.[32] He did not, however, deny that Cyril had on occasion exercised 'accommodation', but he rearranged the chronology, to make Cyril's final word a demand for Theodore's condemnation. Accordingly he criticizes those who appealed to the 'forged' letter in the following terms:[33]

> Ignoring everything that reveals the intention that the holy Cyril had to anathematize Theodore, they use only those statements that were uttered out of accommodation in order fully to draw away from Nestorius' heresy those who were still caught in it and prevent the disorders that they suspected the heretics would foment. Therefore Proclus of holy memory, having received the holy Cyril's letter, as well as many entreaties from the easterners against the anathematization of Theodore and his impious writings, wrote urging them to anathematize Theodore's blasphemies and prove themselves free of any such suspicion. But because they did not respond to the accommodation of Cyril and Proclus of holy memory but on the contrary continued to defend the very blasphemies of Theodore and to say that they were in accord with the writings of the holy fathers, the holy Cyril, seeing that impiety was on the increase and fearing that the more simple-minded would be harmed thereby, was compelled to write books against Theodore and against

32 Ibid., V. 65–7 (*ACO* 4.1, pp. 104–6).
33 Ibid., V. 79 (*ACO* 4.1, pp. 110–1).

his blasphemies and to show even after the death of the same Theodore that he was heretical and impious and a greater blasphemer than the pagans and Jews.

And after reading out excerpts from the Tome to the Armenians, as if it represented not Proclus' first thoughts but his final ones, Ascidas reiterated the same point:[34]

> But if our fathers said anything for the sake of accommodation, in order to separate his defenders at that time from the heresy of Nestorius, yet because they did not accept their words and the time requiring accommodation came to an end, they then proceeded to what is perfect and wrote what was cited above against him and his impious writings even after his death.

What of Theodosius II's intervention, demanding that the dead be left in peace? This was suppressed, and replaced by the text of the edict in which he had condemned Nestorius, with the name of Theodore interpolated.[35] The edict in fact antedated the crisis over Theodore and had nothing to do with it; but, as presented undated in the acts of 553, it was clearly intended to tell the 'true' conclusion to the controversy: the emperor had listened to Cyril and Proclus and condemned Theodore, imposing dire penalties on those who believed, or read, or merely possessed his books.[36]

This was indeed a reshaping of the historical record. But was it a case of conscious and deliberate falsification?[37] The alteration of the text of the edict could be so described, but it may be argued that the version of events presented in 553 was more the fruit of wishful thinking than of deceit, on the following grounds.

(1) None of the letters (around twenty in number) that are our evidence for the course of the controversy over Theodore in the 430s is

---

34 Ibid., V. 85 (*ACO* 4.1, pp. 112,37–113,3).

35 Two versions of the interpolated edict, including Theodore's name, are given in the Acts of 553 – V. 25–6 (*ACO* 4.1, pp. 91–3).

36 For the genuine edict see Millar (2006), 176–8. The Theodosian Code (XVI. 5.66) gives a date of 3 August 435 for its issue, which does not fit easily with the other evidence, as Millar notes. Schwartz (1927, 92, and in *ACO* 1.4, p. xi, n. 1) seems right to dismiss it as inauthentic and to place the edict in its natural context as part of the final clampdown on Nestorianism in 436.

37 See Gray (1997), 193–205 for acute comment on the psychology involved – not sincerity, nor conscious falsification, but self-deceit.

dated. Ascidas and the other bishops did not have before them the reconstruction of the course of events worked out centuries later by Eduard Schwartz and Marcel Richard.

(2) It was surely a correct reading of the evidence to conclude that Cyril and Proclus wished to see Theodore's teaching condemned, and that their adoption (at whatever stage) of a policy of accommodation represented not conviction but a yielding to political pressure. The defenders of the Three Chapters were singularly unconvincing when they argued that Cyril had had no wish to see Theodore condemned.

(3) Even the interpolation of Theodore's name into the edict against Nestorius could claim a grain of justification, on the grounds that its condemnation of 'those everywhere who share in the villainous heresy of Nestorius' could not but include Theodore. The interpolators of Theodore's name may well have persuaded themselves that they were not distorting the meaning of the edict but simply clarifying its implications.

The 'real' truth of history

All the ecumenical councils had a conservative agenda – to rescue the truths of the Christian faith from perverse innovation. Heresy of its very nature was innovative, while the truth had been revealed for all time by Christ and the apostles. This theme may be traced back to the treatment of heretics in the New Testament itself:[38]

> There will be a time when they will not endure sound teaching, but with itching ears they will collect teachers according to their own desires and turn their attention away from the truth and deviate into myths.

It was, however, in reaction to the free creativity of so-called 'Gnostic' theology in the second century that the changelessness of orthodoxy came to be stressed as one of the key attributes by which it could be recognized. This is clearly stated by both Irenaeus of Lyons and Tertullian of Carthage.[39]

The modern historian of Christian doctrine is well aware that the

---

38 2 Tim 4:3–4.
39 Irenaeus, *Adversus haereses* III. 1–4. Tertullian, *De praescriptione haereticorum*.

Christian tradition was less conservative than it claimed to be. The development of the Christian understanding of the great doctrines of the Trinity and of the union of Godhead and manhood in Christ was primarily carried on by theologians, but it could not but find expression in the formal creeds and definitions composed at councils by bishops. But we shall misunderstand the ethos and functioning of councils if we forget that their perceived function was not to advance theology but to protect the Church against novel teaching that distorted the meaning of the creeds. Doctrinal conservatism was not a mere rhetorical claim but a serious commitment, which made it necessary to respond to controversy by looking long and meticulously at what had been defined in the past.

Susan Wessel has brought out very well how an essential contribution to the victory of Cyril of Alexandria over Nestorius was his success in portraying Nestorianism as not an attempted solution to a new problem but a recrudescence of Arianism.[40] Likewise the Chalcedonian Definition insists that it is doing nothing more than protecting the Nicene Creed.[41] It was in the same spirit that the emperor Justinian and the council of 553 presented their work as unadorned fidelity to Chalcedon.

Yet the very purpose of Justinian's edicts and of the council was to correct errors that Chalcedon had made – its failure to take on board the full scope of Cyril's doctrine, its evasion of the question of Theodore's orthodoxy, and its too easy readmission of Theodoret and Ibas. Yet the very notion of 'developing' the work of Chalcedon, let alone 'correcting' it, was alien. The only way to solve the problem of the apparent flaws in the work of Chalcedon was to demonstrate that its work had not been properly understood. The reshaping of the record that I have analysed in this essay presented a perfected and purified Chalcedon, that indeed approved Cyril's Twelve Chapters, that ignored Theodore only because he had already been formally condemned, and that readmitted Theodoret and Ibas not as teachers but as penitents. As for the Letter to Mari the Persian, was it not plain that the fathers of Chalcedon ignored it not because they thought it orthodox but because it was so heretical that they knew it to be a forgery?

A consequence of this interpretation was that the differences between

---

40 Wessel (2004), 189, 218–24. The awareness of the importance of the charge of Arianism and the analysis of Cyril's rhetorical method (190–235) are the strong points in this study.
41 Note how the final section of the Definition forbids the composition of another creed, a reference to the finality not of the Definition itself but of the Nicene Creed.

the situation around 450 and that around 550 were minimized. Aware-ness of the gradual and piecemeal development of late antique Christology, in which the acceptance of Cyril had at first been selective and a distinction had been drawn between Nestorius and more moderate Antiochenes such as Theodore and Theodoret, was replaced by a simpler and more comprehensible story, in which the orthodox had recognized the authority of the Twelve Chapters from the very first, the heretics had been consistently assailed by Cyril, and the battle-lines had always been clearly drawn. We may understand too why Justinian continued to insist that his condemnation of the Three Chapters was necessitated by a still lively Nestorian movement.[42] Nestorianism was far from lively by the time of Justinian, but the shifting complexities of historical reality had to yield before the myth of a timeless and change-less confrontation of truth and falsity, in which the victory of orthodoxy had constantly to be re-enacted.

BIBLIOGRAPHY

Abramowski, Luise (1992), 'The Controversy over Diodore and Theodore in the Interim between the two Councils of Ephesus' = id., *Formula and Context: Studies in Early Christian Thought* (Ashgate, 1992), I.

Acta Conciliorum Oecumenicorum, ed. Eduard Schwartz and others (Berlin, 1914–).

Brock, Sebastian (1981), 'The Conversations with the Syrian Orthodox under Justinian (532)', *OCP* 47: 87–121 = id., *Studies in Syriac Christianity* (Variorum, 1992), XIII.

Chadwick, Henry (2001), *The Church in Ancient Society* (Oxford).

De Halleux, André (1992), 'Les douze chapitres cyrilliens au concile d'Ephèse (430–433)', *RThL* 23: 425–58.

Facundus of Hermiane, *Pro defensione trium capitulorum* and *Contra Mocianum*, CCSL 90A (Turnhout, 1974).

Gray, P.T.R. (1997), 'Covering the Nakedness of Noah: Reconstruction and Denial in the Age of Justinian', *ByzF* 24: 193–205.

Michael the Syrian, *Chronicle. Chronique de Michel le Syrien Patriarche Jacobite d'Antioche (1166–99)*, ed. and trans. J.-B. Chabot, vol. 2 [trans. of VII–XI] (Paris, 1901).

Millar, Fergus (2006), *A Greek Roman Empire: Power and Belief under Theodosius II (408–450)* (Berkeley and London).

---

42 See Acts of 553, I. 7.8 (*ACO* 4.1, p. 10).

Pietri, Luce (1998), *Histoire du Christianisme*, vol. 3, *Les Églises d'Orient et d'Occident (432–610)* (Paris).

Price, Richard and Gaddis, Michael (2005), *The Acts of the Council of Chalcedon*, 3 vols, TTH 45 (Liverpool).

Price, R.M. (2009), *Acts of the Council of Constantinople of 553*, trans. with introduction and notes, 2 vols, TTH 51 (Liverpool).

Richard, Marcel (1942), 'Proclus de Constantinople et le Théopaschisme', *RHE* 38: 303–31 = *Opera Minora* (Turnhout and Leuven, 1977), vol. 2, no. 52.

Schwartz, Eduard (1914), *Konzilstudien*. Schriften der wissenschaftlichen Gesellschaft in Strassburg 20.

—— (1927), *Codex Vaticanus gr. 1431: Eine antichalkedonische Sammlung aus der Zeit Kaiser Zenos*. ABAW.PPH 32.6 (Munich).

—— (1939), *Drei dogmatische Schriften Justinians*. ABAW.PH NF 18 (Munich).

Shestov, Lev (2001), *Afiny i Ierusalim* (St.-Petersburg).

Wessel, Susan (2004), *Cyril of Alexandria and the Nestorian Controversy: The Making of a Saint and a Heretic* (Oxford, 2004).

THE LATERAN COUNCIL OF 649
AS AN ECUMENICAL COUNCIL

Catherine Cubitt

The repercussions of the Council of Chalcedon for both doctrinal questions and religious politics between east and west extended well beyond
the fifth and sixth centuries into the seventh.[1] The monothelete doctrine
which prompted the papal Lateran Council of 649 was but the latest in
a series of attempts by the Byzantine emperors to achieve reconciliation
amongst the dissenting religious groups of the empire. The activities of
the emperor Justinian to enforce doctrinal agreement had rather
provoked disagreement and division, particularly a damaging schism in
the west between the papacy – who had been forced into agreement with
the emperor – and those bishops and areas which refused to accept the
condemnation of the Three Chapters. Thus the aftermath of Chalcedon
continued to shape relations between east and west, with the Byzantine
emperors still seeking compromise and pacification within the east and
the papacy anxious to avoid further schism amongst the western
churches. The theological and linguistic divide between east and west,
manifest in the mid-fifth century, had become wider and deeper by the
seventh.

While the complexities of monotheletism have concerned historians
and theologians rather less than those of miaphysitism, the controversy
is a highly significant one, both theologically and politically.[2] The questions concerning the will of Christ are of central importance to
Christology. Their exposition at the Lateran Council of 649 was extensive and penetrating, and the council itself, as I will argue below, should
be seen as a key moment in relations between the Byzantine emperors
and the papacy.[3]

---

1 *Acts of the Council of Chalcedon*, I, 51–6.
2 See, for example, the treatment of monotheletism and the Lateran Council in Chadwick (2003), 59–64.
3 The *acta* of the council are edited by Rudolf Riedinger in *ACO* II. 1. See also the
   important accounts of Conte (1971, 1989) and now Ekonomou (2007), 113–57, which
   appeared at a late stage in the completion of this essay.

The convocation of the Lateran Council in the middle of the seventh century coincided with the break up of the Byzantine Empire at the hands of the Arabs, after long years of wars with the Persians. The inability of the Byzantines to defend their territory and its loss to non-believers provoked a long crisis in Byzantium in which its failure was interpreted as divine punishment for apostasy.[4] This argument was used by both sides in the doctrinal debates – by the emperors who had sponsored monotheletism as a compromise to win over the miaphysites, and by the dyotheletes themselves. The emperors viewed opposition to monotheletism as treason against the empire, and its opponents were accused of favouring the Arabs.[5] The new doctrine was espoused by the emperor Heraclius, who issued the *Ekthesis* in 638 to impose it. At first, this compromise was successful in placating the miaphysites, until orthodox opposition to the new doctrine was initiated by Sophronius who became patriarch of Jerusalem. As the Arabs conquered more and more of the Middle East, theological controversy raged until the emperor Constans II tried to silence debate by the *Typos*, which forbad any discussion of the issues and rejected the doctrines of both one and two wills.[6]

Papal agreement to the new imperial dogma had been solicited for some time, but after an initial rapprochement the opposition of the popes hardened. The promulgation of the *Typos* in 648 was probably the spur for the convocation of the Lateran Synod in 649, originally planned by Pope Theodore who died before its convocation. Conciliar preparations were then in the hands of the very new Pope Martin, but a major part in these was played by Maximus the Confessor, a disciple of Sophronius, and his followers, largely Greek monks who had fled to Rome in the wake of imperial hostility and Arab attacks on Africa.[7]

Papal defiance of the *Typos* had a predictable effect: as a result, Martin was arrested by an imperial representative in Italy and taken off to Constantinople where he was tried in December 652 and condemned to death. The sentence was commuted to exile, and he died six months later in the Cherson.[8] Maximus was also arrested, tried and exiled in 655

4 See Haldon (1986, 1997), Kaegi (2003) and bibliography contained in these.
5 Brandes (1998).
6 Winkelmann (1987, 2001).
7 See Riedinger (1992) and Allen and Neil (2002), 19–20. A useful introduction to Maximus and his writings can be found in Larchet (2003).
8 *Liber Pontificalis*, ed. Duchesne (1955/1981), I, 336–40, trans. Davis (2000), 70–2. *Narrationes de exilio sancti Papae Martini*, PL 129. 585–604, discussed by Allen and Neil (2002), 22.

(to Bizye in Thrace).[9] However, this did not stop Maximus and his followers from maintaining a propaganda campaign against the heresy, as a result of which in 662 he and his closest followers, Anastasius the Disciple and Anastasius Apocrisiarius, were tried again. This time they were brutally mutilated to prevent any further attempts to propagate their views, and all three died in exile not long afterwards. Martin, Maximus, and his disciples felt the full force of Byzantine displeasure: they were accused of treason and collaborating with the Arabs.[10]

In modern times too the council has provoked lively controversy. Its *acta* survive in Greek and Latin versions. Naturally, since it was a papal council, the Latin *acta* were assumed to have priority, but the preparation of an edition for the *Acta Conciliorum Oecumenicorum* by Rudolf Riedinger revealed otherwise.[11] Riedinger's detailed analysis of the two texts showed that the Greek text was in fact the original and the Latin a translation of this. Riedinger's analyses and their exposition were complex and included computer-based studies of the stylistic idiosyncracies of the two versions. However, clear indicators of the priority of the Greek version can be seen in the way in which many of the biblical quotations in the Latin are in fact translations of the Greek rather than independent use of a Latin Bible. Moreover, Riedinger was able to show through his stylistic analyses that the speeches made in the course of the council by Pope Martin bore all the marks of the Latin translation and could not be considered verbatim records of what he said.[12]

These discoveries led Riedinger to doubt the historicity of the council itself and to suggest that the *acta* were a literary confection, suggesting perhaps that the council never really took place. This hypothesis has proved controversial, and it must be said that Riedinger himself has shifted his position in the course of his numerous publications, and has adopted a less crude position than his earlier description of the proceedings as a forgery. Many scholars, myself included, are reluctant to see the

9 See the records of the trials and exiles of Maximus and his followers in Allen and Neil (2002), 47–119, and for an account of Maximus' trials Haldon (1985) and Brandes (1998).
10 Allen and Neil (2002), 116–19, 150–1. On Pope Martin see the papers in *Martino I Papa* (1992).
11 *ACO* II. 1, and see Riedinger (1976, 1977, 1981), whose important studies are brought together in Riedinger (1998).
12 *ACO* II. 1, Riedinger (1981).

council as simply a sham.[13] The council could have been convened but with all the discussion pre-arranged and 'scripted', or the *acta* could represent an artificial account of what took place, less the formalized minutes of actual debate than a creative and literary composition crafted to convey the doctrinal authority of the meeting. However, it is important to note two points, firstly, that it would have been imperative for the council to have actually pronounced its anathemas on the heretics and their teachings, and secondly, that the *acta* frequently refer to the translation of documents from Greek into Latin before the assembly. On the one hand these statements may be fictions designed to give the appearance of veracity, but on the other they may indicate something of the actual proceedings, suggesting that it took place in Latin or both Latin and Greek.[14]

In fact, many of Riedinger's conclusions were anticipated by Caspar in his 1932 discussion of the council, where he pointed to Greek influence within the Latin text and to the clearly Greek nature of the theological discussion; he highlighted the role of Maximus the Confessor and his followers.[15] Riedinger and others have taken this much further, and it has been shown that Maximus was probably the author of some of the conciliar canons and the compiler of a florilegium of patristic texts. There can be no doubt that Maximus and his followers played a major part in the preparation of the *acta* with their reasoned refutation of the arguments of the monotheletes. Pope Martin may have known little or no Greek, and it is frankly improbable that his careful point-by-point demolition of technical Greek discussion of the will of Christ was all his own work, whether originally created in Latin or Greek.[16]

The council reflects the Mediterranean world of the mid-seventh century – attended by the Italian episcopate, including bishops from Sardinia, Corsica, and Sicily, with submissions from Palestine, Africa

---

13 Riedinger (1976), 37 described the *acta* as a 'purely literary product'. See, also for example, Riedinger's statement (1982), 120, 'What happened in the five days in session in the Lateran Palace in October 649? We do not know, but it is probable that the Latin translation of the text of the *acta* was read out formally by the pope and his bishops.' Ekonomou (2007), 131 (following Conte and Riedinger) regards the proceedings as essentially scripted.

14 See note 19 below.

15 Caspar (1930–3), II, 553–4.

16 Riedinger (1982). Ekonomou (2007), 129 points out that Martin had been *apocrisiarius* in Constantinople and argues for substantial knowledge of Greek on his part, a hypothesis which needs further testing.

and Cyprus.[17] It reflects tensions in that world, not least linguistic ones. The submission of the Greek monks who had fled from Africa is made in Greek, but the letters of the African bishops are drafted in Latin. How far was this a bilingual world? The bishop of Sardinia, Deusdedit of Cagliari, is one of the most prominent individual bishops shown in the *acta*. After the exile of Maximus, his follower Anastasius wrote in his support to the monks of Cagliari, a letter now extant only in a Latin translation but originally drafted in Greek.[18] These monks were presumably a refugee Greek colony, but this correspondence raises the question of the extent to which Greek was known and understood in Sardinia.

There are practical concerns behind the production of the bilingual *acta* which also merit consideration. The monothelete controversy was effectively a Greek controversy, and the majority of the documents produced at the council were already in that tongue. If we take at face value the statements within the council that Greek documents were read out in Latin translation, then embryonic versions of the proceedings already existed in both languages.[19] The final preparation of the bilingual texts was simply a further step. One can also question further the view that in some way the production of the Greek text was disassociated from Martin himself; one might rather see the creators of the bilingual versions as working on behalf of the pope. Perhaps one should associate their production with Maximus' follower, Anastasius Apocrisiarius, who may have played an important role in their composition. I suggest this because we know from subsequent accounts that Anastasius was fluent in both Greek and Latin (while Maximus was not) and that he had been much earlier a papal *apocrisiarius*.[20]

One very important key to understanding the meaning of the *acta* has been provided by Alexander Alexakis in his work on conciliar flori-

---

17 See, for example, the list of bishops subscribing, *ACO* II. 1, pp. 2–7.

18 Allen and Neil (2002), 124–31 with discussion at 37–8; Winkelmann (2001) no. 137; Conte (1989), 162. It is unclear which of the two Anastasii penned the letter – Winkelmann gives Anastasius the Disciple, but Allen and Neil regard the author's identity as uncertain.

19 Documents originally in Latin include the submissions of Maurus of Cesena (*ACO* II. 1, pp. 23–5), the letter of the African bishops to Pope Theodore (pp. 67–71), the letter of Bishop Stephen of Bizacena to the emperor (pp. 75–9), the letters of Bishops Gulosus, Probus and other bishops to Patriarch Paul (pp. 81–95), and the letter of Victor of Carthage to Pope Theodore (pp. 97–103). For an examination of the Greek and Latin texts behind different documents see Riedinger (1980, 1981, 1983).

20 Allen and Neil (2002), 24, 98–9. Winkelmann and others (1998–), I, 79–80, no. 237.

legia.[21] Here he shows how much careful preparation went into the convocation of a major theological council. The Council of Constantinople in 553 was a landmark in this respect in its use of florilegia which must have been put together before the council. He argues that it is clear that the extensive documentation discussed in the course of this council had been organized before the meeting itself. The Council of Constantinople seems to have been a model in this respect for the Lateran Council of 649, which relied on florilegia both of orthodox testimonies and of heretical texts. He regards these two councils – and parts of the Second Council of Nicaea – as 'stage-managed', which seems to me a better description of their proceedings. For these reasons, he contests Riedinger's view that the Lateran Council was a literary fiction and provides it with a meaningful context by comparison with the other great theological councils of the early Middle Ages.

Alexakis's observations reinforce the comparison made by Caspar in 1932 between the Lateran Council and ecumenical councils. Its proceedings were clearly modelled on those of the ecumenical councils and particularly the Council of Constantinople of 553.[22] This conclusion is not simply an observation about form or style, but a significant interpretation of the intentions of Pope Martin and his associates.[23]

The artificiality of the Lateran *acta* need not be a bar to historical enquiry, undermining their use as evidence, but rather it enables us to ask questions about what images of the council and of papal authority were being projected in them. The quasi-ecumenical nature of the council also sheds some light on the vexed question of the Greek *acta*. The composition and publication of these in Greek must echo the *acta* of earlier ecumenical councils which were drafted in this language. While they mimic the proceedings of ecumenical councils, the Lateran Council has not been classed as an ecumenical council. It was not convened by the emperor nor attended by the emperor or his representatives. In Rome in 649, it is Martin who presides over the council and acts usually as the ultimate authority, authorising the production of different witnesses. He convoked the council and played the leading role

21 Alexakis (1996), 16–21. See also *Acts of the Council of Chalcedon*, I, 75–8 for a helpful account of the production of conciliar proceedings.
22 Caspar (1932) and Caspar (1930–3), II, 553–4.
23 See also the discussion of Ekonomou (2007), 117–41, emphasizing the ecumenical nature of the council.

in refuting heretical texts.[24] Convocation of councils in imitation of ecumenical councils was one means by which the new kings of the successor states might take on imperial roles to lend an imperial lustre to their new rulership. One thinks, for example, of Reccared at the Third Council of Toledo in 589, or of Charlemagne at Frankfurt in 794.[25] Martin's role at the council sidesteps imperial authority in a deliberate fashion, just as did his failure to announce his election to the emperor. Indeed, the legitimacy of the council was deeply contested in Constantinople. At Maximus' first trial, his prosecutors attempted to undermine its authority by arguing that it had not received ratification because Martin had been deposed, which Maximus contested.[26] Then in 656 the same question was raised again when Maximus was under pressure in exile from the imperial representative, Bishop Theodosius, to recant. The bishop pointedly rejected the council, stating that 'the synod in Rome was not ratified, because it was held without the order of the emperor.'[27] Maximus retorted on this occasion that councils did not need imperial convocation or ratification to attest to orthodoxy, which was correct: 'What kind of canon declares that only those synods are approved which are convened on the orders of emperors, or that generally speaking synods are convened at all on the order of an emperor?'[28] But the fact that the same objection to the council was made twice is a revealing one, suggesting that tacitly the council might be treated as an ecumenical council and subject to imperial ratification.[29] Writing in Rome after the council, Maximus designated the Lateran Council as the successor to the fifth ecumenical council, the Council of Constantinople of 553, describing it as the sixth council which had pronounced on true doctrine through the inspiration of God.[30]

In the *Commemoratio*, a text composed after the deaths of Martin and Maximus to publicize their sufferings and martyrdoms, Martin is praised for shedding the light of true teaching:

24 For the convocation see *ACO* II. 1; for Martin presiding over the council see opening protocols to each session, 2–3, 31, 111, 177, 247; for condemnation of the heresy see 10–21, 174–5, 182–95, 336–43, 358–65; for the defence of orthodoxy see 252–3.

25 Stocking (2000), 59–60.

26 Allen and Neil (2002), 70–3.

27 Allen and Neil (2002), 88–9, 96–9.

28 Allen and Neil (2002), 88–9.

29 Allen and Neil (2002), 60–1.

30 PG 91. 138–9. On Maximus' conception of Roman authority see Larchet (1998), 125–201, esp. 155–9, and Garrigues (1976).

[Martin fell asleep] after he had brought illumination to the one and only catholic and apostolic, glorious Church of our God, by the all-holy and the true teachings of the synods, I mean the one in Nicaea, and Constantinople, both Ephesus I and Chalcedon, and again in Constantinople at the time of the emperor Justinian, and the sacred and all-pious teachings of all the holy Fathers who are both full of divine wisdom and approved, and our true teachers, as those who wish to read reverently will find in the sacred acts of the holy and apostolic and all-pious synod which was convened by him in Rome.[31]

The emphasis on the orthodox teaching of the ecumenical councils, upheld and reiterated in the Lateran Council, and on Martin's role in convening that council in Rome, is suggestive.

The independent convocation of the council is a mark of Martin's aspirations to action independent of imperial authority, asserting the supremacy of the papacy in matters of faith. This is an implicit denial of imperial authority in doctrinal matters, although the *acta* as a whole are careful never to criticize the emperors directly. The *Ekthesis* and the *Typos* are condemned as the work of the emperor's heretical advisers, the patriarchs of Constantinople.[32] This is an important point: the subsequent trials and interrogations of Maximus return time and time again to the condemnation of the *Typos* as an act which had brought the emperor into disrepute. Maximus was careful to respond that the emperor himself had not been condemned but the document and its originators, the patriarchs.[33]

Nor was the Lateran Council attended by representatives of the universal Church. While it was a large council, attended by over a hundred bishops whose names are listed, these were drawn almost entirely from Italy. And yet, it seems that there is a deliberate attempt within the conciliar *acta* to project both an image of the unity of the Italian church and an image of the universal authority of the pope over the Church and to show his far-flung authority.

The proceedings of the council consist of five sessions. The very first session consisted only of the letter of Maurus of Ravenna delivered by his representatives, giving his excuses for non-attendance and his

31 Allen and Neil (2002), 160–1.
32 *ACO* II. 1, pp. 182–3. At pp. 206–7 Martin says that the *Typos* was composed through the persuasion of Patriarch Paul.
33 Allen and Neil (2002), 66–72, 110–13.

support for orthodoxy, thus indicating the agreement of one of the most important of the Italian bishops.[34] Throughout the council, a handful of Italian bishops make interventions, usually of a perfunctory kind, and these act as signals of the unity of the Italian episcopate behind the pope and in condemnation of the heresy. Moreover, at six moments the whole synod or episcopate speaks like a chorus, a display of the collective nature of conciliar action. The three occasions when the words of the whole synod are reported are in the final sessions when the heretics are anathematized and the canons issued, in the endorsement of the orthodox florilegium and in the condemnation of the *Typos*. [35] The collective rejection of the imperial decree, in contravention of which the council was held, is clearly significant both as an expression of the unanimity of the council and as an avoidance of individual action by Martin himself. Is this image of the unity of the Italian episcopate a conscious counter to the disunity of the Italian church in the Three Chapters controversy?[36]

The second session was occupied by the production of testimonies of support for the papal position by overseas bishops. Here the impression is given of the pope's care for the whole Church, both in the reading out of submissions from all over the empire and also in the rhetoric employed. Letters and reports are read from the papal legate in Palestine, Stephen of Dora, a deputation of Greek monks in Rome (including Maximus and his followers), from the archbishop of Cyprus, an acephalous see, and a number of letters from bishops in Africa.[37] Stephen refers to the responsibility of Peter to act as shepherd of the 'flock of the whole Catholic Church' and describes how Sophronius, the anti-monothelete patriarch of Jerusalem, charged him to travel to Rome, the foundation of orthodox doctrine, from the ends of the earth; he says that he was beseeched by the supplications of bishops and laity of nearly the whole of the east.[38] The letter of the African bishops of Numidia, Mauretania and Byzacena to Pope Theodore is a difficult text, since Riedinger

---

34 *ACO* II. 1, pp. 2–29.

35 'All the bishops': *ACO* II. 1, pp. 28–9, 118–19, 194–5. 'The holy synod': pp. 210–17, 314–21, 364–67.

36 On the impact of this controversy see Chazelle and Cubitt 2007.

37 Submission of Stephen of Dora, *ACO* II. 1, pp. 36–47; of the Greek monks, pp. 50–9; of the archbishop of Cyprus, pp. 60–5; of the African bishops, pp. 66–71, 74–9, 80–95, 98–103.

38 *ACO* II. 1, pp. 38–47, esp. pp. 40, 5 and 42, 4.

has argued that it was composed in Rome using a Roman canon law collection. Even if this is a fabrication in Rome, its depiction of papal authority is valuable – it opens with an image of Rome as a spring from which streams flow, irrigating the Christian world. It goes on to state that actions in the 'remote and distantly-placed provinces' must refer to Rome for their guidance and ratification.[39] In the letter of Bishop Victor of Carthage also to Pope Theodore, Victor describes how the whole world is strengthened and guided by the divinely-inspired teaching of the pope.[40] Martin responds to this letter by emphasizing its message that the cries of nearly all Christendom have been raised by the heresy.[41] There is a counterpoint to these statements in the letters also reported as sent in orthodox protest to the emperor and the patriarchs of Constantinople which refer to the imperial care for the whole Church and to the authority of the councils convened by the emperor, the same institutions which are now responsible for the introduction of novelties and heresy into the Church.[42]

The Lateran Council of 649 was not a mere rhetorical exercise – it was held in defiance of an imperial order forbidding discussion of the will of Christ. The active role of the papacy can be seen in the report of Stephen of Dora, appointed as papal representative in order to counteract the invalid consecrations of the heretical patriarch of Jerusalem, by deposing those ordained by him. Moreover, the council itself was followed by an active programme of dissemination in both east and west. The *Liber Pontificalis* reports that Martin 'made copies and sent them through all the districts of east and west, broadcasting them by the hands of the orthodox faithful.'[43] This intention is made clear in Martin's encyclical and in his letter to the Frankish monk and missionary, St Amandus.[44] Martin not only sent Amandus the conciliar *acta* and papal encyclical but also asked him to inform King Sigibert of the proceedings

---

39 *ACO* II. 1, pp. 66–71, quotation from p. 67, 38.
40 *ACO* II. 1, pp. 98–103, esp. 101.
41 *ACO* II. 1, pp. 104–5.
42 *ACO* II. 1, pp. 72–9, 80–3.
43 Trans. Davis (2000), 71. Duchesne (1955), I, 357: 'Et faciens exemplaria, per omnes tractos Orientis et Occidentis direxit, per manus orthodoxorum fidelium disseminavit'.
44 *ACO* II. 1, pp. 404–21, esp. 413, 'Propterea enim ea quae a nobis pro catholicae ecclesiae synodaliter gesta sunt omnibus direximus...' ('Therefore we have sent to all the things which were enacted by us in the council for the sake of the catholic church'); see Riedinger (1994). For the letter to Amandus, pp. 422–4, see Riedinger (1996).

and convene a council to discuss the heresy.[45] The *Vita sancti Eligii* records similar papal initiatives in the kingdom of Neustria, when Eligius and Audouen of Rouen were selected to report back to the pope. The Council of Chalon, probably held in 650, must have been convened in fulfilment of the papal request for conciliar action and upholds in its very first canon the orthodoxy of the ecumenical councils.[46]

The dissemination of the Lateran *acta* in the east was more problematic because of the political difficulties, but we know that copies circulated amongst Maximus' followers and were used to refute monothelete arguments. Martin sent a copy of the *acta* and the encyclical to Bishop John of Philadelphia.[47] The *Commemoratio* suggests that Pope Martin in Rome asked its author, Theodore Spoudaeus, to spread the text.[48] The disputation between Maximus the Confessor and Bishop Theodosius mentioned above indicates that Maximus actually produced a copy in order to show Theodosius patristic proof texts.[49] And a copy of the *acta* was requested by Maximus' follower, Anastasius Apocrisiarius, in a letter to Theodore of Gangra.[50] Anastasius requests a copy from his fellow dyotheletes travelling in those parts, expressly so that he can use the texts contained within it to refute monothelete teaching. He comments that the persecution of Maximus and his followers has actually served not to suppress their views but to disseminate them more widely: 'while banishing us to different places and regions, they contrive to have the orthodox faith of the holy Fathers, which we too preach, revealed further.' The *acta* in their original Greek version were used as a powerful tool against the monotheletism championed by the emperor. They were cited by Maximus in the course of his trial.[51] Maximus and his followers clearly regarded the *acta* as an important weapon in their fight against the heresy.

This evidence for the deliberate diffusion of the text emphasizes two points. Firstly, it underlines the importance of the bilingual composition

---

45 *ACO* II. 1, pp. 422–4.
46 *Vita Eligii*, pp. 689–93. *Concilia Galliae* (1963), 302–10, with French trans. in *Les Canons des Conciles mérovingiens*, II, 550–65. On papal outreach to Francia see Borias (1987), Scheibelreiter (1992), Wood (2007) and Cubitt (forthcoming), which also discuss the dating of the council and its special link to papal initiatives.
47 Ekonomou (2007), 140.
48 Allen and Neil (2002), 164–5.
49 Allen and Neil (2002), 88–9, 96–9.
50 Allen and Neil (2002), 142–3.
51 Allen and Neil (2002), 60–1.

of the *acta*, showing that the original aim was to produce texts for widespread circulation. Secondly, it reinforces the active intention of the pope and his assistants to attack the imperial position and to marshal as widespread support throughout Christendom against the imperially sponsored heresy. The record of Maximus' first trial in 655 states that one of his prosecutors, 'on hearing that the *Typos* was anathematized throughout the entire west', accused the theologian of bringing the emperor's name into disrepute. In his later interrogation, it is claimed that Maximus was the leader of subversion throughout the east and west.[52] The implications of the anathematization of the heretics at the synod of 649 was to require all orthodox Christians to cease communication with them, as Maximus indeed did in response to the Lateran Council.[53] The convention of the synod, its condemnation of the *Typos* and *Ekthesis* and of the patriarchs, and the publication and dissemination of bilingual *acta* was a highly provocative political act.

Form and content in the Lateran *acta* work closely together. They were composed in Greek and Latin in order to facilitate the widespread diffusion of their decrees. They were deliberately crafted to emphasize the unity of the Christian world in support of the papal dyothelete position and to cast the pope as its Christian leader. Their careful creation drew upon conciliar tradition and reworked it in a dramatically new fashion.[54]

BIBLIOGRAPHY

Primary Sources

Acta Conciliorum Oecumenicorum, Series Secunda (II) 1, *Concilium Lateranense a. 649 celebratum,* ed. Rudolf Riedinger (Berlin, 1984).

The Acts of the Council of Chalcedon, trans. Richard Price and Michael Gaddis, 3 vols, TTH 45 (Liverpool, 2005).

Les Canons des Conciles mérovingiens (VIe–VIIe), ed. Jean Gaudemet and Brigitte Basdevant, 2 vols, SC 353–4 (Paris, 1989).

Concilia Galliae A. 511–A. 695, ed. Charles de Clercq, Corpus Christianorum Series Latina 148A (Turnhout, 1963).

52 Allen and Neil (2002), 108–9.

53 Allen and Neil (2002), 70–1, 88–91.

54 These questions will be further considered in the introduction and translation of the Acts of the Lateran Council of 649 by Richard Price and myself, to be published in TTH. I am grateful to the British Academy and to the Leverhulme Trust for grants which facilitated this research and to Dumbarton Oaks for a Summer Fellowship. I am most grateful to the editors for their comments and guidance.

Le Liber Pontificalis. Texte, Introduction, et Commentaire, ed. Louis Duchesne with additions and corrections by Cyrille Vogel, 3 vols (1955, repr. 1981), Bibliothèque des Écoles françaises d'Athènes et de Rome. Trans. Raymond Davis, *The Book of Pontiffs (Liber Pontificalis)*, TTH 5 (Liverpool, 2000).

Maximus the Confessor and his Companions: Documents from Exile, ed. and trans. Pauline Allen and Bronwen Neil (Oxford, 2002).

Vita Eligii Episcopi Noviomagensis, ed. B. Krusch, MGH, Scriptores Rerum Merovingicarum 4 (1902), 634–76.

Secondary Literature

Alexakis, Alexander (1996), *Codex Parisinus Graecus 1115 and its Archetype*, Dumbarton Oaks Studies 34 (Washington).

Allen and Neil (2002): see Primary Sources, 'Maximus the Confessor and his Companions'.

Borias, P. (1987), 'Saint Wandrille et la crise monothélite', *RBen* 97: 42–67.

Brandes, Wolfram (1998), '"Juristische" Krisenbewältigung im 7. Jahrhundert? Die Processe gegen Papst Martin I. und Maximos Homologetes', *Fontes Minores* 10, 141–212.

Caspar, Erich (1930–3), *Geschichte des Papsttums von den Anfängen bis zur Höhe der Weltherrschaft*, 2 vols (Tübingen).

—— (1932), 'Die Lateransynode von 649', *ZKG* 51, 75–137.

Chadwick, Henry (2003), *East and West: the Making of a Rift in the Church from Apostolic Times until the Council of Florence* (Oxford).

Chazelle, Celia and Cubitt, Catherine, eds (2007), *The Crisis of the Oikoumene: The Three Chapters and the Failed Quest for Unity in the Sixth-Century Mediterranean* (Turnhout).

Conte, Pietro (1971), *Chiesa e Primato nelle Lettere dei Papi del Secolo VII*, Pubblicazioni dell'Università cattolica del S. Cuore, Saggi e ricerche ser. 3, Scienze storiche 4 (Milan).

—— (1989), *Il Sinodo Lateranense dell'ottobre 649 – La nuova edizione degli atti a cura de Rudolf Riedinger*. Rassegna critica di fonti dei secoli vii–xii, Collezione teologica 3 (Vatican City).

Cubitt, Catherine (forthcoming), 'The Lateran Council of 649 and the Western Successor States'.

Ekonomou, A.J. (2007), *Byzantine Rome and the Greek Popes. Eastern Influences on Rome and the Papacy from Gregory the Great to Zacharias, A. D. 590–752* (Lanham).

Garrigues, Juan-Miguel (1976), 'Le sens de la primauté romaine chez Maxime le Confesseur', *Istina* 21: 6–24.

Haldon, John (1985), 'Ideology and the Byzantine State in the Seventh Century: The "Trial" of Maximus the Confessor', in Vavrínek, Vladimir, ed., *From Late Antiquity to Early Byzantium*, Proceedings of the Byzantinological Symposium in the 16th International Eirene Conference (Prague), 87–92.

—— (1986), 'Ideology and Social Change in the Seventh Century. Military Discontent as a Barometer', *Klio* 68.1: 139–90.

—— (1997), *Byzantium in the Seventh Century*, 2nd edition (Cambridge).

Kaegi, W.E. (2003), *Heraclius Emperor of Byzantium* (Cambridge).

Larchet, Jean-Claude (1998), *Maxime le Confesseur, médiateur entre l'Orient et l'Occident* (Paris).

—— (2003), *Saint Maxime le Confesseur* (Paris).

Martino I Papa (649–653) e il suo Tempo (1992). Atti del XXVIII Convegno storico internazionale. Todi, 13–16 ottobre 1991, Centro italiano di Studi sull'alto Medioevo (Spoleto).

Neil, Bronwen (1998), 'The *Lives* of Pope Martin I and Maximus the Confessor: some Reconsiderations of Dating and Provenance', *Byz* 68: 91–109.

Riedinger, Rudolf (1976), 'Aus den Akten der Lateran-Synode von 649', *ByzZ* 69: 17–38 = id. (1998), 3–24.

—— (1977), 'Griechische Konzilsakten auf dem Wege ins lateinische Mittelalter', *AHC* 9: 253–301 = id. (1998), 43–91.

—— (1980), 'Zwei Briefe aus den Akten der Lateransynode von 649', *JÖB* 29: 37–59 = id. (1998), 95–117.

—— (1981), 'Sprachschichten in der lateinischen Übersetzung der Lateranakten von 649', *ZKG* 92: 180–203 = id. (1998), 137–60.

—— (1982), 'Die Lateransynode von 649 und Maximos der Bekenner', in F. Heiner and E. Schönborn, eds. (1982), *Maximus Confessor. Actes du Symposium sur Maxime le Confesseur. Fribourg, 2–5 Septembre 1980*, *Paradosis* 27: 111–21 = id. (1998), 169–79.

—— (1983), 'Papst Martin 1. und Papst Leo I. in den Akten der Lateran-Synode von 649', *JÖB* 33: 87–8 = id. (1998), 201–2.

—— (1994), 'Die lateinischen Übersetzungen der Epistula Papst Martins I (CPG 9403) und der Epistula Synodica des Sophronios von Jerusalem (CPG 7635)', *FilMed* 1: 45–69 = id. (1998), 301–25.

—— (1996), 'Wer hat den Briefe Papst Martins I an Amandus verfaßt?', *FilMed* 3: 95–104 = id. (1998), 329–38.

—— (1998), *Kleine Schriften zu den Konzilsakten des 7. Jahrhunderts* (Turnhout).

Scheibelreiter, Georg (1992), 'Griechisches-lateinisches-frankisches Christentum. Der Brief Papst Martins I. an den Bischof Amandus von Maastricht aus dem Jahre 649', *Mitteilungen des Instituts für Österreichische Geschichtsforschung* 100: 84–102.

Stocking, R.L. (2000), *Bishops, Councils and Consensus in the Visigothic Kingdom, 589–633* (Ann Arbor).

Stratos, A.N. (1968–80), *Byzantium in the Seventh Century*, 5 vols (Amsterdam).

Winkelmann, Friedhelm (1987), 'Die Quellen zur Erforschung des monergetisch-monotheletischen Streites', *Klio* 69: 515–59.

—— and Ralph-Johannes Lilie, Claudia Ludwig, Thomas Pratsch and Iles Rochow (1998–), *Prosopographie der mittelbyzantinischen Zeit. Erste Abteilung (641–867)*, 6 vols, in progress (Berlin).

—— (2001), *Der monenergetisch-monotheletische Streit* (Frankfurt am Main).

Wood, Ian (2007), 'The Franks and Papal Theology, 550–660', in Chazelle and Cubitt (2007), 23–41.

THE QUINISEXT COUNCIL (692)
AS A CONTINUATION OF CHALCEDON

Judith Herrin

In the study of the Fourth Ecumenical Council of Chalcedon, the canons attached to it are frequently neglected. This may be because no discussion of them is recorded in the official acts of 451. Nonetheless, in the oldest Latin version and the Greek manuscript tradition of the Acts of Chalcedon the twenty-seven canons are inserted as 'the seventh act', as if they formed part of the agreed record of the council.[1] The debate over Canon 28, which is numbered to follow on from the other 27, forms the seventeenth session in the Greek acts and the sixteenth in the Latin.[2] The canons became part of the ecclesiastical law of the Church and are cited in sixth-century lists.

The purpose of this short article is two-fold: to examine the fate of Canon 28, which confirmed the standing of Constantinople as the leading patriarchal see in the ecclesiastical hierarchy of the east, with an authority comparable to that of Old Rome, and to trace the continuity of concern about particular features of clerical life which feature in the 27 canons. Since the Fifth and Sixth Ecumenical Councils of 553 and 680/1 were devoted to matters concerning the 'mystery of the faith', rather than ecclesiastical legislation, the gathering summoned by Justinian II in 692 was the first to devote itself to canonical legislation for 240 years.[3] Because it met under the dome (*troullos*) of an audience

---

1 For an introduction to the complex history of the canons see Price and Gaddis (2005), III, vii–viii, 67, 92–3.
2 In the later Latin tradition the 27 canons immediately precede discussion of Canon 28. This discussion clearly took place in an unofficial fashion and was later reported to the final session of the council. In similar fashion, the 27 canons may have been presented though not recorded in the course of the council's meetings.
3 Full text in Mansi, XI, 928–1006; Rhalles–Potles (1852), II, 295–550 (with twelfth-century commentaries); Joannou (1962), I/1, 101–241 (with Latin and French translations); Troianos (1992), 46–113; Nedungatt–Featherstone (1995), 45–185 (with English translation); Ohme (2006) with revised Greek text and German translation; Nedungatt–Agrestini (2006) with revised Latin translation, 219–93. Reference to 'the mystery of the faith' at Rhalles–Potles, II, 298; Nedungatt–Featherstone, 51; Ohme (2006), 166. In subsequent notes reference will be made to the Nedungatt–Featherstone Greek text and English translation.

hall in the Great Palace of the emperors of Constantinople, it is identified in the manuscript tradition by the name *in Trullo*. Because it was
perceived as a completion of the Fifth Council of 553 and the Sixth of
680/1, it was also known as the *Penthekte, Quinisextum* or 'Fifth-Sixth'.[4]
Although separated from Chalcedon by nearly two and a half centuries,
its 102 canons were conceived as a continuation of the rulings issued at
Chalcedon in 451.[5]

Of course, many other methods of ensuring ecclesiastical discipline
had intervened during the long gap from 451 to 692, notably imperial
legislation and collections of canon law. But in their address to Emperor
Justinian II, the bishops in 692 stated clearly that their role was inspired
by the need for regulations which might raise the people 'to a better and
loftier life' and prevent 'the royal priesthood' from being 'torn asunder
and led astray through the many passions resulting from indiscipline'.[6]
In this function they explicitly followed the example of the first four
ecumenical councils and proceeded to issue their own canons. Together
with the address to the emperor and a list of episcopal signatures, these
are the only records that survive.[7]

From the fifth to the seventh century certain features of conciliar
procedure remained the same. All universal gatherings were
summoned by the emperor (Marcian, Justinian I and Justinian II), in
conjunction with the patriarch of the day (Anatolius, Eutychius and
Paul), since they were held in Constantinople or its close environs. In
all these councils representatives of the bishop of Rome were given
precedence, seated on the emperor's right hand; they were the first
clerics to sign all documents, ahead of the easterners. At most meetings,
lay figures played a major part in the direction of the sessions and
ensured that imperial concerns dominated the proceedings. No record
survives of those officials who in 692 performed the role of Anatolius,
magister militum, Palladius, praetorian prefect of the east, and Vinco-
malus, master of the divine offices, in 451. But thirteen high-ranking
secular and military figures were in charge of the Sixth Ecumenical
Council in 680/1 and may have been in office eleven years later to

---

4　Nedungatt–Agrestini (2006), 205–6.
5　Ibid. 208–9, showing how the Council *in Trullo* continued the work of Chalcedon by
　specifying the councils and canons approved, which totalled 643.
6　Rhalles–Potles (1852), 298; Nedungatt–Featherstone (1995), 52; Ohme (2006), 166.
7　Ohme (1990) on the list of episcopal signatures.

manage the Council *in Trullo*.[8] Under such imperial guidance, the bishops of the Council *in Trullo* displayed a self-conscious awareness in maintaining direct continuity with the work of previous councils, which they cited in their introductory letter and in the first two canons.[9]

At Chalcedon three laws drafted by Emperor Marcian were introduced during the sixth session, when they were read out by Veronicianus, secretary of the sacred consistory, for the council's approval. The emperor wished the issues addressed to be enshrined in ecclesiastical as well as civil law. Following acclamation by the bishops, these matters were entrusted to Patriarch Anatolius, who issued them as Canons 3, 4, and 20 of the list of 27 probably agreed at a session not formally recorded in the acts of the council.[10] What the emperor had perceived as a need to control monks and monasteries (which were to be placed under episcopal authority), to curb monks or clerics who took secular jobs, and clerics who attempt to move from church to church, was thus incorporated in canon law.[11] It was at the end of the same sixth session that the emperor instructed the bishops to remain in council, and 'in the presence of our most magnificent officials [to] move whatever proposals you wish… None of you is to leave the holy council until definitive decrees have been issued about everything.'[12] This indicates two methods by which canons originated: they might be proposed by the emperor, or bishops could bring their concerns for definitive resolution to the highest authority in the Church. The remaining canons attached to Chalcedon probably originated in common anxieties shared by many of the bishops present. Whatever their origin, the rulings issued by universal councils became binding on all Christians.

In 451 the bishops continued their work for another week, holding ten more sessions devoted to problems of seniority between sees and rivalry between bishops that had been addressed to the emperor. Marcian had decided to pass them on to the council, which thus took responsibility for establishing the independence of the see of Jerusalem from Antioch,

8   These officers signed the *acta* ahead of all the bishops, for example, at the final session in 681. Three held high-ranking military positions; three were legal specialists; five were patricians of ex-consular rank, and the last was in charge of the emperor's private dining room: see Riedinger (1992), II, 752–5.

9   Nedungatt–Featherstone (1995), 45–69.

10 The letter authorizing the circulation of the canons is now lost, see Grumel (1932), 55, no. 127. Most of Anatolius' official documents are not preserved, cf. nos. 128–32.

11 Price and Gaddis (2005), II, 242.

12 Ibid. II, 243.

the restoration of Bishops Theodoret and Ibas, and the resolution of a number of disputes. These sessions are numbered VII–XVI in the Latin manuscript tradition, and VIII–XVII in the Greek tradition (because the 27 canons were inserted as Session VII).

The status of Rome and Constantinople

On 1 November 451 the final session of the Council of Chalcedon met to discuss a canon approved by 182 bishops at an informal meeting the previous day. The Roman representatives had declined to attend this meeting as they had no mandate to discuss additional issues; they announced that they considered the proceedings 'to have been transacted in contravention of the canons and ecclesiastical discipline'; the archdeacon of Constantinople immediately denied this and assured the council that 'nothing was transacted in secret or in a fraudulent manner'.[13] When the acts of the previous meeting were read, it was clear that the new canon relied on the Council of the 150 Fathers (Constantinople 381) to claim Constantinople's status as second only to Rome, because it was the imperial city. New Rome was to share the same privileges as Senior Rome;[14] Emperor Theodosius had insisted upon this promotion which placed Constantinople ahead of the other eastern patriarchates.

The reading of this text provoked an angry retort from Lucentius, one of the papal representatives, who suggested that those bishops who had signed the text must have done so under duress. When this was denied, he pointed out that the new document relied on the authority of the Council of Constantinople (381) and was trying to set aside the Council of Nicaea, which had given 'Senior Rome' highest status and honour. In addition, he drew attention to the fact that the decrees of the 150 Fathers of 381 were not included among the recognized conciliar canons.[15] Although Constantinople did not contest the primacy of Old Rome, the Roman legates claimed that the hierarchy established in 325 was under threat. The relevant canons were then read – Canon 6 of Nicaea followed by the *synodikon* of Constantinople with its three canons.

13 Ibid. III, 75.
14 Ibid. III, 86–7. See the whole session, 73–91, and commentary, 67–73.
15 Ibid. III, 84. The canons of Constantinople (381) were apparently not recorded in the list of canons cited at Chalcedon and were quoted from another document – the *synodikon* of 381, ibid, III, 86–7.

Both sides agreed that Constantinople frequently exercised the right to consecrate metropolitan bishops in the eastern provinces. Indeed, Eusebius of Ancyra complained that extremely high fees had been demanded for this act, which made the consecration appear rather too close to a purchase fee (simony);[16] he was one of the ten metropolitans directly affected by the new canon who had not signed it the previous day. The secular officials then summed up, saying that 'primacy and exceptional honour should be reserved for the most God-beloved archbishop of Senior Rome according to the canons,' and that Constantinople New Rome would enjoy the same privileges of honour, and the power to consecrate the metropolitans of Asiana, Pontica and Thrace, but not their suffragan bishops. While those present approved of this conclusion, Lucentius insisted that if the canon was maintained, his formal protest against it should be recorded in the minutes. He considered it an insult to the see of Rome and pointed out that only the bishop of Rome, 'that apostolic man the pope of the universal church', had authority to decide on such a matter.[17] The council then disbanded.

When Pope Leo I received notification of the work of the council, he understood that Canon 28 posed a threat to the standing of his see. Letters from the authorities in the east, both imperial and patriarchal, urged him to sign the document, but he refused. When he responded to the emperor, it was to stress that the apostolic foundation of Rome set it apart from all others.[18] He noted pointedly that Patriarch Anatolius should not covet what was not his – 'Let him not disdain as unworthy the Imperial City which he cannot make into an apostolic see' – and denounced his shameless cupidity.[19] In his response to Anatolius, Leo repeatedly stressed the authority of the Council of Nicaea, denounced the 'reprehensible innovation contrary to the Nicene decrees' introduced at Chalcedon, and praised Antioch as another foundation of St Peter, which should never fall below its rank as third in the patriarchal hierarchy, junior only to Rome and Alexandria.[20] Only ten months later,

---

16 Ibid. III, 90. Eusebius had been consecrated in Constantinople by the patriarch.
17 Ibid. III, 90–1. Dvornik (1958), 82–5, 91–6, with detailed discussion of the stress laid by papal legates on the apostolic character of the see of Rome.
18 *Ep.* 104 of 22 May 452 to Emperor Marcian, *ACO* 2.4, pp. 55–7, Price and Gaddis, III, 142–5. Cf. Dvornik (1958), 96–105.
19 Price and Gaddis, III, 144.
20 *Ep.* 106, *ACO* 2.4, pp. 59–62, trans. Price and Gaddis, III, 146–50, cf. Dvornik (1958), 98–9.

in March 453, did he send his acceptance of the Acts of Chalcedon; in a letter to the council fathers he again stressed the inviolable decrees of the Council of Nicaea, and condemned the 'vicious ambition' and 'vainglorious pride' of the bishop of Constantinople.[21]

Canon 28 was to have a fascinating history. In the east it took its place among the canons issued at Chalcedon and was reproduced in later Greek records. Lists of canons already circulated, and one had been cited during the council proceedings, for instance in session XI when two canons of the council of Antioch of *c.* 330 were read out and identified as numbers 95 and 96 of this list. Again, in Session XIII the fourth canon issued by the First Ecumenical Council was quoted although it was incorrectly identified as number 6.[22] From these citations it is clear that the council had a book, *biblion,* containing a list of canons, starting with those of Nicaea; the bishops knew the contents of this list and could appeal to specific canons in support of their claims. They also cited additional material, such as the creed and canons of the Council of Constantinople of 381, from a separate codex.[23]

The most influential of these lists was the *Syntagma kanonon,* originally compiled at Antioch by Bishop Meletius (362–81), which consisted of canons numbered in a continuous series. It included the rulings issued by the ecumenical councils and the most significant local fourth-century councils (Ancyra, Neocaesarea, Gangra, Antioch and Laodicea). After 451 the canons issued at Chalcedon were added to it, and in the early sixth century the imperial chancellery added those of Sardica (342/3) and 133 canons of Carthage (419). The oldest surviving witnesses to this *Syntagma kanonon* are a Syriac translation made after 501 for the church of Hierapolis and a later Coptic translation.[24] By this process of dissemination throughout the Greek east, the *Syntagma kanonon* was evidently regarded as an authentic and uniformly binding list of canons.

---

21 *Ep.* 114 to the council fathers, *ACO* 2.4, 70–1, trans. Price and Gaddis, III, 153–4; and *ep.* 115 to the emperor, *ACO* 2.4, 67–8, trans. Price and Gaddis, III, 151–2.

22 Price and Gaddis, III, 10–11, 29; all three related to the consecration of bishops and were cited by rivals to the see of Ephesus. See L'Huillier (1996), 206–7; Di Berardino (1992), 141–2.

23 Price and Gaddis, II, 12–13, and III, 86–7, where the *synodikon* of 381 was cited.

24 Turner (1929/30), 9–20. *Pace* Dvornik (1958), 82, who claims that Canon 28 was not included in any Greek collections before the *Syntagma in 14 Titles* of the late sixth century, it must have been in the earlier witness now lost, because it was included in these translations.

In the west the situation was somewhat different. The canons of Nicaea were recognized everywhere as the foundation of ecclesiastical law, and those issued at Sardica were frequently associated with the First Ecumenical Council. In addition to the fourth-century councils held in the east, the rulings of Carthage (419) and the letters recording the fifth-century dispute over Apiarius were included in canonical collections. In Rome and Carthage these were kept up to date by the addition of later material – papal and episcopal letters.

In the course of the fifth century, however, these Latin lists were rivalled by three independent translations of Greek collections probably made in Rome.[25] One of these, the so-called *Prisca* version, is marked by its omission of the canons of Nicaea (which were so well known that it was not necessary to include them), its much fuller version of the canons of Sardica, taken from the original Latin record, and its inclusion of Canon 28 of Chalcedon.[26] So despite the fact that the other two Latin translations ignored Canon 28, through the *Prisca* translation it became known in some parts of the west. Further, the third canon of Constantinople (381), which established the superiority of Constantinople over the sees of Antioch, Alexandria and Jerusalem, and was cited in Canon 28, was included in all three new Latin versions.[27]

Nonetheless, when Pope Hormisdas (514–23) commissioned the Scythian monk Dionysius Exiguus to make an accurate translation of all recognized canonical material from the Greek original texts, one of his aims was to revise the *Prisca* version, considered unsatisfactory;[28] and Dionysius did not include Canon 28 of Chalcedon. His collection, which became the authoritative western list of canons, began with the first 50 of the 85 Apostolic Constitutions, 165 canons from fourth-century ecumenical and eastern councils, and 27 from Chalcedon, plus 21 from Sardica and 138 from Carthage, a total of 430.[29] To these recognized canonical rulings, Dionysius then added selections from 38 decretal letters written between the pontificates of Siricius (384–99) and Anastasius II (died 498). At least 460 letters existed in the Roman chancery of the time, and how Dionysius chose the texts he included is not made clear; but the effect was to raise papal responses to specific problems, in

25 Turner (1928/9), 340–2.
26 Turner (1929/30), 10–17.
27 L'Huillier (1996), 212; Turner (1928/9), 339–40.
28 Gallagher (2002), 3–10.
29 Gallagher (2002), 11–12; Gaudemet (1985), 136.

letters addressed to individual bishops, to the level of canons. Dionysius arranged the decretals in chronological order and according to particular topics, and listed them in one numerical sequence, following the system that was already familiar from canonical collections in Greek.

Among the letters that Dionysius chose were those of Pope Innocent I (401–17) which drew attention to the foundation of the Church of Antioch by St Peter, thus stressing the significance of an apostolic foundation, which Constantinople lacked. The primacy of Rome over all other churches was similarly emphasized. Problems over the calculation of Easter also featured in Dionysius' list, including letters by Cyril of Alexandria and Innocent I on how the date should be calculated so that all Christians could celebrate the most important feast of the Church on the same Sunday. This issue fitted with Dionysius' understanding of the difficulties of predicting correct future dates of Easter, based on his study of the Great Paschal Cycle of 532 years, which had been developed in Alexandria. It may reflect a period of negotiation between Constantinople and Rome in which the translations of the bilingual Scythian monk played a significant role.[30]

Despite his efforts to bring east and west into closer agreement, Dionysius omitted Canon 28 of Chalcedon from his list although he must have known that many Greek lists included it. He nonetheless included the third canon of Constantinople (381), which gave the imperial city a superior status to Alexandria and Antioch, the ruling on which the Greek bishops at Chalcedon in 451 drew for support for the claims made in Canon 28.[31] This was regularly repeated in Greek canonical and civil legislation, for instance in Novella 131 issued by Justinian I in 545.[32] Eventually, at the Fourth Lateran Council of 1215 it was accepted in Rome, in order to ensure the authority of the then Latin patriarch of Constantinople.[33]

In 692, however, the issue was still a delicate one which the Council in Trullo addressed in Canon 36. This reasserts the equal privileges of Old Rome and New Rome, and ranks New Rome/Constantinople ahead of Alexandria, Antioch and Jerusalem. In support of this position the Council in Trullo quotes the legislation of the 150 fathers of 381 and the

30 Gallagher (2002), 15.
31 Dvornik (1958), 50–53, 56.
32 Gallagher (2002), 22, n. 70.
33 Canon 5 of 1215, see Tanner (1990), I, 236.

630 fathers of Chalcedon.[34] It does not mention the primacy of honour which is due to the heirs of St Peter who hold the see of Rome, and thus avoids the issue of apostolic foundation, which would rank the eastern sees of Antioch (founded by Peter) and Alexandria (by the Evangelist Mark) ahead of Constantinople. Although emperors and bishops of the 'ruling city', as Constantinople was called, had accumulated many apostolic relics to enhance its position, the tradition that St Andrew had founded the see was a later invention. It was based on a legend that the apostle Andrew, Peter's brother, had passed through Byzantium during his missionary activity and ordained one Stathys as bishop in the city, a legend that was later accepted in both east and west.[35]

Developments in Eastern Canon Law

Turning now to the second aspect of this paper, I wish to examine the development of canon law between the Councils of Chalcedon and Trullo, to draw attention to the persistence of abiding concerns and the growth of new ones. From the citation of canonical material at Chalcedon, as we have seen, a list of early canons existed which numbered them consecutively starting with the twenty issued at Nicaea in 325. In the east under the influence of Justinian's legislative activity this list was reorganized into a collection, *Synagoge,* in 60 titles, which no longer survives. It was, however, used by John Scholasticus, a priest at Antioch who later became patriarch of Constantinople (565–77), when he made his own *Synagoge* in 50 titles. This decisive development in the east created a systematic counterpart in Greek to the collection of Dionysius.[36]

John's compilation established a list of canons accepted in the east, starting with all the 85 Apostolic Constitutions, the canons of the ecumenical councils and other eastern councils (all those included by Dionysius in his collection), plus the eight attributed to the Council of Ephesus (which dealt with its problems), and 68 regulations from St Basil taken to be canonical. In the east these were granted the same

---

34 Rhalles–Potles (1852), II, 387; Ioannou (1960), 170; Nedungatt–Featherstone (1995), 114; Ohme (2006), 128; commentary in Ohme (1995), 316–17.

35 Dvornik (1958), 138–80. It would be interesting to investigate whether the use of the legend could be related to Canon 36 of the Council *in Trullo.*

36 Beck (1959), 144–6, 423; Macrides (1990), 64–7; Gallagher (2002), 20–1.

status as papal decretals in the west. Finally, John added 87 excerpts from the Novels of Justinian, which reinforced canonical requirements.[37]

Unlike the edition of Dionysius, John arranged the material at his disposal by topic, starting with the honour due to the patriarch and continuing through a wide range of disciplinary matters to the date of Easter. But both collections drew on almost identical conciliar regulations; the only major difference lay in Dionysius' elevation of papal decretals to canonical status, paralleled by John's citation of the rulings of St Basil and laws of Justinian. Although this material had often developed from local disputes, by the end of the sixth century it had been integrated into two distinct traditions, which laid the basis for a divergence between eastern and western Christendom, in Greek and Latin respectively. The linguistic difference further encouraged independent developments of canon law in east and west. John's *Synagoge* provided the basis for the first coherent body of civil and ecclesiastical law (*nomos* and *kanon*), called the *Nomokanon in Fifty Titles,* made in the late sixth century. It was further developed by the addition of imperial legislation, local councils and patriarchal decisions.[38] Similarly, in the west papal decrees, local councils and authoritative statements by recognized authorities like St Isidore of Seville expanded to form a specifically western equivalent. The two remained unaware of each other and built on their own traditions.[39]

This division of Christendom into two legal systems was deepened by theological developments of the sixth and seventh century, which originated in the Greek east. Justinian's condemnation of the theological texts known as the Three Chapters provoked opposition in the west. The later efforts of Emperors Heraclius and Constans II to reunite Christian groups that remained divided by the definition of Chalcedon embroiled Pope Honorius (625–38) and his successors in a series of debates over the energies and wills of Christ. After considerable discussion, Pope Martin I decided to condemn these eastern doctrines, and the Lateran Council of 649 initiated a 30-year schism (see Catherine Cubitt's article in this volume).

So in 678 when Constantine IV sent letters inviting Pope Donus to attend a universal council in Constantinople designed to end the schism,

---

37 Gallagher (2002), 23–5 provides an abridged list of the contents; cf. Beck (1959), 423.
   Humfress (2004) demonstrates the Christianization of the law.
38 Gallagher (2002), 37–49.
39 Ibid. 49–84.

he initiated an important new phase in east/west relations.[40] The emperor was determined to reunite the churches on the basis of an orthodox interpretation of the natures, energies and wills of Christ. In the process, the eastern Church had to acknowledge its own support of unorthodox views, which were condemned as heretical at the Sixth Ecumenical Council of 680/1. Patriarchs Sergius, Pyrrhus and Paul, who had formulated these views, and Pope Honorius who had agreed with the definition of monotheletism, were identified as those responsible for the introduction of the error.[41] In preparing the western defence of orthodoxy, Pope Agatho (678–81) drew heavily on the Lateran Synod and used its arguments to correct the heresy of the eastern Church.

Since the Sixth Ecumenical Council did not issue any canons, eleven years later the young emperor Justinian II (685–95) and Patriarch Paul III (688–94) summoned the bishops back to Constantinople in order to review ecclesiastical legislation.[42] Pope Sergius (687–701) reportedly sent his representatives from Rome and the eastern patriarchates attended, so that the gathering, which eventually numbered 220 bishops, had a universal character.[43] Many of the eastern bishops brought their particular problems to the capital for resolution. Although the acts of the council have not survived, from the bishops' address to the emperor, their subscriptions and the list of 102 canons it is possible to analyse what took place under the dome of an audience chamber within the Great Palace. The rulings reflect the advance of Islam in the 640s, which had removed the provinces of Egypt, Palestine and Syria from imperial control, and Slavic invasions of the Balkans, with references to 'barbarian incursions' traditional in conciliar records.[44] These were said to have forced bishops to flee from their sees, or to have promoted an inappropriate adaptation of Christian customs among those who remained under barbarian control.[45] They suggest that several partici-

40 See the imperial *sacra* sent to the synod of Rome, Riedinger (1992), II, 856–67.
41 The *acta* are edited by Riedinger (1992).
42 Grumel (1932), 126, no. 317, text lost; see Herrin (1987), 284–5.
43 Mansi, XI, 929–88 includes the list of 227 signatories, which begin with the emperor and six secular officials, on which see Ohme (1990). Ohme (2006), 12, 25–6, points out that despite claims in the *Liber Pontificalis* official Roman legates in the strict sense did not participate.
44 Peri (1995).
45 Can. 12 (bishops in Africa and Libya continuing to cohabit with their wives after ordination), Nedungatt–Featherstone, 82–3; Can. 18 (clerics who have abandoned their sees, 'on the pretext of barbarian incursions'), ibid. 93–4; Can. 30 (priests in barbarian lands) ibid, 104–5; Can. 37 (bishops unable to take up residence in their sees), ibid.

pants seem to have requested guidance on how to look after their Christian flocks who found it difficult to sustain the faith under Arab rulers or Slavic pressures.

Nonetheless, a persistent anxiety about ancient problems of church discipline runs through the canonical material, and can be traced back to Chalcedon. All but six of the 27 canons of 451 are repeated in one form or another in 692:[46] these six relate to the secular activities of clerics (3 and 7), to the ordination of priests without designating them to a particular church (6), to clerics who take their legal cases to civilian courts (9), and to clerics or laymen who accuse bishops or clergy without having their characters investigated (21). Presumably, these issues were no longer considered relevant in the late seventh century. The sixth is Canon 26 of Chalcedon which ordered bishops to appoint clerical administrators (*oikonomoi*) to manage their property: this had become standard, so there was no need to repeat it. The concerns behind the remaining 21 canons issued at Chalcedon were reformulated at Trullo, sometimes in an oblique fashion, but occasionally directly, for example in the case of women abducted on the pretext of marriage (Chalcedon 27, Trullo 92). The marriage of monks or nuns, the marriage of lower clergy with heretical Christians, the activities of vagabond monks, priests who perform the liturgy in another city without the bishop's permission, who try to make their ecclesiastical institutions independent of episcopal control, or try to take over a bishop's property after his death, or even conspire against their bishops, were issues that continued to preoccupy the ecclesiastical authorities. Basic problems, such as the preservation of the hierarchy of each diocese and episcopal control of monasteries, had to be addressed again in 692.

In addition, the Council *in Trullo* raised a number of interesting new issues, which seem to be directed against specific developments in the Church (whether these derived from Armenian, Jewish or Roman tradition), and a wide range of non-Christian activity which might mislead the simple-minded (*haplousteroi*).[47] In condemning these incorrect notions, the bishops revealed what was happening in certain regions of the Christian *oikoumene* – telling evidence of developments in popular

115–16. Can. 39 is specifically concerned with Bishop John of Cyprus, who took refuge in Hellespontus when the island was occupied by barbarians (ibid. 117–18).
46 See the table at the end of this article.
47 Herrin (1987), 285–6. For a detailed analysis of what 'average' Christians knew of theology see now Baun (2007).

belief and practice, as well as serious errors in theology. Their disap-
proval preserves information which would otherwise have remained
hidden, and is all the more precious for historians of Church history and
canon law.

Here I shall summarize the major features of these new regulations.
Three are directed against the influence of Armenian practices, which
are to be avoided, such as eating eggs and cheese on Saturdays and
Sundays in Lent (Canon 56), restricting the choice of priests to particular families (33), or bringing animals to be slaughtered outside churches
on the occasion of feasts (*matah*) (99).[48] The last two are both associated
with Jewish customs, which are also condemned in Canon 11, where the
practice of Judaizing is spelled out: attending Jewish festivals, using
Jewish doctors, going to the baths with Jews, or socializing with them in
any way.[49] The bishops of 692 distanced themselves from the Roman
custom of strict clerical celibacy, which it contrasted with the eastern
tradition of clemency and compassion concerning the marriage of lower
clergy, even those who had married a second time (Canon 3).[50] Again in
Canon 13 they instructed lower clergy who were married to remain with
their wives; only those who were promoted to episcopal rank were
obliged to separate from them.[51] In Canon 55 they disagreed with the
Roman custom of fasting on Saturdays in Lent.[52] And in Canon 36 they
reasserted the hierarchy of the pentarchy according to the Second and
Fourth Ecumenical Councils, viz. that Constantinople (New Rome) was
'to enjoy equal privileges to those of the see of the older Rome... coming
second after it, followed by Alexandria, Antioch and Jerusalem'.[53] Here
the canons of Constantinople (381) and Chalcedon (451) were cited.

These so-called anti-Roman canons reflected differences which had
developed in the course of the previous three centuries. While the claim
that Old and New Rome had equal privileges still rankled with western
theologians, it dated back to the Second Ecumenical Council. Habits of
fasting and clerical marriage had slowly solidified into distinct practices
that divided east and west. Later the type of Eucharistic bread would
become even more important. Clerical celibacy remained a major

48 Nedungatt–Featherstone, 137–8, 110–11, 179–80; Ohme (2006), 79.
49 Nedungatt–Featherstone, 81–2.
50 Ibid. 69–74. Clerics already married for the second time were to separate from their
   wives and do penance, Ohme (2006), 137–44.
51 Nedungatt–Feathersone, 84–7.
52 Ibid. 136–7.
53 Ibid. 114. See Ohme (2006), 22–30, 128.

problem even into the early period of the eleventh-century reforms: in 1049 Pope Leo IX presided at a Roman synod which tried to impose stricter observance by insisting that all clerics from the rank of subdeacon upward should not be married.[54] This in effect recognized that many junior clerics were married, as in the east, and that celibacy had been regularly avoided. Even in the thirteenth century, Byzantine critics pointed to western bishops who kept concubines or employed female 'housekeepers' for the same purpose.[55]

More significant for the eastern bishops in 692 were a series of pagan practices documented by canons directed against inappropriate activities which Christians were ordered to avoid, such as allowing people to celebrate the New Year with public dancing, cross-dressing, and wearing ancient theatrical masks, or invoking the name of Dionysus when pressing the grapes and pouring the wine into jars, or lighting fires at the new moon and jumping over them.[56] Law students are singled out for their inappropriate celebrations at the completion of their studies by dressing up in strange costumes and going in rowdy processions to the Hippodrome, and adopting pagan customs such as predicting the future, or swearing by the ancient gods.[57] Ancient prohibitions against clerics and laymen collecting or maintaining prostitutes had to be repeated.[58] The bishops also approved canons designed to improve the moral standing of the clergy and dedicated monks and nuns, for instance, Canon 77 which forbids clerics and ascetics, as well as laymen, to bathe with women in the public baths.[59]

In addition, there is much about those simple-minded people who might be misled by certain practices and must be protected. The activities targeted for condemnation include: reading apocryphal martyr stories in church, uttering prophecies in a feigned state of possession, consulting those (diviners, seers, magicians) who claim to predict the future, good luck and bad, by interpreting clouds, genealogies, or using the hairs of a bear's back, and the wearing of charms and phylacteries.[60]

---

54 Brundage (1995), 39–40.
55 Herrin (2007), 303–4.
56 Nedungatt–Featherstone, Cann. 62 and 65, pp. 142–4, 147–8.
57 Ibid. Can. 71, pp. 152–3; Can. 94, pp. 173–4. Cf. Can. 51, pp. 132–3; Can. 61, pp. 140–2; Can. 62, pp. 142–4.
58 Ibid. Can. 86, pp. 166.
59 Nedungatt–Featherstone, Cann. 40–49, pp. 119–31, and Can. 77, pp. 158; see Ohme (2006), 95–7.
60 Nedungatt–Featherstone, Can. 63, pp. 144; Can. 60, p. 140; Can. 61, pp. 140–2.

Men and women, lay and clergy, are all condemned for celebrating the birth of Christ with inappropriate cakes baked for the Sunday after the Nativity,[61] for behaving inappropriately in church, by selling goods inside churches, or bringing animals into church (except in the case of encountering very bad weather on a journey), or profaning the sacred space by living in church with one's wife.[62] People making fancy plaits of their hair that might seduce others were condemned.[63] The bishops also decreed that the cross was never to be set in the floor of churches where it might be trodden on, and forbade anyone from destroying worn-out copies of the Bible, unless they were utterly ruined by worms or dampness or something else. In particular, no one was to give such texts to the perfume dealers, who would presumably scrape off the text and perhaps reuse the parchment, thus showing dishonour to Holy Scripture.[64]

Special measures were directed against women who provided or used substances to obtain an abortion, or even those who talked in church.[65] And anyone who accompanied young girls in the ritual to adopt the monastic life was instructed not to allow them to come to the ceremony dressed in their finest clothes and jewelry.[66] Several other canons were designed to improve popular behaviour in church. No laity were to receive the Eucharist in a golden or silver bowl rather than in the cupped hand.[67] Clergy and laity alike were enjoined not to let three weeks go by without attending church on Sunday.[68] No one was to have their children baptized in private chapels;[69] and priests were only permitted to celebrate the liturgy in such chapels within houses with the permission of the local bishop.[70]

Finally, there are two new and now famous art-historical matters – Canon 82 against showing Christ in his symbolic form as the Lamb of God (his human form is to be preferred as a reminder of the Incarnation, which permits humans the possibility of salvation), and Canon 100 against permitting any type of painting which might arouse wrong feel-

---

61 Ibid. Can. 79, pp. 159–60.
62 Ibid. Can. 76, pp. 157–8; Can. 88, pp. 168–9; Can. 97, pp. 178–9.
63 Ibid. Can. 96, pp. 177–8.
64 Ibid. Can. 73, p. 155; Can. 68, pp. 150–1.
65 Ibid, Can. 91, p. 171; Can. 70, p. 152; Herrin (1992).
66 Nedungatt–Featherstone, Can. 45, pp. 126–8.
67 Ibid. Can. 101, pp. 181–3.
68 Ibid. Can. 80, pp. 160–1.
69 Ibid. Can. 59, p. 139.
70 Ibid. Can. 31, p. 106.

ings in people.[71] Whether this is a reference to images of the ancient gods or mythological characters, secular portraits of prostitutes, or erotic paintings, the bishops felt it necessary to spell out the dangers.[72]

Although there is no record of how these issues were brought to the attention of the bishops, some must certainly have emanated from groups concerned about foreign invasions and unfamiliar or inappropriate behaviour for Christians. Some seem to have been generated in the capital city, rowdy law students for instance (no other law schools were open), where references to methods of foretelling the future connected with the Hippodrome imply a Constantinopolitan origin. But many could apply to any part of the now reduced Byzantine empire – canons against remarriage before the death of a husband is confirmed, against the marriage of godparents with their godchildren, or against men spending the night in convents or women in male monasteries. The bishops were clearly concerned to reform irregularities and enforce a more Christian morality.

While Rome initially rejected the canons of 692 because of the three critical of Roman primacy and other customs, after Pope Constantine's 710 visit to Byzantium the western church did accept them, although they were never widely diffused. Ohme suggests that Roman hostility may in fact have been provoked by the transfer of the diocese of East Illyricum to Constantinople, which is reflected in the loss of status of its bishops. Thessalonica, which had held the position of vicar of the see of Rome in 680/1 and therefore signed the acts immediately after the patriarch of Constantinople, was in 692 placed below the new see of Nea Justinianopolis, created for the refugee Church of Constantia in Cyprus.[73] Many of the canons clearly related to eastern problems (there were few Armenians in the west, and no known additions to the *Trisagion* hymn). Others were directed against stronger pagan practices than survived outside the empire. Yet those directed to the protection of the simple-minded often find a parallel in the acts of western church councils, which similarly try to prohibit ancient customs and ways of predicting the future.[74] The issues that most worried the bishops of 692

---

71 Ibid. Can. 82, pp. 162–4; Can. 100, pp. 180–1.
72 Ohme (2006), 63; Brubaker (1998), (2006); Herrin (2007), 99–100, 103.
73 Ohme (2006), 13–16, and 27–8, which emphasizes that this new ranking order of the bishops from East Illyricum may be the first sign of the transfer, normally attributed to Emperor Leo III in the early eighth century.
74 See for instance Munier (1963); Brundage (1995), 22–6.

were shared with most Christian authorities in the west.

So far from constituting a decisive breaking-point between east and west, the Council *in Trullo* confirmed most of the canons which were shared in both halves of Christendom. It added concerns which the west could ignore as inapplicable, and emphasized many which were all too familiar in regions under papal control.[75] Nonetheless, it remained a singularly Greek council, and when western councils passed legislation against similar activities they did not cite the eastern equivalents. The so-called 'anti-Roman' canons have been re-evaluated and can now be interpreted in the light of traditional eastern claims for the parity of Old and New Rome, with the primacy of honour reserved to the former. This more ecumenical view is probably closer to the intentions of Patriarch Paul III and Justinian II, who seem to have supported Rome's control over the west against separatist claims made by Ravenna in the late seventh century.

Trullo also continued the tradition of Chalcedon in attempting to legislate for the entire world of Christendom, however divided it was by linguistic and other factors. At this rather critical point in east/west relations, it was important to restate Christian unity against the depredations of the new monotheistic revelation of Islam as well as the continuing appeal of Judaism. As Alexandria, Antioch and Jerusalem had all been overrun, Rome and Constantinople were the sole surviving patriarchal sees and had to take greater responsibility for Christians now living under Islamic rule. Their co-operation was confirmed at the Second Council of Nicaea (787) after the schism caused by Byzantine iconoclasm and again in 869/70 at the Fourth Council of Constantinople. In this way, Trullo played a significant role in sustaining Christian unity and legislation that applied to all believers everywhere.[76]

75 Among the many direct parallels between Trullan canons and those of seventh-century Merovingian church councils, see the issues of episcopal control over chapels in private villas, inappropriate singing in church, and wandering monks, Gaudemet–Basdevant (1989), Chalon Can. 14, p. 556; Chalon Can. 19, p. 568; Losne Can. 19, p. 582, frequently repeated.

76 I thank Richard Price and Mary Whitby for their assistance in correcting and improving the text.

APPENDIX: THE CANONS OF CHALCEDON (451)
COMPARED TO THOSE OF TRULLO (692)

Chalcedon 1: one sentence confirmation of earlier canons.
Trullo 1: long definition of faith, confirming earlier councils.

2: against simony. Cp. Trullo 22 and 23.

3: against clerics who lease estates for sordid gain and engage in secular business, taking on management of estates.

4: against monks (*vagantes*) who travel around, disrupting churches and try to set up their own monasteries, which must be subject to the bishop; no slave to enter a monastery against the wish of his master. Cp. Trullo 42.

5: against monks who move from city to city. Cp. Trullo 17.

6: against ordaining any cleric without specifying a particular church.

7: against clerics/monks who take on state service or a secular dignity.

8: against clergy of almshouses, monasteries and *martyria* who try to become independent of the bishop's control. Cp. Trullo 31.

9: against clergy who take cases to civil courts.

10: against clergy who try to enrol in churches of two cities for empty honour. Cp. Trullo 17.

11: against poor and those in need of assistance who try to travel with systatic letters of recommendation, which are only for honourable people. Ordinary letters or ecclesiastical certificates of peace are enough. Cp. Trullo 17.

12: against dividing ecclesiastical provinces into two, thus creating two metropolitan sees in each province (this did not affect grants of honorary metropolitan status). Cp. Trullo 36, 39.

13: against clerics performing the liturgy in another city unless they have systatic letters from their own bishop. Cp. Trullo 17, 20.

14: against lower clergy, who are allowed to marry, marrying heretics, and what is to be observed in the baptism of their children. Cp. Trullo 72.

15: against women being ordained deaconess before the age of 40. Cp. Trullo 14, 40.

16: against dedicated virgins and monks who marry. Cp. Trullo 44.

17: ecclesiastical dioceses to follow civilian regulations, and bishops to possess rural parishes unless disputes arise within 30 years. Cp. Trullo 38, 25.

18: against clerics or monks who conspire against bishops. Cp. Trullo 34.

19: metropolitans to call assemblies of bishops twice a year to settle any matters. Cp. Trullo 8.

20: against clerics trying to get appointed to churches in other cities, unless they have been driven out of their homelands. Cp. Trullo 17, 37 with references to 'barbarian incursions'.

21: against clerics or laymen who accuse bishops or clergy without having their characters investigated.

22: against clerics who on the death of a bishop try to seize his property. Cp. Trullo 35.

23: against clerics or monks who come to Constantinople with no commission from the bishop. Cp. Trullo 17.

24: monasteries once consecrated must remain in perpetuity together with their property. Cp. Trullo 49.

25: against metropolitans who delay the consecration of bishops longer than three months. Cp. Trullo 19.

26: bishops must appoint administrators *(oikonomoi)* from the clergy to manage their property.

27: against any who abduct women on the pretext of marriage, and those who assist them. Cp. Trullo 92.

28: giving equal status to the sees of Old Rome and New Rome while reserving the primacy of honour to the see of St Peter. Cp. Trullo 36.

BIBLIOGRAPHY

Alberigo, Giuseppe, ed. (2006), *Conciliorum Oecumenicorum Generaliumque decreta*, vol. 1, *The Oecumenical Councils from Nicaea I to Nicaea II (325–787)* (Turnhout).

Baun, Jane (2007), *Tales from Another Byzantium: Celestial Journey and Local Community in the Medieval Greek Apocrypha* (Cambridge).

Beck, Hans-Georg (1959), *Kirche und theologische Literatur im byzantinischen Reich* (Munich).

Brubaker, Leslie (1998), 'Icons before Iconoclasm?', *Settimane di Studio* (Spoleto), 45: 1215–54.

—— (2006), 'In the beginning was the Word. Art and Orthodoxy at the Council of Trullo (692) and Nicaea II (787)', in Andrew Louth and Augustine Casiday, eds, *Byzantine Orthodoxies* (Aldershot), 95–101.

Brundage, J.A. (1995), *Medieval Canon Law* (London).

De Clercq, Carlo, ed. (1963), *Concilia Galliae 506–695*, CCSL 148A (Turnhout). With French trans. in Gaudemet–Basdevant (1989).

Di Berardino, Angelo, ed. (1992), *Encyclopedia of the Early Church* (Cambridge).

Dvornik, Francis (1958), *The Idea of Apostolicity in Byzantium and the Legend of the Apostle Andrew*, Dumbarton Oaks Studies 4 (Cambridge MA).

Gallagher, Clarence (2002), *Church Law and Church Order in Rome and Byzantium* (Aldershot).

Gaudemet, Jean (1985), *Les sources du droit de l'Eglise en Occident du IIe au VIIe siècle* (Paris).

Gaudemet, Jean and Basdevant, Brigitte (1989), *Les canons des conciles mérovingiens (VIe–VIIe siècles)*, SC 353–4 (Paris).

Grumel, Venance, ed. (1932), *Les regestes des actes des patriarches de Constantinople*, vol. 1 (Kadiköy/Istanbul).

Herrin, Judith Herrin (1987), *The Formation of Christendom* (Princeton).

—— (1992), '"Femina byzantina": the Council in Trullo on Women', in *Homo Byzantinus. Papers in Honor of Alexander Kazhdan*, ed. Anthony Cutler and Simon Franklin, *DOP* 46 (1992), 97–105.

—— (2007), *Byzantium: The Surprising Life of a Medieval Empire* (London).

Humfress, Caroline (2004), 'Law and Legal Practice in the Age of Justinian', in Michael Maas, ed. *The Cambridge Companion to the Age of Justinian* (Cambridge), 161–80.

Joannou, Périklès-Pierre (1960), *Discipline générale de l'église antique*, vol I/1: *Les canons des conciles écumeniques* (Rome).

L'Huillier, Peter (1996), *The Church of the Ancient Councils: the disciplinary work of the first four oecumenical councils* (Crestwood, NY).

Macrides, Ruth (1990), 'Nomos and Kanon on paper and in court', in Rosemary Morris, ed., *Church and People in Byzantium* (Birmingham), 61–85.

Mansi, J.-D., ed. (1901), *Sacrorum Conciliorum Nova et Amplissima Collectio*, vol. XI (Florence 1765; Paris and Leipzig 1901).

Munier, Charles, ed. (1963), *Concilia Galliae 314–506*, CCSL 148 (Turnhout), with French trans. by Jean Gaudemet, SC 241 (1977).

Nedungatt, Georges and Agrestini, Silvano (2006), 'Concilium Trullanum', in Alberigo (2006), 203–93.

Nedungatt, George and Featherstone, Jeffrey, eds. (1995), *The Council in Trullo Revisited, Kanonika* 6.

Ohme, Heinz (1990), *Das Concilium Quinisextum und seine Bischofslist. Studien zum Konstantinopoler Konzil von 692* (Berlin–New York).

—— (1992), 'The Causes of the Conflict about the Quinisext Council: New Perspectives on a Disputed Council', in Patsavos (1992), 17–43.

—— (1995), 'Die sogennanten "antirömischen Kanones" des Concilium Quinisextum (692) – Vereinheitlichung als Gefahr für die Einheit der Kirche', in Nedungatt–Featherstone (1995), 307–21.

—— (1998), *Kanon Ekklesiastikos. Die Bedeutung des altkirchlichen Kanonbegriffs* (Berlin/New York).

—— (2006), *Concilium Quinisextum. Das Konzil Quinisextum*, Greek text with German translation, Fontes Christiani 82 (Turnhout).

Patsavos, L.J., ed. (1992), *Greek Orthodox Theological Review* 40, nos. 1–2 (an entire issue dedicated to the Council *in Trullo*).

Peri, Vittorio (1995), 'Le Chiese nell'Impero e le Chiese "tra i barbari". La territorialità ecclesiale nella riforma canonica trullana', in Nedungatt–Featherstone (1995), 198–213.

Price, R.M. and Gaddis, Michael (2005), *The Acts of the Council of Chalcedon*, 3 vols, TTH 45 (Liverpool).

Rhalles, G.A. and Potles M., eds. (1852) *Syntagma ton theion kai hieron kanonon*, vol. 2 (Athens).

Riedinger, Rudolf, ed. (1992), *Concilium Universale Constantinopolitanum Tertium. Acta Conciliorum Oecumenicorum*, Series Secunda, vol. 2 (Berlin).

Tanner, Norman, ed. (1990), *Decrees of the Ecumenical Councils* (Greek and Latin texts with English translation) (London/Washington DC).

Troianos, S.N. (1992), *He Penthekte Oikoumenike Synodos kai to nomothetikon tes ergon* (Athens).

Turner, C.H. (1928/9 and 1929/30), 'Chapters in the History of Latin MSS of Canons', V–VI, 'The Version called Prisca', *JTS* 30 (1928–9), 337–46; ibid. 31 (1929–30), 9–20.

ACCLAMATIONS AT THE COUNCIL
OF CHALCEDON

Charlotte Roueché

One of the more startling aspects of the conciliar acts is the regular recording of acclamations. To a modern reader, they appear intrusive and inappropriate, not least because in modern writing-based societies, cheering and shouting by groups has become increasingly marginalized: it is associated with disorder and disruption, even if it has an established role in certain situations, such as sporting events. This sense of what is appropriate is also influenced by a modern belief in the value of individual commitment. To a modern reader, the statements attributed to the individual bishops seem more significant than the 'shouts' of the group as a whole. But in a pre-individual society, such shouts have a very different significance.

Acclamations can be found throughout the ancient Near East, and in both the Jewish and the Graeco-Roman tradition. Their primary function must be one of communication in a non-literate form. In both cultures they seem to be closely associated with religious practice. When the people of Ephesus were being encouraged to oppose the Christian apostle Paul, the crowd in the theatre was encouraged to shout the cult acclamation 'Great is Artemis of the Ephesians'. This will have been a familiar chant from their normal religious ceremonies; it is therefore understandable that they proceeded to repeat the acclamation over a period of two hours.[1] The fullest account of this aspect of acclamations is still the study, written in 1920 by Peterson, of the acclamation 'One God', a pre-Christian acclamation which was enthusiastically adopted by Christian assemblies, and can be found in the conciliar acts, e.g. at Chalcedon, εἷς θεὸς ὁ τοῦτο ποιήσας ('It is the one God who has done this', Chalcedon VI. 13).[2]

---

1 Act. Ap. 19:23–41, with Robert (1982), 55–7.
2 Peterson (1920). See also Edessa, First report, meeting of 12 April (Doran 2006, 139), meeting of 14 April (ibid. 141), Second Report (ibid. 148), and the acts of 536, *ACO* 3, p. 85.18–19, etc.

In all these situations the role of acclamations is seen as positive and reinforcing: the verbs used in the ancient texts, translated as shouting or crying out, have an inappropriately negative connotation in English. But the liturgies of the churches have retained that role for acclamations, although a modern description would perhaps use the term 'chant'; even the simplest of rituals has retained the function of 'amen'. This reflects the most essential function of acclamation, as an expression of assent. It also expresses that assent as shared and unanimous. In a recent study, Angelos Chaniotis has pointed to the importance of such ritual vocalism in confirming the bonds both among participants and between them and the divinity in Greek religious rituals.[3]

But acclamations also had a long history of secular usage, firstly as an indication of assent. Documents record decrees as being approved by acclamation – so the councillors 'shouted in support', *epeboesan*, at Tyre in 174 A.D.[4] or *epephonesan* at Oxyrhynchus in 192.[5] The formality of this process is confirmed by an inscription from Mylasa, where the acclamations, in Greek, are preceded by the Latin formula 'succlamatum est'.[6] The simplest acclamation was simply one of assent – in Latin *placet*; this is found, for example, in the Acts of the Council of Sardica in 343, where assent is invited by the phrase: *Si hoc omnibus placet*, followed by *Synodus respondit: Placet*.[7] But another way to express such assent was to pick up a proposed phrase – for example ἄξιον, 'worthy', as in the later church liturgies. This kind of acclamation underpinned the awarding of honorific epithets and titles, such as *philopatris*, patriotic, or *ktistes*, founder, in the east;[8] John Chrysostom describes the acclamation of a benefactor in the theatre, ἅπαντες κηδεμόνα καλοῦντες.[9] Similarly in Rome Livy can conceive of Camillus being acclaimed as *Romulus ac pater patriae, conditorque* (5.49.7). Under the empire, emperors came to be acclaimed regularly by the Senate – so Pliny, *Panegyricus* 75.2.

From this process it was a short step to election to offices of real power. Already in republican Rome the title of Imperator was granted

3 Chaniotis (2006), 226–30.
4 *OGIS* 595.
5 Hunt and Edgar (1934), 241.
6 *IMylasa* (Blümel, 1987–8) 605.
7 Mansi III, 23B, 23D, 24C, cf. 23A.
8 On this procedure see Robert (1965), 215–16.
9 *De inan. glor.* 4, with Robert (1960), 569–73.

by *conclamatio*.[10] The kings of ancient Israel were acclaimed,[11] and mediaeval kings were to adopt the practice.[12] By the third century acclamations formed part of the process of appointing a pope (Eusebius, *Hist. Eccl.* 6.29), and they were to become standard in the appointment of bishops during the fourth century (Augustine, *ep.* 213). The origins of acclamations in religious ritual gave them extra significance, and they were seen as reinforcing authority, not least by being unanimous: such unanimity could be interpreted as a mark of divine inspiration, both within religious rituals (as emphasized by Chaniotis), and also beyond them. Thus Apuleius can write of unanimous acclamations as seen to be inspired: *consensum publicae vocis pro divino auspicium interpretatur* (Apuleius, *Apol.* 73). Cassius Dio can use similar language of acclamations in the Circus Maximus in 192: οὕτω μὲν ἔκ τινος θείας ἐπιπνοίας ἐνεθουσίασαν (Dio 75.4.5). This made them all the more valuable in conferring office: Eusebius writes of the election of Pope Fabian, 'The whole people, as if moved by one divine spirit, with all enthusiasm and one voice cried out in agreement, "Worthy".'[13]

Moreover, the process was not one of simple indications of assent, or the monosyllabic awarding of titles. The acclaiming crowd could pick up on a preceding phrase; they could also produce an extended phrase – such as 'Great is Artemis of the Ephesians'. Already in the first century AD crowds at Rome could respond to the news of Germanicus' restored health with the acclamation *Salva Roma, salva patria, salvus est Germanicus* (Suetonius, *Gaius* 6.1). This is also illustrated in the record of the meeting in 178 of a religious confraternity devoted to Dionysus, at Athens. Here statutes are proposed and validated by a show of hands, but this is followed by acclamations: 'Long live our priest Herodes! Now we are happy! Now our Bacchus Club is the first among all (Bacchic) clubs! The vice-priest has done a find job! Let the stele be made' (*IG²* 1368, trans. Chaniotis). In 438 the Senate greeted the issuing of the Theodosian Code not with simple indications of assent, but with a series of complex phrases; the documents record how many times each acclamation was repeated (*Cod. Theod., Gesta senatus*). Similarly, the account of the election of Augustine's successor as bishop of Hippo

10 Caesar, *Bell. Civ.* II. 26.1; Tacitus, *Annales* III. 74.6.
11 Saul, 1 Samuel 10.24; Solomon, 1 Kings 1.39.
12 The fundamental study is still Kantorowicz (1946).
13 ἐφ' ᾧ τὸν πάντα λαόν, ὥσπερ ὑφ' ἑνὸς πνεύματος θείου κινηθέντα, προθυμίᾳ πάσῃ καὶ μιᾷ ψυχῇ ἄξιον ἐπιβοῆσαι, Eusebius, *Hist. Eccl.* VI. 29.3.

enumerates the repetitions of acclamations: 'The people shouted, "To God be thanks! To Christ be praise" (this was repeated twenty-three times). "O Christ, hear us; may Augustine live long!" (repeated sixteen times). "We will have thee as our father, thee as our bishop" (repeated eight times)' (Aug., *ep.* 213).

Their role in religious practice, together with their usefulness to the rulers, therefore conferred authority on acclamations; and their widespread use meant that they could express not just consent but also complex expressions of approval – and of opinion. The best known example of the use of acclamations by an assembly to obtain a demand is probably to obtain a punishment – thus the shouts of the crowd in the Gospel accounts of the trials of Jesus, or the use of the phrase *Christianos ad leones*, 'Christians to the lions'.[14] These accounts, of course, reinforce a modern sense of acclamations as disruptive and malign; but it is clear that they were used in a variety of settings. The acts of the church councils provide the richest source of accounts of acclamations in their entirety. The Acts of Chalcedon are important in this regard; but one of the fullest collections has also just been translated into English. This is the record, only found in Syriac, of gatherings in Edessa, in 449, which was read into the minutes of the Robber Council of Ephesus, later that year, including extensive listings of the acclamations used.[15] The formulaic shape – and rhythm – of the phrases could be used to structure a wide range of requests.

This can be illustrated by examining a set of acclamations inscribed in the late third century in a rural settlement in the territory of Termessus in Lycia; these honoured a certain Hermaius, a local chieftain and 'brigand-chaser', asking for him to be kept in office in the territory:[16]

> Let him who (acts) on behalf of the city reside/remain!
> Let him who (acts) on behalf of peace remain!
> This is of benefit to the city.
> A decree for the brigand-chaser!
> Let the well-born brigand-chaser guard the city!
> Let him who has killed brigands guard the city!
> Let him who has often acted as *ekdikos* for the city guard the city!

14 See Potter (1996).
15 The Syriac text with a German translation is in Flemming (1917), now translated into English by Doran (2006), 133–88.
16 Ballance and Roueché (2001), 87–112.

Let him who has acted as *ekdikos* for the city remain!
Let him who has ... sent *annona* remain!
Let him who (acts) on behalf of peace remain!
Let Hermaius remain, let the son of Askoureus remain!
Hermaius son of Askoureus as brigand-chaser as long as we live!
Let him remain so that we can live!
Let him remain according to the order of the governor!
Let him who has often saved the city remain!
Let him who has sent supplies to the city remain!

This particular text lacks the opening phrases. A more complete, although less complex, set of acclamations was inscribed in the early sixth century at Aphrodisias in Caria, each on one of the twenty columns of a stoa which had been restored by a local benefactor, Albinus:[17]

i: God is one, for the whole world!
ii: Many years for the emperors!
iii: Many years for the eparchs!
iv: Many years for the Senate!
v: Many years for the metropolis!
vi: PERDE[18] Albinus – up with the builder of the stoa!
vii: Lord, lover of your country, remain for us!
viii: Your buildings are an eternal reminder, Albinus, you who love to build.
ix: [...] Albinus *clarissimus.*
x: PERDE Albinus, behold what you have given!
xi: The whole city says this: Your enemies to the river! May the great God provide this!'
[xii is lost.]
xiii: Up with Albinus *clarissimus,* to the Senate!
xiv: [? ...] envy does not vanquish fortune.
xv: Up with Albinus, the builder of this work also!
xvi: You have disregarded wealth and obtained glory, Albinus *clarissimus.*
xvii: Albinus *clarissimus,* like your ancestors a lover of your country, may you receive plenty.
xviii: Providing [?a building] for the city, he is acclaimed [?in it also].
xix: With your buildings you have made the city brilliant, Albinus, lover of your country.

17 Roueché (2004), no. 83.
18 The word or name PERDE is clear, but its meaning is very uncertain.

xx: The whole city, having acclaimed (you) with one voice, says: 'He who forgets you, Albinus *clarissimus,* does not know God.

There are several patterns that can be detected in the two sets of inscribed acclamations and in the conciliar acclamations. Firstly, it is common to start with statements of orthodoxy and loyalty: so Aphrodisias, nos. i–v, and at Edessa.[19] Only after such expressions of loyalty does the series of requests begin. There are stock phrases. Some are very widespread – so 'many years' (Albinus i–v; Chacedon VI, 15) 'so-and-so is victorious' (the term which gave its name to the great Nika riot of 532 in Constantinople); 'up with so and so', and some a little less common, but still widespread: 'may he reside/remain' is used of Hermaius and Albinus. Secondly, there is a basic structure of using repetitions and variation, such as the repetition of 'Albinus *clarissimus'* in a variety of phrases, or, at Edessa, 'Let our lords learn this! Let the prefects learn this! Let the master learn this! Let the Senate learn this!'[20] Another method to make the acclamations flow more easily is to change one half of a sentence, and then the other: so A + B, A + C, A + D, then D + E, D + F: this can be seen in the acclamations for Hermaius. There is also the occasional recurrence of an earlier line, almost like a refrain: 'Up with Albinus'.

Requests are expressed in standard ways. One is the dative of direction or purpose: 'A decree for the brigand-chaser! Your enemies to the river! Albinus to the senate!' At Edessa, 'The hater of Christ to the wild beasts! The party of Hiba to the stadium! An orthodox bishop for the metropolis!'[21] Another recurrent pattern is the phrasing, 'He who does so and so, let him …' : of Hermaius, 'Let him who has often saved the city reside!'; at Edessa, 'Whoever loves Hiba is a Satan';[22] at Aphrodisias, 'He who forgets you, Albinus *clarissimus,* does not know God!'

All this demonstrates a widespread range of formulae and structures which made it possible to concert and organize acclamations, to great effect. To be effective, however, there were two further requirements. Firstly, they needed to be recorded verbatim. One aspect of this is the increased use of improved systems of stenography during the third and

19 First report at the meetings on 12 April (Doran 2006, 139), 14 April (ibid. 141); second report (ibid. 148).
20 First report, 14 April (Doran 2006, 142).
21 First report, 14 April (Doran 2006, 142–3).
22 Doran (2006), 176.

fourth centuries, to which the acts of the councils bear striking witness. The records therefore existed.

Even more importantly, they needed to be accepted as having some kind of status, as a real expression of opinion. In 331 Constantine issued a law arranging for acclamations of governors, probably by provincial assembles, to be reported to the central government by the praetorian prefects and vicars: *praefectis praetorio et comitibus, qui per provincias constituti sunt, provincialium nostrorum voces ad nostrum scientiam referentibus.*[23] But an increasing tendency to record acclamations, and to inscribe them, can already be detected in the third century. The acclamations for Hermaius included a request which must have been forwarded to a senior authority. It seems very likely that, as so often with imperial legislation, Constantine was legislating to confirm a practice which was already developing, of using acclamations to support petitions.

It is therefore unsurprising that, from the fourth century onwards, we find acclamations inscribed and recorded in detail. I have argued elsewhere that in the secular world this reflects, and reinforces, a process by which powerful individuals could bypass the normal civic structures in their relationship with the populace and with the imperial authorities.[24] The authority of such procedures must come from the fact that they appear to confirm unanimity, which they therefore emphasize: so at Aphrodisias 'the whole city' acclaims (xi, xx); exactly the same phrase is used at Edessa.[25] In the church councils, the acclamations are required to confirm the full involvement of all those present in the unanimous decisions which were required; and that therefore offers an opportunity for those wishing to express opinions. One request of the Egyptian bishops at Chalcedon is, precisely, that their acclamations should be forwarded to the emperor: τὰς φωνὰς τῶι βασιλεῖ, 'our words to the emperor' (Chalcedon I. 173).

The acts therefore show how acclamations had a significant role to play in the authentication of authority, ecclesiastical as well as secular. Augustine describes the situation when he talks of the election of his successor, Eraclius, in 426: 'The notaries of the church are, as you observe, recording what I say, and recording what you say; both my address and your acclamations are not allowed to fall to the ground. To

23 *Cod. Theod.* I. 16.6, whence *Cod. Just.* I. 40.3.
24 Roueché (2007), 183–92.
25 Second report (Doran 2006, 149).

speak more plainly, we are making up an ecclesiastical record of this day's proceedings; for I wish them to be in this way confirmed so far as pertains to men'.[26] At both Hippo and Chalcedon, the *gesta* of the meeting are composed of both the sermon or the addresses and the acclamations: both are essential to the conclusions. This helps to explain the careful recording of the acclamations at a variety of assemblies; just as the acclamations from the meetings at Edessa were read into the minutes at Ephesus in 449, similar collections of acclamations, from meetings held in 518 at Constantinople, at Apamea, and at Tyre, were preserved and read into the minutes of the council of 536.[27] These cases illustrate very clearly how the respect for acclamations, and the need for the authority which they conveyed, could empower assemblies who wished to make their views felt. The conciliar acts, taken with the epigraphic record, provide a good understanding of the processes of a very important institution in ancient life, which also had a great influence on the development of the liturgies of the churches.[28]

BIBLIOGRAPHY

Ballance, M. and Roueché, C. (2001), 'Three inscriptions from Ovacik', in Harrison, R.M., *Mountain and Plain: From the Lycian Coast to the Phrygian Plateau in the Late Roman and Early Byzantine Period* (Ann Arbor), 87–112.

Blümel, Wolfgang, ed. (1987–8), *Die Inschriften von Mylasa* (Bonn).

Chaniotis, Angelos (2006), 'Rituals between Norms and Emotions: Rituals as Shared Experience and Memory', in E. Stavrianopoulou, ed., *Ritual and Communication in the Graeco-Roman World*, Kernos Supplement 16 (Liège), 211–38.

Doran, Robert (2006), *Stewards of the Poor: The Man of God, Rabbula, and Hiba in Fifth-Century Edessa* (Kalamazoo).

Flemming, Johannes (1917), *Akten der ephesinischen Synode vom Jahre 449. Abh. der kön. Gesellschaft der Wissenschaften zu Göttingen*, Philologisch-historische Klasse, NF 15.1.

Hunt, A.S. and Edgar, C.C. (1934), *Select Papyri* II (Harvard).

26 Augustine, *ep.* 213, 'A notariis ecclesiasticis excipiuntur quae dicitis; et meus sermo et vestrae acclamationes in terram non cadunt. Apertius ut dicam, ecclesiastica nunc gesta conficimus: sic enim hoc esse, quantum ad homines attinet, confirmatum volo.'

27 *ACO* 3, pp. 71–7, 85–7, 102–3.

28 For further studies on acclamations see Roueché (1984, 1999), and, most recently, Wiemer (2004).

Kantorowicz, Ernst (1946) *Laudes Regiae* (Berkeley).

Mansi, J.-D., ed., *Sacrorum Conciliorum nova et amplissima collectio*, ed. J.-D. Mansi, 31 vols (Florence and Venice, 1759–98; Paris and Leipzig, 1901–6).

Peterson, Erik (1920), *Heis theos : epigraphische, formgeschichtliche und religionsgeschichtliche Untersuchungen* (Göttingen).

Potter, D. (1996), 'Performance, power and justice in the High Empire', in W. J. Slater, ed., *Roman Theater and Society*: *E. Togo Salmon Papers* (Ann Arbor), vol. 1, 129–60.

Robert, Louis, (1960) *Hellenica* XI–XII (Paris).

—— (1965) *Hellenica* XIII (Paris).

—— (1982), 'La date de l'épigrammatiste Rufinus. Philologie et réalité', *CRAI* (1982) 50–63, 55–7, = *Opera Minora Selecta* V (1989), 129, 777–90, 782–4.

Roueché, Charlotte (1984), 'Acclamations in the later Roman empire: new evidence from Aphrodisias', *Journal of Roman Studies* 74, 181–99.

—— (1999), 'Looking for Late Antique ceremonial: Ephesos and Aphrodisias', in H. Friesinger and F. Krinzinger, eds. (1999), *100 Jahre Österreichische Forschungen in Ephesos. Akten des Symposions Wien 1995* (Archäologische Forschungen 1, DenkschrWien 260) (Vienna), 161–8.

—— (2004) *Aphrodisias in Late Antiquity,* Online second edition available at http://insaph.kcl.ac.uk/ala2004

—— (2007), 'From Aphrodisias to Stauropolis', in R. Salway and J. Drinkwater (eds.) *Wolf Liebeschuetz Reflected* (London), 183–192.

Wiemer, H.-U. (2004), 'Akklamationen im spätrömischen Reich. Zur Typologie und Funktion eines Kommunikationsrituals', *Archiv für Kulturgeschichte* 86: 27–73.

AN UNHOLY CREW? BISHOPS BEHAVING BADLY AT CHURCH COUNCILS

Michael Whitby

The acts of church councils offer us an exceptionally rich source of information about the utterances and behaviour of large numbers of bishops while engaged in one of their most important duties, namely the collective establishment of orthodoxy and the identification of heresy. They provide examples of Christian leaders in action, not only of individual bishops who in their own cities would be regarded as leaders but in the context of an ecumenical council were overshadowed by their metropolitans or the patriarchs or other key figures prominent in a particular debate, but also of a small number of international leaders. Although the absolute accuracy of council records is open to challenge, with the impossibility of verbatim precision, especially during heated moments, being acknowledged by those responsible for attempting to produce the records,[1] the general impression of the tone and conduct of debates is beyond challenge, while the subscriptions by individual bishops to various decisions also offer insights into how the participants wished their involvement to be registered and remembered.

Episcopal behaviour has recently been the subject of two illuminating studies. The first, by Claudia Rapp,[2] identifies different strands of episcopal authority – spiritual, ascetic and pragmatic –, probes how these were combined to legitimate that authority, and considers how bishops as men of power operated within the evolving economic and social structures of their cities. Theological debates are an area which Rapp specifically chose not to treat (p. 22), and so council acts do not contribute to the evidence through which she investigates 'the realities

---

1 As the senior notary, Aetius, admitted when challenged about the accuracy of his record of Flavian's proceedings against Eutyches in 448: Acts of Chalcedon 1. 767, 792, *ACO* 2.1, pp. 170–1, 173; see also Ste. Croix (2006) 307–8. Some acts appear to be an artful composition reflecting how a council wished to present itself rather than a straightforward factual record; see Thomas Graumann's discussion of the acts of the first session of Ephesus I, pp. 27–43 above.

2 Rapp (2005).

of episcopal office' (p. 20). Rather, Rapp's picture of 'holy bishops' is constructed from patristic works on the qualities and duties of bishops and from hagiographies of those most renowned for their holiness. Although it is useful to identify what types of behaviour were being held up as models, there are obvious dangers in this approach that the ideal or exceptional will supplant the average,[3] and that the silent majority of bishops, about whom a name is often the limit to our knowledge, will be overshadowed by the holy elite or their idealized representation. The second study, by Michael Gaddis, devotes one chapter to bishops in a broader-ranging study of justified religious violence, with particular attention to the operation of the councils of Second Ephesus and Chalcedon.[4] Not surprisingly, the picture of episcopal behaviour that emerges appears very different from Rapp's, but there are certain similarities in that Gaddis also focuses on a limited selection of bishops, those at the centre of proceedings (and much of the discussion concerns the trio of Cyril, Nestorius and Dioscorus), and the misbehaviour of a Dioscorus can be dismissed as characteristic of a false rather than an ideal bishop. In the light of these contributions, it is worth reflecting on the evidence that the council acts provide for a broader range of episcopal conduct.

A first point to consider is the general tone of conciliar proceedings. Reading the acts of First and Second Ephesus, or of Second Constantinople, makes clear that very serious issues were under discussion and that on occasions feelings ran high, but the overall impression is that debates were conducted in a reasonably orderly fashion. Acclamations are reported as representing the views of the whole council, e.g. 'Dioscorus and Cyril have one faith. This is what the entire council believes,' or are presented as statements rather than chants, e.g. 'The holy council said: "And the ecumenical council believes likewise".'[5] Even the climax of the drama at Second Ephesus, when Dioscorus pronounced judgement against Flavian of Constantinople and Eusebius of Dorylaeum, thereby prompting Flavian to appeal to Pope Leo through his representative, appears to proceed smoothly: Hilary, the Roman deacon who was representing Leo, responded '"*Contradicitur*", which means, "An objection is lodged"', but the council then went on to

---

3 As Rapp notes on occasion, e.g. 294–5.
4 Gaddis (2005), ch. 8.
5 Acts I. 226, 228, *ACO* 2.1, p. 101, both from Second Ephesus as read out at Chalcedon. Translations are from Price and Gaddis (2005).

record the views of all the bishops in favour of the judgement.[6] From the subsequent testimony of participants when these proceedings were read out at Chalcedon, it emerges that the deliberations at Second Ephesus had been joined at this stage by armed soldiers and a large gang of monks led by the zealot Barsauma, with Dioscorus standing on his footstool to summon these reinforcements.[7] Hilary later alleged that Dioscorus had attempted to prevent him from leaving the session, and an inscription in the baptistery at St John Lateran in honour of his 'liberator', John the Evangelist, is plausibly connected with his escape from being forced to participate in Flavian's condemnation.[8] None of this drama is present in the original written record, and uproar is most easily identified only through subsequent references.[9]

By contrast, proceedings at Chalcedon, especially when Dioscorus or Theodoret is the subject of discussion, appear exceptionally noisy, even chaotic. It seems that a certain level of noise was required to demonstrate the will of the whole council: thus at the second session, in response to demands that excluded bishops should be reinstated, the Constantinopolitan clergy shouted, 'Only a few are clamouring. The council is not speaking,' which sparked opposed chants between the eastern (= Syrian) and Illyrican bishops demanding the exile or restoration of Dioscorus.[10] It was very rare for the presiding officials to intervene to check the noise, the most decisive case being near the start of the first session when the decision of the *magister militum* Anatolius and his colleagues to admit Theodoret of Cyrrhus as accuser of Dioscorus generated fierce denunciations from the Egyptian contingent and their supporters from Illyricum and Palestine, which were opposed by chants against Dioscorus by the eastern bishops. Theodoret's enemies attempted to appeal to the orthodoxy of Emperor Marcian and Empress Pulcheria, but the presidents firmly stamped their authority on proceedings: 'These vulgar outbursts are not becoming to bishops, nor useful to either party. Allow everything to be read. ... Allow, rather, the hearing to be conducted according to God, and permit everything to be read in order'.[11]

---

6 Acts I. 964–1066, *ACO* 2.1, pp. 191–4 and 2.3, pp. 238–52.
7 Acts I. 851, 858, *ACO* 2.1, pp. 179–80.
8 *Inscriptiones Latinae Christianae Veteres* 980 (I, p. 183).
9 E.g. Acts I. 803, 808, *ACO* 2.1, pp. 174–5, from the Acts of Second Ephesus, referring back to Flavian's investigation of Eutyches.
10 Acts II. 35–44, *ACO* 2.1, pp. 279–80.
11 Acts I. 35–46, *ACO* 2.1, p. 70.

The distinct nature of the record of Chalcedon requires explanation. Gaddis sees the preservation of dissonant voices as contributing to the establishment of the absolute accuracy of the acts, which would serve to validate the council as a restoration of law and order after the disruptions of Second Ephesus; on this view Chalcedon represents the triumph of the establishment, with the unprecedented acceptance by the Church of secular control of proceedings being the price which bishops were prepared to pay to be released from Dioscorus' violent tyranny at Second Ephesus.[12] This, however, fails to recognize the strength of Marcian and Pulcheria's determination to control the council, even against the wishes of many, perhaps the majority of bishops. Ste. Croix's analysis of the links between the presiding officials, in particular the senior official Anatolius, and Theodoret of Cyrrhus reveals that the rehabilitation of the deposed bishop had been a priority from the very conception of the council, even though there were probably few bishops outside the diocese of Oriens who would have supported this action if it had not been perceived to chime with imperial wishes.[13] The production of a new definition of the faith was certainly opposed fiercely by the bishops when it was first mooted by the imperial commissioners at the second session: 'This is what we all say. What has already been expounded is sufficient. It is not permissible to produce another exposition. ... We will not produce a written exposition. There is a canon which declares that what has already been expounded is sufficient. The canon forbids the making of another exposition. Let the [will] of the fathers prevail.'[14] After a small drafting group had produced an initial definition, the imperial commissioners backed reservations expressed by the papal representatives and some eastern bishops, in spite of the fact that the majority of bishops were chanting, 'The definition has satisfied everyone. Our statements to the emperor. This is the definition of the orthodox... Another definition must not be produced. Nothing is lacking in the definition.'[15] Although bishops shouted that those wanting further change were Nestorians, this opposition collapsed in the face of a threat to transfer the council to Italy, and a new drafting group quickly produced an acceptable version.[16]

---

12 Gaddis (2005), 310–11.
13 Ste. Croix (2006), 285–94.
14 Acts II. 5, 7, *ACO* 2.1, p. 274.
15 Acts V. 11, 18, *ACO* 2.1, p. 320.
16 See further Ste. Croix (2006), 284–5.

A further probable example of imperial wishes determining actions without regard to episcopal preferences is the invitation to Nestorius to attend the council, a proposal so contentious that the ecclesiastical historian Evagrius rejected it as slander by the anti-Chalcedonian Zachariah.[17] It is difficult to believe that the bishops who found it difficult to accept Theodoret into their presence would have sought the much more disruptive attendance of Nestorius, but one can see how this might have boosted the reputation of the imperial pair who could present themselves as the agents for the re-establishment of complete harmony in the Church.[18] Only Nestorius' opportune death in Egypt, shortly after he had received the summons, avoided an awkward scene.[19] The imperial commissioners might direct episcopal decisions even on quite minor matters: thus at the eleventh session, when the dispute between Bassianus and Stephen over the right to the see of Ephesus was being decided and it became clear that both individuals had supporters,[20] the commissioners intervened to state that in their view both competitors had transgressed, so that a new appointment must be made. Although the commissioners were careful to express deference to the verdict of the council,[21] there was no doubt now about the outcome and the secular advice was duly endorsed by the bishops.

Chalcedon needs to be seen as a council whose key decisions had been determined in advance by Marcian and Pulcheria, with the bishops meeting to deliver the appropriate episcopal approval, whereafter they could resolve various lesser ecclesiastical issues. Very few bishops could have been entirely happy with the outcome, certainly not the papal representatives, even though Chalcedon endorsed the Tome of Leo, since papal claims to universal authority were compromised, nor the leading bishops of the eastern empire who had to sign up to a new definition contrary to their clear intentions. Although the council cleverly presented itself as steering a compromise doctrinal course between the

---

17 Evagrius, *Hist. Eccl.* II. 2, trans. Whitby, p. 62.
18 See further Ste. Croix (2006), 280–1.
19 Zachariah, *Hist. Eccl.* III. 1, trans. Hamilton and Brooks, p. 42. Rufus, *Plerophories* 33, 36; *PO* 8, 1911, pp. 76, 84–5.
20 Bassianus received two clear endorsements, from the bishops of Bizye and Juliopolis as well as general chanting (Acts XI. 40–1, 46, *ACO* 2.1, pp. 409–10), whereas Stephen had one indirect endorsement phrased in terms of the reputation of Flavian of Constantinople, who had consecrated him, while the Constantinopolitan contingent naturally backed the decision of their former leader (Acts XI. 43–4, *ACO* 2.1, p. 410).
21 Acts XI. 47, *ACO* 2.1, p. 410.

extremes of Nestorius' presentation of Christ as a mere man and Eutyches' rejection of the full humanity of Christ, in reality it was little different from Second Ephesus in endorsing the triumph of one particular viewpoint:[22] compromise came later as, between the late fifth and the seventh centuries, successive emperors attempted to identify a means to reconcile the vehement divisions aroused by the council.[23]

Marcian and Pulcheria wanted to emerge from the council as the saviours of the Church, the new Constantine and Helena in the words of acclamations which greeted their presence at the sixth session,[24] comparisons which would probably have been known in advance to appeal to imperial vanity. Against this background, the reporting of episcopal misbehaviour at the council is unlikely to have been an accident, but Gaddis' suggestion that this was intended to validate the accuracy of the record is implausible. It is likely that this departure from convention was also part of the imperial project for the council. The bishops themselves would scarcely have benefited from this publicity for their riotous conduct, any more than British Members of Parliament, whose boorish rowdiness was long concealed from public gaze by the traditions of parliamentary reporting in Hansard and the conventions of the parliamentary lobby, had their collective reputation enhanced when television cameras were permitted into the House of Commons. To the extent that the text of the extremely long acts became public knowledge, their revelation of the realities of episcopal debate is more likely to have raised the credit of the secular authorities, who had steered discussions towards appropriate conclusions without infringing the liberty of the bishops to indulge in their characteristic intemperance. The Acts of Chalcedon introduce a period in which emperors, following the problems that Theodosius II experienced with the councils at Ephesus that he had entrusted to episcopal control, took charge of attempts to reach doctrinal unity, from the encyclical letter of Leo requesting views on Chalcedon and Timothy Aelurus, through Zeno's *Henotikon*, to the theopaschite, Three Chapters, and aphthartodocete initiatives of Justinian. The Acts of Chalcedon demonstrated that bishops could not be trusted to look after the business of the Church, especially on important matters.

Another type of poor behaviour to emerge from the acts, one at odds

---

22 *Contra* Gaddis (2005), 299, 310.
23 For subsequent developments see Frend (1972).
24 Acts VI. 11, *ACO* 2.1, p. 351.

with the ideal image of bishops as principled leaders in matters of faith, is the failure of numerous bishops to defend their beliefs: over 100 bishops present at Second Ephesus also participated at Chalcedon, or were represented there by deputies, but only Dioscorus stuck to his views, since most of his non-Egyptian supporters abandoned him during the first session and even some of his Egyptian bishops were prepared to anathematize Eutyches at the fourth session.[25] One line of defence was ignorance of the issues. This was the first excuse advanced by Theodore of Claudiopolis in a long justification for his change of heart at Chalcedon: 'Dioscorus and Juvenal and all those who signed first had, as orthodox, been entrusted by the master of the world with passing judgement in matters of faith. Plotting nefariously among themselves, they made us act as judges, who were sitting in all innocence as men ignorant of the affair.'[26] It might seem surprising that the people responsible for guiding local communities in matters of faith should express such reservations about their own capacity, and when the same argument was used at the fourth session by the group of thirteen Egyptian bishops, who were attempting to avoid committing themselves to an anathema of Eutyches, they incurred some mockery: 'Cecropius the most devout bishop of Sebastopolis said: "They don't know what they believe. Are they now willing to learn?"... Paschasinus, Lucentius and Boniface, the most devout representatives of the apostolic see, said through Paschasinus: "Having grown old as bishops in their churches for so many years till this time, are they still ignorant of the orthodox and catholic faith, and expect to depend on the judgement of another?"'[27] On the other hand, it is a reminder that, although the ideal was for bishops to be educated and confident leaders of their communities,[28] many had probably received no more than a modest education and so relied on doctrinal experts such as Cyril, Theodoret or Dioscorus for guidance through the minefields of current debate.

A second line of defence was intimidation by Dioscorus. Theodore of Claudiopolis also exploited this option: 'They brought us blank sheets – Dioscorus and Juvenal – accompanied by a mob of disorderly people, with a mass of them shouting and making a tumult and disrupting the council... They made a sport of our lives.'[29] The composition of the mob

25 Acts IV. 42, *ACO* 2.1, p. 308.
26 Acts I. 62, *ACO* 2.1, p. 76.
27 Acts IV. 36, 38, *ACO* 2.1, p. 308.
28 Rapp (2006), ch. 6, esp. 178–83.
29 Acts I. 62, *ACO* 2.1, p. 76.

is subsequently clarified by Basil of Seleucia, 'Armed soldiers burst into the church, and there were arrayed Barsauma and his monks, *parabalani*, and a great miscellaneous mob,'[30] while Marinianus of Synnada states, 'The counts entered, and they led in the proconsul with fetters and with a great crowd...'[31] Theodore attempted to justify his apparent cowardice by parading his concern for all those whom he had baptized: they would be ruined if his refusal to acquiesce in Dioscorus' designs led to him being branded a heretic, since this would invalidate their membership of the Church.[32]

A third defence was respect for authority. This was advanced by Basil of Seleucia: in spite of his prominence as one of the six bishops excluded at the end of the first session of Chalcedon for their role in controlling proceedings at Second Ephesus, he was not quite of the stature of Juvenal of Jerusalem or Thalassius of Caesarea in Cappadocia. On being challenged by Dioscorus for showing respect to human beings while rejecting the faith, Basil responded, 'If I had been up before secular officials, I would have borne witness; after all, I displayed boldness of speech at Constantinople. But if one is judged by one's father, one cannot defend oneself. Death to a child who defends himself against his father!'[33] When the imperial commissioners then remarked that Basil had earlier been relying on the defence of compulsion, his potential embarrassment was avoided by an outbreak of chanting from the eastern bishops, 'We all sinned, we all beg forgiveness.'[34]

These defences, however, do not entirely conceal signs of subservient adaptability to the currently prevailing point of view. Both Basil of Seleucia and Aethericus of Smyrna were in the embarrassing position of having participated in Flavian of Constantinople's sessions where Eutyches was examined, then of justifying at Second Ephesus their support for his condemnation, and finally explaining these changes at Chalcedon in the face of challenges from Dioscorus and limited sympathy from the imperial commissioners. Aethericus first alleged, in a disjointed

---

30 Acts I. 851, *ACO* 2.1, p. 179. *Parabalani* were volunteers originally devoted to the care of the sick, but increasingly used to intimidate opponents. See Kazhdan (1991), III, 1582.

31 Acts I. 861, *ACO* 2.1, p. 180.

32 Zachariah, *Hist. Eccl.* III. 1 (trans. Hamilton and Brooks, p. 46) alleges that Amphilochius of Side only subscribed to the Chalcedonian definition because Aetius, archdeacon of Constantinople, hit him over the head.

33 Acts I. 180, *ACO* 2.1, p. 94.

34 Acts I. 183, *ACO* 2.1, p. 94.

exchange with Dioscorus at Second Ephesus, that his verdict at Constantinople had been a confused response to a request from Flavian shortly after he had arrived to join the hearings, but then at Chalcedon he denied this exchange without being able to provide specific corroboration for his version.[35] At Ephesus Basil asserted, quite possibly correctly, that the record of the Constantinople hearings did not preserve his full contribution,[36] but at Chalcedon relied on the allegations of intimidation noted above to justify this change. Aethericus and Basil had particularly difficult trajectories to explain, but there will have been many others whose changes of heart were no more reputable. According to Theodore of Claudiopolis, of the 135 participants at Second Ephesus, 42 had been ordered to remain silent, only 15 were in Theodore's group of opponents or doubters, while all the remainder were with Dioscorus and Juvenal.[37] The Egyptian bishops mocked such cowardice, 'A Christian fears no one. An orthodox fears no one. Bring fire, and we shall learn. If they had feared men, they would never have been martyrs.'[38] A century later the clergy of Milan, writing to Frankish envoys on their way to Constantinople with reference to the Three Chapters controversy, contrasted the subservience of eastern bishops with the rectitude of their western opponents: 'For there are Greek bishops who have rich and opulent churches, and cannot bear even a two-month interruption in the conduct of church business; for this reason, as required by the situation and the will of the princes, they assent without questioning to whatever is asked of them. When the African bishops mentioned above reached the imperial city, they began to press them, now by blandishments and now by threats, to give their assent to the condemnation of the chapters. But when this pressure failed utterly…'[39]

The Egyptians at Chalcedon, however, proved to be no braver than their opponents, when they had their own chance to display *parrhesia* in support of their beliefs. At the fourth session, a group of thirteen former supporters of Dioscorus attempted to avoid his downfall by petitioning the emperor with a statement of orthodoxy in terms of Nicaea, Athanasius and Cyril.[40] Under challenge by the council, they reluctantly agreed

---

35 Acts I. 308–29, *ACO* 2.1, pp. 118–19.
36 Acts I. 545–6, *ACO* 2.1, pp. 144–5. Cf. I. 791, 798, *ACO* 2.1, pp. 173–4.
37 Acts I. 62, *ACO* 2.1, p. 76.
38 Acts I. 64, *ACO* 2.1, p. 76.
39 Schwartz (1940), 20, *PL* 69. 114C–119A, trans. Price (2009), I, 166–7.
40 Acts IV. 19–62, *ACO* 2.1, pp. 306–10.

to pronounce an anathema against Eutyches, but then balked at the demand to subscribe to the Tome of Leo, stating that they could not do this without the approval of their archbishop – a post which had to be filled following the deposition of Dioscorus. Initially they cited the canons of Nicaea, which had confirmed the authority of Alexandria over bishops in Egypt, but then pleaded more desperately that they would be driven from their province, and finally that they would be killed, if they ignored Egyptian custom in this. The bishops, and especially the papal representatives, were not swayed by these arguments, but the imperial commissioners acceded and permitted them to remain in Constantinople until a replacement for Dioscorus had been chosen. The Egyptians' fears were probably not excessive, as the fate of Dioscorus' imperially-approved successor, Proterius, demonstrates: during the uncertainty caused by the death of Marcian in 457, he was dragged from his baptistery and torn to pieces by a mob who had not forgiven him for betraying Dioscorus after Chalcedon. This passage is a useful reminder that individual bishops could not necessarily dominate their own cities, especially in matters of religion, if there was strong opposition within their region from monks or other clergy. Even a bishop as powerful and resourceful as Juvenal of Jerusalem might not be able to hold his own: Juvenal was the most high profile turncoat at Chalcedon, having supposedly promised before setting out for the council not to abandon Dioscorus' position, but before he could return to Palestine a monk named Theodosius had rushed back to the province to proclaim the bishop's treachery; Theodosius then secured appointment as bishop and begun to ordain episcopal supporters, a challenge which took two years and considerable imperial military support to suppress.[41]

The wider population might take some notice of what bishops did and said at church councils. For the majority of bishops their main contribution to a council was their availability as lobby fodder, numbers who could lend greater weight to decisions by their mere presence, vociferous during chanting but individually silent, except for the occasions when they were required to state their opinion in sequence. It is easy to skip over these long series of expressions of support, for explicit disagreement such as the papal legate Hilary declared at Second Ephesus is extremely rare. On occasion, indeed, one bishop might be deputed to deliver the verdict for a group, which might be regional or might simply

41 Zachariah, *Hist. Eccl.* III. 3–9, trans. Hamilton and Brooks, pp. 49–56. Evagrius, *Hist. Eccl.* II. 5, trans. Whitby, pp. 78–80.

be those bishops who happened to be sitting together at the meeting, as occurred when judgements were delivered on the dispute over the bishopric of Ephesus between Bassianus and Stephen;[42] occasionally several bishops are reported by one of their number to hold the same view,[43] and a clear verdict on issues of secondary importance might be made by supporting acclamations from 'all the most devout bishops' after an appropriate number of senior bishops had pronounced.[44] It was, however, expected that a bishop should normally formulate a declaration before subscribing to a decision, as Dioscorus urged when defending his conduct of Second Ephesus: 'Since they are making an accusation that they were given a blank sheet to sign, who then composed their declarations? I ask your magnificence to make them answer.'[45] One response would have been that a sequence of formulaic declarations had also been devised in advance by Dioscorus and his supporters, but the fact that the imperial commissioners evaded the challenge by insisting that the reading of the acts should continue might suggest that Dioscorus had identified a weakness in the defence of the inconsistent bishops.

In spite of the prevalence of formulae and the rarity of outright disagreement, minor variations in expression could be significant, and so they deserve attention. With regard to the case of Ibas of Edessa in the tenth session, a first issue to be decided was whether the proceedings against Ibas at Second Ephesus should be read out. Although a substantial portion of the first day's events at Ephesus had been read into the record of the first session at Chalcedon, in response to a suggestion from the presiding officials it was now decided that the council was not to be mentioned again and its proceedings to have no force.[46] First the papal representatives stated that the proceedings had been nullified by Pope Leo, with the exception of the legitimacy of Maximus of Antioch who had been received into communion by Leo. Then Anatolius of Constantinople rehearsed the same points, but while he noted Leo's acceptance of Maximus, which served to obscure the fact that Anatolius had consecrated Maximus in somewhat contentious circumstances, the rectification of the errors of Ephesus is not attributed

42 Acts XI. 40–41, *ACO* 2.1, pp. 409–10.
43 E.g. Acts X. 174, *ACO* 2.3, p. 490: six named bishops.
44 E.g. Acts X. 179, *ACO* 2.1, p. 401.
45 Acts I. 65, *ACO* 2.1, pp. 76–7.
46 Acts X. 143–60, *ACO* 2.1, pp. 397–8.

to the pope. Juvenal of Jerusalem came third with a simple statement that the emperor should decree his preference, and of the other 12 bishops whose opinions are recorded three explicitly related their opinion to that of Juvenal and one paraphrased his opinion without naming him, four referred more vaguely to the views of the fathers or archbishops, Eunomius of Nicomedia stated that he would support the decision of the council, ignoring the fact that he was one of those responsible for constructing that decision, while the last individual bishop to be named in the sequence, Cecropius of Sebastopolis, bluntly stated, 'We ought not to mention that council.' Stephen of Ephesus briefly rehearsed the views of Anatolius, perhaps because the matter concerned his own see, while Peter of Corinth noted that he had not participated at Second Ephesus, being the first of the bishops who could register this excuse. In this sequence there is clearly an issue over how much credit Leo is to be accorded in developments, but many bishops are content to follow the views of predecessors with minor changes of vocabulary so that a change of emphasis by one bishop may then be picked up: the switch from references to Juvenal's opinion to the more general 'declarations of the fathers' was initiated by Constantine of Bostra, who may well have had little liking for the ambitions of his powerful neighbour.[47]

This verdict on Second Ephesus was not contentious, but rather more was at stake in the main decision on Ibas which immediately followed.[48] The papal representatives set the tone by referring to 'the verdict of the most devout bishops', a reference to the judgement of Photius and Eustathius at Tyre, which had in fact been more of a compromise than a demonstration of Ibas' innocence, and also declared that the infamous letter (to Mari the Persian) was orthodox; they also referred the matter of Ibas' successor at Edessa, Nonnus, to decision by the Church of Antioch. Next, Anatolius of Constantinople was a bit more circumspect, referring to 'the reading of all the accompanying material', which implicitly included the letter, and noting that he had held suspicions which were now being set aside because Ibas had signed up to the decisions of Chalcedon and the Tome of Leo; he ended by mentioning the issue of Nonnus. Third, Maximus of Antioch followed the papal envoys in referring to the orthodoxy of the letter, the only subsequent bishop to do so, and then explained how a decision would be reached about Nonnus, thereby removing that particular issue from subsequent opinions.

47 Acts X. 153, *ACO* 2.1, p. 398.
48 Acts X. 160–81, *ACO* 2.1, pp. 398–401.

Juvenal of Jerusalem came fourth, and, as befitting one of Ibas' bitterest opponents, his verdict is distinctive: 'Divine Scripture orders the receiving back of those who repent, which is why we also receive people from heresy. I therefore resolve that the most devout Ibas should receive clemency, also because he is elderly, so as to retain the episcopal dignity, being orthodox.'[49] A judgement of orthodoxy could scarcely be more damning. Thalassius of Caesarea then put proceedings back on the expected track by referring to Photius and Eustathius and Ibas' willingness to anathematize heretical views, and this established a trend for the following speakers, so that individual bishops began simply to agree to the decision of the council or of the holy fathers. The only minor interruption was when Eunomius of Nicomedia mentioned Ibas' attacks on Cyril of Alexandria, noting that he had corrected these errors in his subsequent statements,[50] but the sequence of straightforward support was promptly restored.

A parallel case to that of Ibas was the full rehabilitation of Theodoret which occupied the brief eighth session.[51] As with Ibas, the papal envoys initiated the record of views by noting that Pope Leo had welcomed Theodoret back into communion some time previously, and that Theodoret's current written and verbal anathemas of Nestorius and Eutyches had merely confirmed the rectitude of that decision. The papal view of the council as a mechanism to endorse Pope Leo's views was, unsurprisingly, not picked up by any of the subsequent speakers. Maximus of Antioch, speaking third, was the most effusive in affirming Theodoret's orthodoxy, which had, apparently, been evident to him from the very beginning, a surprising assertion for someone who had been consecrated during Theodoret's exclusion from his see, but perhaps necessary now that Maximus would have to deal closely with Theodoret as the most influential bishop within the diocese of Oriens. Juvenal of Jerusalem, who came next, is even more revealing, managing a terse, 'I too agree with the resolution of the most God-beloved Anatolius archbishop of Constantinople';[52] alone out of the bishops who

---

49 Acts X. 164, *ACO* 2.1, p. 399.
50 Acts X. 173, *ACO* 2.3, p. 490. This statement is supplied from the Latin version of the Acts, having been excluded at some stage from the Greek Acts which attach Eunomius to the six bishops in §174 (*ACO* 2.1, p. 400): see Price and Gaddis (2005), II, 308, n. 125.
51 Acts VIII. 16–25, *ACO* 2.1, pp. 369–70.
52 Acts VIII. 19, *ACO* 2.1, p. 369.

spoke he could not bring himself to mention his doctrinal enemy by name, even though he could not avoid participating in his return.

The key decision on the first day of Second Ephesus, about the deposition of Flavian and Eusebius, produced a range of episcopal responses. The sequence was initiated by Juvenal with a specific endorsement of the judgement of Dioscorus against them, referring to their changes to the faith established at Nicaea and the turmoil which they had caused.[53] Another enthusiast was Uranius of Hemerium in Osrhoene, who suggested that 'they ought not only to be deprived of ecclesiastical rank but also subjected to the sword; for those who see their predecessors incurring such a penalty will necessarily be deterred from such an attempt. Because therefore Flavian and Eusebius have transgressed them [the mandates of Nicaea and First Ephesus], I pronounce that they are excluded from episcopal dignity and are worthy of misfortunes beyond counting.'[54] At the opposite extreme from this endorsement of the virtues of capital punishment were the statements of a few bishops who expressed regrets. Eusebius of Ancyra began his opinion by pronouncing, 'I have always loved mercy', Julian of Tavium was clearer, 'It is with profound regret that I make this sad pronouncement, for such is the rule of the wise', while Epiphanius of Perge was more vehement, 'Execrable was this to me. I too, while lamenting in my soul, concur with the condemnation...'[55] Whether such sympathy was genuine cannot be established, but it deserves note even if it merely expressed the humanity which milder bishops felt they ought to articulate. One Egyptian bishop, Zeno of Rhinocolura, adopted this line, which Dioscorus might not have wanted to hear, though balancing it against the greater wickedness and impiety of Flavian and Eusebius: 'We ourselves, who follow the rules of compassion and brotherly love, assent while lamenting to the just judgement promulgated against them.'[56]

The intervention of the Egyptian contingent is of some interest, since they were the last block of bishops to have the chance to contribute their opinions, and by this stage a number of the statements had become brief and formulaic. By contrast, the first of the Egyptians, Theopemptus of

53 Acts I. 966, *ACO* 2.1, p. 192.
54 Acts I. 1009, *ACO* 2.3, p. 244, §1012. From §971 the Greek version of the Acts only records the names of the speakers, but their individual contributions are preserved in the Latin Acts: Price and Gaddis (2005), I, 345, n. 503.
55 Acts I. 969, 981, 1018, *ACO* 2.1, p. 192; *ACO* 2.3, p. 241, §984, p. 245, §1021.
56 Acts I. 1060, *ACO* 2.3, p. 251, §1063.

Cabasa, pronounced the second longest judgement of the whole sequence, a strong statement of support for the position of his metropolitan: 'War is serious when waged by open enemies, but is still more grievous when waged by false friends and deceivers, for they cause harm by pretence, drawing the most simple away from piety and distancing them from the doctrines of the church'; this continues with assertions about the heresy of both Flavian and Eusebius, 'formerly a wrong appointment as bishop of the city of Dorylaeum', before concurring with the council's verdict.[57] This rhetorical *tour de force* was only surpassed by the next but one speaker, John of Hephaestus: 'If a divine sentence from the Saviour declared that he who causes one of the little ones to fall incurs a most grievous penalty, what worthy of their impiety should be suffered by those who at this time have thrown almost the whole world into confusion and given confidence, as far as they could, to those who follow the doctrines of Nestorius? In addition they have given pagans and Jews the opportunity to deride and denigrate the Christian faith, as if our orthodox and unimpeachable faith were unknown until today, when in fact this faith was defined by the holy fathers at Nicaea through the Holy Spirit, and was sealed a short time ago in this metropolis also.'[58] John had not quite reached the mid-point of his harangue. Theodulus of Tesila in Cyrenaica endorsed scriptural violence against the guilty: 'It would have been better for the former bishops Flavian and Eusebius if they had not been born, but to have millstones hung around their necks and be thrown into the sea, because they have caused simple souls to transgress.'[59] Although many Egyptians dutifully supported Dioscorus with standard statements, there also appears to have been competition among some bishops to attract attention through the diversity and ingenuity of their intervention.

When the time came to pass judgement on Dioscorus at Chalcedon, there were very few bishops who were prepared to depart from the explicit condemnation initiated by the papal representatives. Of the bishops who delivered anything more than bland assent, only Amphilochius of Side and Epiphanius of Perge appear less than enthusiastic: 'It was not my wish to cut off any member whatsoever of the church, particularly one of rank. But because Dioscorus, formerly bishop of the great city of Alexandria, in addition to the charges that

57 Acts I. 1043, *ACO* 2.3, p. 248, §1046.
58 Acts I. 1045, *ACO* 2.3, p. 249, §1048.
59 Acts I. 1057, *ACO* 2.3, p. 251, §1060.

certain persons have brought against him, refused to present himself when summoned for a third time by the holy and ecumenical council and brought down the sentence of the council on his own head, he has only himself to blame.'[60] Amphilochius appears to have been unhappy with the Chalcedonian definition, which he refused to endorse when consulted by Emperor Leo in 458;[61] a story in Rufus' *Plerophories* (85) might indicate that he and Epiphanius had been expected to show greater support for Dioscorus, so their regretful endorsement of the deposition, with the emphasis on the three summons rather than any other wrong-doing, was intended to be a deliberate signal.

It is easy to see how high-level rivalry between major sees or contentious issues relating to prominent bishops might generate divergences, but there are also interesting differences in the responses to some of the more specific difficulties which Chalcedon was required to address after the weighty doctrinal and disciplinary matters had been handled. The dispute between Stephen and Bassianus over who should hold the see of Ephesus had occupied the eleventh session on 29 October, with one important issue being who had the right to consecrate the individual, since the see of Constantinople had been attempting to secure recognition for its rights over the metropolitan see of the province of Asia. On the following day, the twelfth session opened with a grumble from the presiding officials about how the prolongation of the council was impinging on public business.[62] At once Anatolius of Constantinople and the papal representatives gave a clear steer that both claimants should be ejected because of their uncanonical route to the bishopric, but that both also deserved continuing support from the Church of Ephesus. Maximus of Antioch, however, stated that clemency suggested that, in spite of the wrong-doing, one of the competitors should be selected by the provincial bishops. The next three speakers ignored this diversion, but then Julian of Cos returned to Maximus' line that, in spite of the canonical irregularity, the Council of Asia should select which was to remain in post. Eusebius of Dorylaeum promptly stressed the breach of the canons, while Diogenes of Cyzicus responded by upholding the superior knowledge of the provincial bishops. In spite of this disagreement, which was clear even if not directly antagonistic, a

60 Acts III. 96.22–23, *ACO* 2.3, p. 309, §94.22–3. Again the full statements of Amphilochius and Epiphanius have to be supplied from the Latin Acts.
61 Evagrius, *Hist. Eccl.* II. 10, trans. Whitby, p. 92.
62 Acts XII. 2, *ACO* 2.1, p. 412.

subsequent bishop could state, 'I too agree with the decrees of the most holy bishops before me.' Diogenes had the last word, responding to the positive general chant of 'This is a pious proposal. This is according to the canons', with the less enthusiastic, 'It is better than the others.'[63] The issue of Constantinople's expansion of control influenced these comments, with even Maximus, who had been consecrated by Anatolius, supporting those who wished to keep this in check; for the time being the weight of opposition to Constantinople's ambitions deferred a decision on this matter, though within two more days the imperial capital had secured its wishes, to be enshrined in the contentious Canon 28.

There are occasions when variation seems to have had little point. Discussion of the case of Athanasius of Perrhe at the fourteenth session involved the reading of proceedings at a local synod in Antioch in 445. On that occasion 23 bishops had offered an opinion about Athanasius' failure to appear, and, although there was no disagreement about the issues or verdict and the speakers drew on common themes of letters of excuse, guilty conscience, failure to respond to three summons, and friendship with the presiding bishop, they managed to express their views in different ways without precise verbal overlap.[64] There seems to be deliberate avoidance of exact repetition in this first round of responses,[65] but shortly after, when the same bishops were asked about the related issue of the content of certain letters from Athanasius, their inventiveness had dwindled and half resorted to statements along the lines of, 'I too have come to the same opinion.'[66] A third round of decision-making initially prompted diversity of expression, but this tailed off towards the end.[67]

Bishops were on display at church councils, in the first instance to their fellow bishops, but then indirectly to wider audiences through the reports which other attendees would broadcast or through dissemination of the acts. Most attention would naturally focus on the metropolitans and other leaders, but even a lowly bishop might want to point out back home how he had contributed to discussions. The acts of councils present invaluable information, and the Acts of Chalcedon in

---

63 Acts XII. 19, 23–4, *ACO* 2.1, p. 414.
64 Acts XIV. 38–60, *ACO* 2.1, pp. 429–30.
65 Two of the bishops resorted to generic agreement with the holy council/fathers, but that still leaves a considerable display of diversity.
66 Acts XIV. 76–95, *ACO* 2.1, pp. 433–4.
67 Acts XIV. 123–48, *ACO* 2.1, pp. 436–40.

particular, since these do not seem to have undergone a smoothing process to reduce the discordances and disruptions of passionate debate and also preserve discussions on a series of relatively local issues which did not usually reach an ecumenical council. If the bishops emerge as less than perfect, that should be no surprise: episcopal susceptibility to human failings is evident from a range of sources – the letters of Sidonius Apollinaris on competition for office in fifth-century Gaul, or of Pope Gregory on disputes in Dalmatia and Italy in the 590s, accounts of personal as well as regional rivalries in the fifth-century church historians, or Procopius of Caesarea's allusion (*Wars* II.7.17) to the flight of Bishop Ephraem from Antioch in 540. Even the *Life* of Theodore of Sykeon, which attempts to present an ideal image of its honorand, provides enough information for the modern reader to infer that the great ascetic was not completely successful as a bishop. Equally, Dioscorus whose ruthless pursuit of doctrinal victory as well as Egyptian supremacy emerges from the council acts, could be presented in hagiography as an unbending pillar of orthodoxy, while in the mainstream Chalcedonian tradition the bishops whose imperfections have been reviewed above became the 630 holy fathers who, with divine inspiration, had defined the true faith.

BIBLIOGRAPHY

Acta Conciliorum Oecumenicorum, ed. Eduard Schwartz and others (Berlin, 1914–).

Evagrius, *Ecclesiastical History*, trans. Michael Whitby, TTH 33 (Liverpool, 2000).

Frend, W.H.C. (1972), *The Rise of the Monophysite Movement: Chapters in the History of the Church in the Fifth and Sixth Centuries* (London).

Gaddis, Michael (2005), *There is No Crime for Those Who Have Christ: Religious violence in the Christian Roman Empire* (Berkeley).

Inscriptiones Latinae Christianae Veteres, ed. Ernst Diehl, 3 vols (Berlin, 1925–31).

Kazhdan, A.P. (1991), *The Oxford Dictionary of Byzantium*, 3 vols (Oxford).

Price, Richard and Gaddis, Michael (2005), *The Acts of the Council of Chalcedon*, TTH 45 (Liverpool).

Price, R.M. (2009), *Acts of the Council of Constantinople of 553*, trans. with introduction and notes, 2 vols, TTH 51 (Liverpool).

Rapp, Claudia (2005), *Holy Bishops in Late Antiquity. The Nature of Christian Leadership in an Age of Transition* (Berkeley).

Schwartz, Eduard (1940), *Vigiliusbriefe*. SBAW.PH, Heft 2 (Munich).

Ste. Croix, G.E.M. de (2006) 'The Council of Chalcedon' (with additions by Michael Whitby), in id., *Christian Persecution, Martyrdom, and Orthodoxy*, ed. Michael Whitby and Joseph Streeter (Oxford), 259–319.

(Ps.-)Zachariah of Mitylene, *Historia Ecclesiastica*. Trans. F.J. Hamilton and E.W. Brooks, *The Syriac Chronicle known as that of Zachariah of Mitylene* (London, 1899; New York, 1979).

INDEX

Acacius of Constantinople (d. 489) 21, 115
acclamations 169–77
    at Aphrodisias, Caria 173–5
    at Athens 171
    at church councils 170–6, 179, 188
    at Chalcedon 16, 18, 74, 78–82, 87, 92,
        96, 100, 122, 150, 169–76, 183
    at Ephesus against St Paul 169
    at Ephesus I (431) 33 n. 16, 38–9
    at Ephesus II (449) 14, 58, 62, 172–6
    at Mylasa 170
    at Oxyrhynchus 170
    at Rome 170–1
    at Sardica 170
    at Termessus (Lycia) 172–3
    at Tyre 170
    patterns in 171–4
Acta Conciliorum Oecumenicorum
    (*ACO*), *see* Riedinger, Schwartz
acts (*acta*), conciliar
    authority of 87–90
    circulation of 32, 41, 48, 66–7, 92, 119,
        142–4
    editing of 27–8, 32–43, 46–9, 61, 94–
        105, 135–7, 144
    read out at councils 29–31, 42–3, 74,
        85–6
    see also councils, and individual
        councils
Aethericus of Smyrna (at Chalcedon)
    185–6
Aetius, archdeacon of Constantinople (at
    Chalcedon) 79 n. 34, 80, 185 n. 32
Africans and Lateran Council (649) 136,
    141
Agatho (pope 678–81) 158
akephaloi ('headless'), rejectors of both
    Chalcedon and the *Henotikon* 115
Albinus of Aphrodisias, acclamations for
    173–4
Alexakis, Alexander 4, 137–8
Alexandria, Council of (338) 9 n. 6
Alexandrian 'School', a problematic
    term 108–12
Amphilochius of Side (at Chalcedon) 185

n. 32, 192–3
Anastasius I (emperor 491–518) 65
Anastasius II (pope 496–8) 154
Anastasius Apocrisarius (d. 662) 135–7,
    143
Anastasius the Disciple (*fl.* 650) 135–7
Anathemas, Twelve, *see* Cyril of
    Alexandria, Third Letter to Nestorius
Anatolius of Constantinople (d. 458)
    at Chalcedon 75–80 and n. 35, 84–5,
        95–9, 150 and n. 10, 188–90, 193–4
    and Pope Leo 19, 72, 152–3
Anatolius, *magister militum praesentalis*,
    chairman at Chalcedon 73–84, 94–9,
    104, 122
    see also commissioners, imperial
Anthimus of Constantinople (*fl.* 536) 66
Antioch, Councils of: (325) 93, (*c.* 330)
    153, (341), 72 n. 13, (445) 194
Antiochene 'School', a misleading term
    108–11
Aphrodisias (Caria), *see* acclamations
Apiarius, dispute over, in canonical
    collections 154
Apollinarius, Apollinarianism 12–17,
    112–14
Apostolic Constitutions, in canonical
    collections 154–6
Arianism 9–11, 130
Arles, Council of (314) 2
Armenian traditions in the canons of
    Trullo 159–60, 163
Ascidas, *see* Theodore Ascidas
Asiana, authority of see of
    Constantinople in 83–4, 193
Assyrian Church of the East, *see* Church
    of the East
Athanasius of Alexandria 2, 9–13, 110–12
    On the incarnation 111–12
    version of Nicene creed 29 n. 27
Athanasius of Perrhe (at Chalcedon) 194
Athens, *see* acclamations
Atticus of Nicopolis (at Chalcedon) 119
Augustine of Hippo, and acclamations
    172–6